Meditations on the Apocalypse

Meditations on the Apocalypse

A Psychospiritual Perspective on the Book of Revelation

F. Aster Barnwell

ELEMENT
Rockport, Massachusetts • Shaftesbury, Dorset
Brisbane, Queensland

© 1992 F. Aster Barnwell

Published in the U.S.A. in 1992 by
Element Inc.
42 Broadway, Rockport, MA 01966

Published in Great Britain in 1992 by
Element Books Limited
Longmead, Shaftesbury, Dorset

Published in Australia in 1992 by
Element Books Limited for
Jacaranda Wiley Ltd
33 Park Road, Milton, Brisbane, 4064

All rights reserved. No part of this book may
be reproduced or utilized, in any form or by any
means, electronic or mechanical, without permission
in writing from the publisher.

Cover design by Jim Wasserman
Cover illustration *The New Jerusalem* by Gustave Doré
Designed by Nancy Lawrence
Typeset in Garamond by BP Integraphics Ltd.,
Bath, Avon, England
Printed in the United States of America by
Edward Brothers Inc.

Library of Congress data available
British Library Cataloguing–in–Publication data available

ISBN 1-85230-363-8

Dedicated to the memory of my late father,
Robert Charles Barnwell
(1914–1990)

Acknowledgments

I gratefully acknowledge the contributions of the following persons:

Dr. Peter Roche de Coppens for his friendship and encouragement, and whose relentless efforts on my behalf were instrumental in getting this book into print.

Donald R. Gordon, who first read the manuscript and offered valuable criticism and encouragement.

I also acknowledge with gratitude the Unseen Influences and the many personal lessons that "conspired" and orchestrated events to bring these ideas into form.

Table of Contents

		Page
	List of Figures and Tables	xiii
	Introduction	1
Chapter 1	**The Book of Revelation: A Window on the Soul**	7
	Overview	7
	Astrology as a Key to Interpreting Revelation	8
	The Astrological Evidence	9
	The Four "Beasts" as Interpreted by Christian Theologians	13
	Other Layers of Knowledge in Revelation	14
Chapter 2	**Astrological Symbolism in the Bible**	15
	Christian Opposition to Astrology	15
	Astrological References in the Old Testament	15
	Astrology in the New Testament	18
Chapter 3	**Basic Concepts of Astrology**	22
	The Zodiac and the Twelve Signs	22
	Basic Sign Characteristics	23
	The Meaning of the Elements	24
	The Meaning of the Qualities	24
	The Meaning of the Polarities	25
	The Interaction of Elements, Qualities, and Polarities	25

		Picture Symbols for the Twelve Signs	25
		The Annual Cycle of Zodiacal Signs	26
		Geographical Factors Behind the Derivation of the Signs	26
		Earth-Centered and Sun-Centered Views of the Earth–Sun Orbital Relationship	27
		The Dynamic Relationship Between the Signs and Seasons	30
Chapter 4		**Representations of the Twelve Zodiacal Sign Energies in Revelation**	32
		The Four Beasts and the Fixed Sign Energies	32
		The Result of Misuse of the Fixed Sign Energies	32
		The "Themes" of the Fixed Signs	34
		The Energies of the Four Mutable Signs as Featured in the Four Horsemen	36
		The White Horse and Rider	37
		The Red Horse and Rider	38
		The Black Horse and Rider	39
		The Pale Horse and Rider, and Companion	40
		Powers of the Horsemen	41
		Themes of the Mutable Signs	42
		The Energies of the Four Cardinal Signs as Featured in the "Two" Witnesses	42
		Powers of the Witnesses	46
		Themes of the Cardinal Signs	47
Chapter 5		**The Problem of Duality as the Foundation of Revelation's Psychology of Transformation**	49
		Overview	49
		The Duality Problem	50
		Beyond Duality: Entering the New Jerusalem	53
		The Six Psychological Principles at the Basis of the Twelve Zodiacal Signs	55
		The Dynamic Interplay of the Six Psychological Principles Behind the Twelve Zodiacal Signs	57
		Aries–Libra: Polarity of Being and Accommodating	57
		Taurus–Scorpio: Polarity of Domination and Obligation	58
		Gemini–Sagittarius: Polarity of Thinking and Understanding	59
		Cancer–Capricorn: Polarity of Belonging and Consecration	60
		Leo–Aquarius: Polarity of Will and Intuition	60
		Virgo–Pisces: Polarity of Verification and Acceptance	62
		A Note on the Self	62

Chapter 6	Time, Space, and Process: The Utilization of Time and Numbers in Revelation as Metaphors for Psychospiritual Integration	64
	The Year and the Zodiac	64
	The Decanate Concept as the Building Block for Revelation's Time–Space Creations	68
	The Twenty-four Elders	70
	The Number 1,260 as a Symbol for the Process of Psychospiritual Integration	72
	The Number 666 as Symbolic of Aborted Psychospiritual Integration	74
	The Similarity Between the Concept of Psychospiritual Integration and the Process of *Kundalini* Awakening	76
Chapter 7	Revelation's Perspective on the Forces that Define the Psyche of Man	78
	Overview	78
	Two Conflicting Dynamics of Consciousness: The Woman in Labor and the Dragon	78
	The Battle in Heaven	81
	Persecution of the Woman by the Dragon	83
	The Beast from the Sea	85
	The Beast from the Earth	88
	The Image Made to the Beast from the Sea and the Mark of the Beast	90
	The Alternative to the Mark of the Beast	93
Chapter 8	Seven Churches, Seven Cities, Seven Planets: Factors Connecting the Seven Churches to the Zodiac	95
	Overview	95
	The Cities of the Seven Churches as the Relevant Points of Focus for the Seven Letters	96
	Astrological Factors Connecting the Seven Cities	97
	General Outline of Available Evidence to Support the Affinities of Cities and Zodiacal Signs	98

	The Relationship Between "Ruling Planets" of Astrological Signs and the Seven Cities	99
Chapter 9	**The Principles Linking Specific Cities to Specific Zodiacal Signs**	103
	Introduction	103
	The City of Ephesus: Embodiment of the Cancer–Capricorn Principle	103
	The City of Smyrna: Embodiment of the Virgo–Pisces Principle	106
	The City of Pergamum: Embodiment of the Gemini–Sagittarius Principle	110
	The City of Thyatira: Embodiment of the Aries–Libra Principle	113
	The City of Sardis: Embodiment of the Leo–Aquarius Principle	116
	The City of Laodicea: Embodiment of the Taurus–Scorpio Principle	119
	The City of Philadelphia: Embodiment of the Consciousness Beyond Duality	122
Chapter 10	**The Pattern of the Letters**	127
Chapter 11	**The Ephesus Letter: Instructions on Integrating Cancer–Capricorn Energy**	130
	The Letter	130
	King James Version	130
	Revised Standard Version	130
	Interpretation	131
	Introduction	131
	Address	134
	Criticism and Threat	136
	Encouragement and Promise	137
Chapter 12	**The Smyrna Letter: Instructions on Integrating Virgo–Pisces Energy**	139
	The Letter	139
	King James Version	139
	Revised Standard Version	139

	Interpretation	140
	Introduction	140
	Address	141
	Criticism and Threat	143
	Encouragement and Promise	144
Chapter 13	**The Pergamum Letter: Instructions on Integrating Gemini–Sagittarius Energy**	146
	The Letter	146
	King James Version	146
	Revised Standard Version	146
	Interpretation	147
	Introduction	147
	Address	147
	Criticism and Threat	148
	Encouragement and Promise	152
Chapter 14	**The Thyatira Letter: Instructions on Integrating Aries–Libra Energy**	155
	The Letter	155
	King James Version	155
	Revised Standard Version	156
	Interpretation	156
	Introduction	156
	Address	159
	Criticism and Threat	160
	Encouragement and Promise	162
Chapter 15	**The Sardis Letter: Instructions on Integrating Leo–Aquarius Energy**	165
	The Letter	165
	King James Version	165
	Revised Standard Version	165
	Interpretation	166
	Introduction	166
	Address	167
	Further Criticism and Threat	169
	Encouragement and Promise	170
Chapter 16	**The Laodicea Letter: Instructions on Integrating Taurus–Scorpio Energy**	173
	The Letter	173
	King James Version	173
	Revised Standard Version	174

Interpretation	174
Introduction	174
Address	176
Criticism and Threat	177
Encouragement and Promise	179

Chapter 17   The Philadelphia Letter: Insight into the Consciousness Beyond Duality   182

The Letter	182
King James Version	182
Revised Standard Version	183
Interpretation	183
Introduction	183
Address	184
The Promise in lieu of Criticism	186
Encouragement and Concluding Promise	188

Chapter 18   Experiencing the Totality of Ourselves: The Book of Revelation as a Record of Christian Spiritual Initiation   192

Spirit of Truth	192
Spiritual Initiation	194
Expansion of Consciousness	195

Chapter 19   Progressing from the "Lower" to the "Higher" Self   199

The Lower Self	199
First Level of the Lower Self	199
Second Level of the Lower Self	200
Third Level of the Lower Self	201
The Levels of the Higher Self	202
Fourth Level of Consciousness or First Level of the Higher Self	203
Fifth Level of Consciousness or Second Level of the Higher Self	204
Sixth Level of Consciousness or Third Level of the Higher Self	205
Seventh Level of Consciousness or Fourth Level of the Higher Self	208

Notes	212
Bibliography	221

List of Figures and Tables

		page
Figure 1-1	The Four "Beasts"	12
Figure 2-1	Woodcut Depicting the Zodiac	18
Figure 3-1	Picture Symbols for the Twelve Signs	27
Figure 5-1	A Dramatization of the Problem of Opposites	50
Figure 6-1	Thirty-six Decanates of the Zodiac	69
Figure 6-2	The Twenty-four "Elders" and the Four Beasts	71
Figure 8-1	Relationship Between Astrological Signs, Planets, Cities, and Churches	102
Figure 9-1	The Ephesian Artemis	104
Figure 11-1	The Seven Chakras	137
Table 2-1	Apostles' Names and Their Meaning	20
Table 3-1	Classification of the Signs According to Elements, Qualities, and Polarities	23
Table 3-2	The Elements and Their Correspondence in Physics and Psychology	24
Table 3-3	The Qualities and Their Correspondence in Physics and Psychology	25
Table 3-4	Characteristics of the Twelve Signs	26
Table 3-5	Picture Symbols and Glyphs of the Signs	28
Table 3-6	Cycle of Zodiacal Signs	29
Table 4-1	Themes of the Fixed Signs	34
Table 4-2	Themes of the Mutable Signs	42
Table 4-3	Themes of the Cardinal Signs	47
Table 5-1	The Relationship Between the Praises to the Lamb and the Signs of the Zodiac	52
Table 5-2	The Results of Failure at Integrating the Energies of the Zodiac	53
Table 5-3	The Six Psychological Principles Behind the Twelve Zodiacal Signs	55
Table 7-1	The Coalition of Forces that Define the Psyche of Man	93

Table 8-1	The Relationship Between the Seven Cities and the Twelve Signs of the Zodiac	98
Table 8-2	The Relationships Between Signs and Planets	100
Table 8-3	The Seven Cities and Their Planetary Influences	101
Table 10-1	The Letters and Their Structural Components	128
Table 10-2	The Relationship Between the Introductions and Promises	129
Table 11-1	The Seven *Chakras*	133
Table 19-1	Properties of the Various Levels of Being	203

Introduction

My interest in the Book of Revelation was sparked in the summer of 1979 as the result of a challenge I accepted from the late Dr. Carl Gustav Jung. At the time, I was reading Jung's autobiography, entitled *Memories, Dreams, Reflections*, when the following statement in the book caused me to take offense:

> *I will not discuss the transparent prophecies of the Book of Revelation because no one believes in them and the whole subject is felt to be an embarrassing one.*[1]

I felt that this was a brash statement, to say the least, even if it was coming from one as eminent as Jung himself. The statement set off a chain of combative questions in my mind:

> *What does he mean by calling the Revelation prophecies transparent?*
>
> *What does he mean when he says that no one believes in the Revelation prophecies?*
>
> *How can anyone judge the authenticity of anything on the basis of whether or not people believe in it?*
>
> *Should not understanding be a precondition for belief?*
>
> *How can we expect people to make an intelligent statement of belief or disbelief with respect to something they may not understand?*

Since it did not appear as if there was going to be an end to my inner dialogue, I decided to end the inner quarrel with Jung once and for all by studying Revelation for myself.

At this time of my life, I was deeply involved in a spiritual enquiry as a result of several mystical experiences that brought about a change in my life and perception of reality. One consequence of this change in consciousness was the kindling of a religious fervour within me and an awakened interest in scriptures and spiritual writings of all faiths. I discovered that scriptural writings that were difficult to understand previously now made perfect sense.

When I began reading Revelation, I felt an excitement as things began to make sense to me. I discovered that Revelation was heavily overladen with astrological symbolism, so much so that to understand this document at all, one would of necessity have to be familiar with the language and meaning of the zodiac—the basic underpinning of astrology. With an understanding of astrology, I possessed the conceptual tools to pry meaning and relevance out of Revelation's complex orchestra of symbols. I had read Revelation previously only to be stymied by its complexity. Furthermore, available commentaries and explanations were little help as they were too concerned with interpretations at a literal level.

As I drew upon the astrological understanding I had acquired and applied it to Revelation, I felt this book to be yielding its secrets, and inviting me into its secret depths. On many occasions when I would be at a loss to find a suitable explanation to some aspect of Revelation, I would experience breakthroughs—from either the outer or inner spheres. The outer sphere breakthroughs sometimes took the form of finding some bit of knowledge in a book that would help put some aspect of Revelation into perspective; the inner sphere breakthroughs would typically consist of an imbuing of understanding that would just flood my consciousness. At various times, I would feel suffused with understanding at a nonverbal level.

My studies were facilitated by a new aspect of consciousness that had emerged as a result of earlier mystical breakthroughs. I had developed a feeling akin to a new faculty. If I ardently desired to know the answer to a spiritual or philosophical problem, I would sit with the question until something emerged in consciousness at a feeling level that would "answer" the question. Actually, I would experience this feeling state as a resolution to my question and would then attempt to articulate my answer at a cognitive, verbal level. Usually, I would test my "answer" by searching for anything that seemed contradictory to it from amongst the many insights I had already synthesized and held to be valid. It was then my task to find the concepts, words, and analogies to relate what I was experiencing at an inner level. In particular, the discipline I had to observe was that of research to find corroborating evidence to intuitive truths—to bridge inner and outer.

When I encountered concepts that were difficult to understand and interpret, I exercised patience by assuring myself that Revelation was written to be understood, and that what seemed incomprehensible to me was not a result of the material being faulty, but because

I lacked the required background or understanding. By observing this practice, I was able to make a deeper and deeper penetration into the meaning of Revelation.

During my studies, I often reflected on the coincidences that brought me to the point of taking on this project. Four years previously, when I began my quest for self-understanding, I took up the study of astrology. The subject of astrology came up in discussions I had had with several different people, leading me to surmise that I might gain some insight into the unfolding pattern of my life at that time. I consulted two astrologers within the course of a few weeks. The insights I gained into my own nature and perspective on life so convinced me of the validity of astrology as a tool for self-understanding that I decided to study the discipline on my own—the next three years were spent on an intense study.

Astrology, as I newly discovered it, provides an additional scope to present-day social sciences for understanding and communicating information on the dynamics of the human psyche and its relationship to the Cosmos. It is, therefore, an ancient spiritual psychology and is virtually light years away in sophistication and meaningfulness from the daily horoscope column found in most daily newspapers. Coincidental with my astrological studies I had embarked on a regular habit of meditation, contemplation, and Hatha Yoga. I had become interested in psychology aided significantly by the *Collected Works of Jung*, mythology, Eastern philosophy, works on certain mystical and parapsychological phenomena, e.g., Edgar Cayce, the Seth books by Jane Roberts, Swedenborg, plus various other works and authors concerned with human spiritual and psychological possibilities.

By the time I was well into writing up my findings, I realized that the statement of Dr. Jung that offended me was not necessarily meant by him to cast aspersions on the Bible. I did not realize at the time I took offense and accepted a personal challenge from him that he himself had grappled with the Book of Revelation and had published his thoughts in *Answer to Job*. When I realized this, I understood that his comments could have been an expression of his own exasperation at making sense of this most enigmatic book. But by this time the "damage" had been done, and it was impossible to turn back.

Once I began to make some inroad into Revelation, I realized that my new adventure was already foreseen at a preconscious level. Just a few days before I discovered the "offending" statement in Jung's autobiography, I had had a dream that served to alert me to the significance of what I was to discover about the Book of

Revelation. In my dream, I was showing a companion some framed, color photographs that I had taken. I was very excited by my own handiwork and moreso by the brilliance of the colors and the life-like appearance of the images in the photographs. As I continued to look at the pictures, I gave in to a wave of exuberance and thought: "What a good photographer I am!" I was overwhelmed by the three-dimensional characteristics of the pictures and found that element more interesting than any other. The more I looked at the pictures, the more they seemed like a miniature, three-dimensional world. I turned to my companion and said proudly, "I took these pictures in a dream." Having said this, my jubilation changed to puzzlement as this thought formed and dominated my consciousness: "How can I take pictures of scenes in a dream unless the dream itself is real?" It was in this state of puzzlement that I awoke.

It was only after my excursion into the mystery of Revelation began to bear fruit, that the meaning of my dream became clear to me. It occurred to me that the Book of Revelation was a "dream" of sorts—I was now engaged in taking "pictures" and "framing" them in the contemporary language of the psychology of transformation. It also became evident that what Revelation presents to us is the *Real* side of life—the side that is hidden from our physical senses. Thus, to get a grasp on the principles that are embodied in its symbolism and give expression to them in contemporary terms is indeed an act of taking pictures from a dream, a "dream" that just happens to be *Real*.

I find it necessary to be cautious here and quickly add that I am not claiming "revelation status" for the insights that I am now sharing in this work. The dream I refer to was only a way of alerting me to the insights that were soon to result from my persistent enquiry into Revelation. If I could attribute this work to any single, personal characteristic, it would be the eclecticism that I have espoused with regard to spiritual matters. It was this that was bearing fruit.

Now, I would like to explain how I approached the task of interpreting the symbols in Revelation. First, I approached it with an open mind—a mind free of all preconceived ideas as to what its many symbols mean. My approach to these symbols was to not attempt an interpretation as they were encountered. Indeed, it was not my objective to find a one-to-one correspondence between each symbol and something in the outer world, but to find meaning in the sense of personal relevance.

Second, as my understanding about Revelation was emerging at a feeling level, I "measured" this against all my beliefs and against all that I held as Truth. As a consequence, I had to modify some of my previously held beliefs. At the same time, my own sense of Truth—i.e., what I had already proven by experience to be Truth—helped to guide my enquiry by providing me with parallels, similarities, and correspondences between the symbols in Revelation and systems of knowledge beside Christianity.

Third, as my understanding of Revelation's message increased at an integral level, I was able to place an interpretation on individual symbols. For me, this ensured that the individual symbols take their meaning from the overall message of Revelation rather than vice versa. This is where my knowledge of astrological/zodiacal symbolism proved valuable. In its application to Revelation, astrology provides us with the symbolic system to decode its language. It enables us to translate from a setting involving time and events to the timeless setting dealing with principles.

Without the key that astrology provides, the information Revelation presents to us will appear distorted when we attempt to interpret it in terms of our familiar logic. We will become baffled looking for explanations that make sense to us and that are compatible with our understanding of life as we experience it. Success at interpreting Revelation will elude us until we change our perspective from a temporal to a spatial one. With such a change of perspective, we will find Revelation to be more of a multitiered map of the human soul or psyche, rather than as a scenario of future world events. As such, it is a window on the journey of the soul. By "soul," I do not mean some fixed entity, but an arena of existence where the purpose of human life and the metaphysical causes of human problems and conflicts become apparent—or "visible."

Once we make this shift in perspective, we are able to understand Revelation's message in relation to ourselves. Where previously we were satisfied to interpret its symbolism and concepts as part of an independent whole without personal relevance, we can now recognize ourselves in these symbols and thus establish a direct relationship with them. Not only that, but as we see ourselves reflected here, we become able to deepen this relationship with that which we seek to understand. This deepening takes place because Revelation consists of several overlays, each of which has to be conceptually peeled off before we get its full message. As we do so, we are brought face to face with hidden aspects of our own nature. Eventually, this relationship goes beyond the level of intellectual understanding to the core of our sense of subjective identity. Through this process, a marriage of the conscious and unconscious aspects of the psyche is effected.

It is my belief that Revelation was produced and written with the purpose of leaving a record of spiritual initiation of a Christian genre. An initiation is a direct experience of what life is about behind the surface level of consciousness, and in a sense, it is an encounter with the various hidden aspects of our nature and *Real*ity. Initiations serve to lead us to wholeness by presenting us with the opportunity to reclaim those parts of ourselves that have been repressed, whether consciously or unconsciously. This is the sense in which an understanding of Revelation serves as an *initiation*, because, in bringing its message down to the level of personal relevance, it leads to a fundamental change in the way we perceive and relate to Ultimate Reality.

As a final word, I would like to assure the reader that for he/she to derive full benefit from the information provided in this book, it is not a prerequisite that he/she believe in the efficacy or appropriateness of astrology. It is sufficient that the framework that astrology provides enables us to derive meaning and relevance out of the heretofore difficult to understand world of Revelation and place it in a contemporary setting.

Chapter 1

The Book of Revelation:
A Window on the Soul

Overview

The Book of Revelation has earned itself the epithet, "The Apocalypse"—a term that literally means "the end"—because it has been thought by many people to offer a preview of the events leading up to the end of the world. Revelation does indeed deal with "the end," but not in the historical sense of the word. Its sense of "end" has to do with a change of relationship—a reorientation from a temporal and ephemeral frame of reference to one that is spatial and eternal. Revelation is a window, offering a "behind the scenes" view of the forces and processes that give the life impulse in mankind its psychological and cultural expression. As such, it is an exposé on the journey of the soul, that arena of existence where the metaphysical causes of human problems and conflicts become apparent—or "visible."

The information Revelation presents to us has an order and logic of its own that gives it an "other worldliness." If we try to interpret this information in terms of our familiar logic, it will appear distorted. We will become baffled looking for explanations that make sense to us, that are compatible with our understanding of life as we experience it. Success at interpreting Revelation will elude us until we change our perspective from a linear or temporal one to a spatial one. With this change, we will find Revelation to be a map of the multilayered structure of the human soul or psyche, rather than a scenario of future world events.

A spatial perspective allows us to understand Revelation's message in relation to ourselves. Where previously we were satisfied to interpret its symbolism and concepts as part of an autonomous whole without personal relevance, we can now recognize ourselves in these symbols and thus establish a direct relationship with them. Not only that, but as we see ourselves reflected here, we become able to deepen this relationship with what we seek to understand. This deepening takes place because Revelation consists of several overlays, each of which has to be conceptually peeled off before we get its full message. As we do so, we are brought face to face with hidden aspects of our own nature. Eventually, this relationship goes beyond the level of intellectual understanding to the core of our sense of subjective identity. Through this process, a marriage of the conscious and unconscious aspects of the psyche is effected.

Astrology as a Key to Interpreting Revelation

Astrology assists us in changing our perspective on life from a linear or temporal one to a spatial one. It helps us to understand the impulses that cause us to act and express ourselves in our characteristic ways. With knowledge of this kind we are better able to relate the events in our lives to their hidden causes—i.e., causes as they exist in subconscious impulses and tendencies—and therefore, are better able to see ourselves in the context of causes and effects.

We should exercise some caution by realizing that the application of astrology to Revelation does not mean that whatever goes by the title of astrology today is compatible with the spiritual understanding of it. For example, astrology, as it is found in the horoscope section of most daily newspapers, represents a most degenerate exploitation of the discipline. Unlike these "horoscopes," serious astrology does not deal primarily with the prediction of events in one's life—much less that one-twelfth of the world's population can be accurately portrayed by any one prediction! It is not that prediction of this sort is not useful. When it does take place, it is useful in assisting the individual to become alert to the cyclical opportunities for growth. By taking advantage of these opportunities, by striking while the iron is hot, as the saying goes, one becomes better able to participate in the advancement of his or her consciousness.

Naturally, the spiritual quality of astrology varies with the spiritual development of the one who set him/herself up as the astrologer, just as in psychology or psychiatry. Just as in these disciplines, too, the therapist can only help others in relation to his or her own psychological development. Similarly, we find various schools of astrology, some even carrying names that closely resemble those of the various schools of psychology: humanistic astrology, conventional astrology (which is expressed mainly as character analysis and closely parallels industrial psychology), cosmobiology, harmonic astrology, gestalt astrology, and so on.

Standing head and shoulders above these brands of astrology is an approach that regards the discipline in "its highest and truest function in human affairs." For an insight into how this type of astrology is practiced, we turn to an exposition provided by Dane Rudhyar. This individual has been credited, more than any other, with the reformulation of many astrological ideas so that the disciple could keep pace with the growing psychological needs of mankind. He says:

Astrology, in so far as it is based on astronomical data, deals also with objective time and its cycles. But astrology is not merely a study of celestial cycles in themselves; it is a technique of interpretation of the meaning of these cycles with reference to the possibilities for growth in individuals. It does not aim merely at telling what will happen at a definite moment of objective time. Its essential purpose—when true to its highest and truest function in human affairs—is to indicate the possibilities for individual development inherent in the significant turning points in the cycle of human life....

He continues:

Astrology can be understood as a technique for the discovery of one's own individual structure of being. And this structure is the foundation of individual immortality; for immortality is the power to dwell in a world of one's individual making, and to hold the structure of that world intact (and one's creative thought-powers firmly established within it), even against the shock of the disintegration of the biological organism, which we call death. Immortality is the victory of subjective duration over objective time. It is the triumph of the consciousness of being a whole with a unique identity over the consciousness of being merely a part of the human species subject to generic and social patterns of living and behavior.[1]

If we were to translate Rudhyar's expressions into terms that are more familiar, we would say that astrology represents a set of techniques that can allow an individual to gain some objective knowledge about himself and, on the basis of that objective knowledge, dedicate himself to a program of growth and expanding consciousness. In other words, with such knowledge about oneself as is obtained from astrological analysis, a person can come to know his or her individual life purpose and how to fully utilize the powers available to make this purpose a reality.

The Astrological Evidence

The first proving ground for the application of astrological understanding in Revelation is the fourth chapter where John is taken by an angel to the "Throne Room" in Heaven. Here, he finds the "Lamb," a symbol for Christ, on the throne surrounded by a host of attendants. These attendants are described as four "Beasts" and twenty-four gold-crowned "elders." The four Beasts are described in the King James version of the Bible as a Lion, a Calf, a Man, and an Eagle. These symbols, when found together, represent that grouping of zodiacal signs known as the "fixed quality," namely, Leo (Lion), Taurus (Bull), Aquarius (Man), and Scorpio (Eagle).

We will now turn to the fourth chapter of Revelation where the scene is described:

> *After this I looked, and, behold, a door was opened in heaven: and the first voice which I heard was as it were of a trumpet talking with me; which said, Come up hither, and I will show thee things which must be hereafter.*
>
> *And immediately I was in the spirit; and, behold, a throne was set in heaven, and one sat on the throne.*
>
> *And he that sat was to look upon like a jasper and a sardine stone; and there was a rainbow around about the throne, in sight like unto an emerald.*
>
> *And round about the throne were four and twenty seats; and upon the seats I saw four and twenty elders sitting, clothed in white raiment; and they had on their heads crowns of gold.*
>
> *And out of the throne proceeded lightnings and thunderings and voices; and there were seven lamps of fire burning before the throne, which are the seven Spirits of God.*
>
> *And before the throne there was a sea of glass like unto crystal: and, in the midst of the throne, and round about the throne, were four beasts full of eyes before and behind.*
>
> *And the first beast was like a lion, and the second beast like a calf, and the third beast had a face as a man, and the fourth beast was like a flying eagle.*
>
> *And the four beasts had each of them six wings about him; and they were full of eyes within: and they rest not day and night, saying, Holy, holy, holy, Lord God Almighty, which was, and is, and is to come.* Rev. 4:1–8

The presence of these four Beasts in Revelation is more than coincidental. They are also found in the Old Testament book of Ezekiel. There the prophet Ezekiel relates a vision in which images appeared to him featuring a Man, a Lion, an Ox, and an Eagle.

> *Now it came to pass in the thirtieth year, in the fourth month, as I was among the captives by the river Chebar, that the heavens were opened, and I saw visions of God.*
>
> *In the fifth day of the month, which was the fifth year of King Jehoiachim's captivity, the word of the Lord came*

expressly unto Ezekiel the priest, the son of Buzi, in the land of the Chaldeans by the river Chebar; and the hand of the Lord was there upon him.

And I looked, and behold, a whirlwind came out of the north, a great cloud, and a fire infolding itself and a brightness was about it, and out of the midst thereof as the colour of amber, out of the midst of the fire.

Also out of the midst thereof came the likeness of four living creatures. And this was their appearance; they had wings ...

As for the likeness of their faces, they four had the face of a man, and the face of a lion, on the right side; and they four had the face of an ox, on the left side, they four also had the face of an eagle. Ezekiel 1:1–6, 10

It should be noted that except for the substitution of "calf" for "ox" in the King James version, the arrangement of these four Beasts in Revelation is identical to that found in Ezekiel. The Revised Standard version uses "ox" for both the Revelation and Ezekiel versions.

As mentioned before, these four "Beasts"—the Lion, the Bull (or Ox), the Man, and the Eagle—are symbols used in astrology to represent the zodiacal signs of Leo, Taurus, Aquarius, and Scorpio. This arrangement is demonstrated in Figure 1-1.

The symbols for Taurus, Aquarius, and Scorpio may sometimes show very slight variations in astrological usage, but their essential characteristics remain unchanged. For example, Taurus is referred to as the Bull, Aquarius as the Water Bearer—a human figure—and Scorpio as an Eagle—though Scorpio is sometimes represented by both the Eagle and the Scorpion or the Scorpion alone. The Scorpion symbol is the lower psychic expression of Scorpio, while the Eagle is the higher. Astrologers who are spiritually oriented regard the energy of Scorpio as symbolically represented by the Eagle. For example, Manly P. Hall, in his book *The Secret Teachings of All Ages*, says:

Probably the rarest form of Scorpio is that of an Eagle. The arrangement of the stars of the constellation bears as much resemblance to a flying bird as to a scorpion. Scorpio, being the sign of occult initiation, the flying eagle—the king of birds—represents the highest and most spiritual type of Scorpio, in which it transcends the venomous insect of the earth.[2]

Similar thoughts about the relationship of the Eagle, as a symbol to Scorpio, are expressed by Elisabeth Haich in her book *Initiation*. She writes:

The sign of the Scorpion-Eagle represents the great turning point when the

12 MEDITATIONS ON THE APOCALYPSE

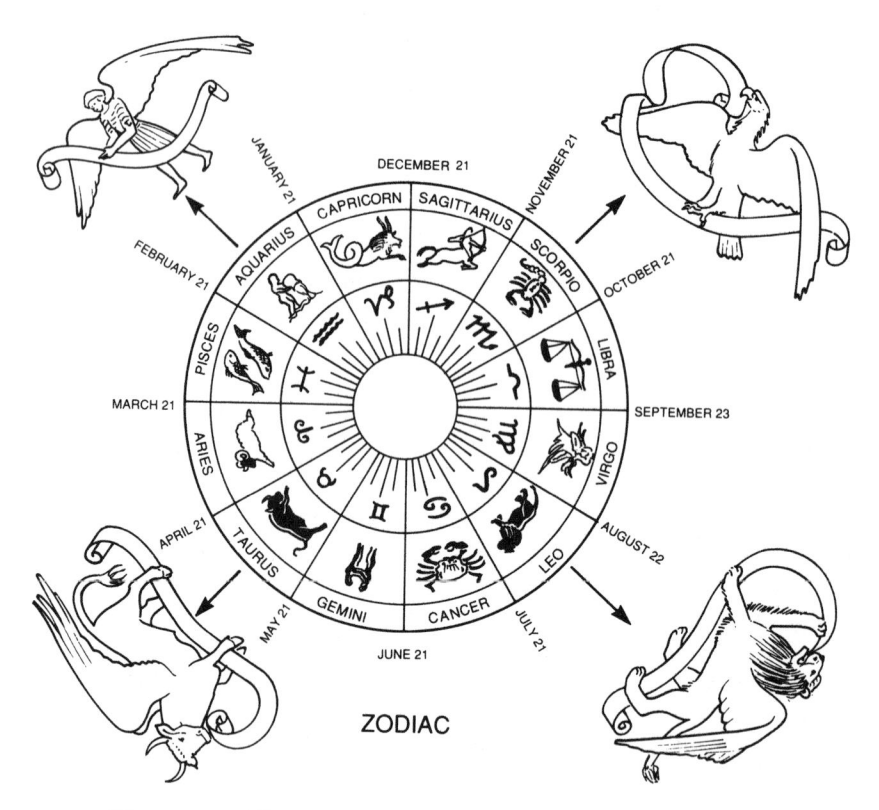

Figure 1.1 *The Four "Beasts"*

crawling worm is transformed into a high-flying eagle, redeemed, a being that has awakened and become conscious in the divine self. The worm—Scorpion—must kill itself in order to become an eagle. That's why this constellation has a double name. In its unredeemed condition it is called Scorpion after the animal that can kill itself with its own sting; in its redeemed condition it is called Eagle, symbolizing the free soul flying high above the material world like the divine falcon, Horus.[3]

The appearance of these four zodiacal (or astrological) symbols in Revelation and Ezekiel means that Christianity is sharing a religious motif common to the Wisdom Traditions of Egypt and Babylon. For example, the Lion, Bull, Man, and Eagle comprise the body of the Sphinx found at the entrance of the Great Pyramid of Giza—a pyramid considered to have functioned as a place of *initiation* into the mysteries of the soul. The Sphinx is composed of the head of a *Man*, the body of a *Bull*, the claws of a *Lion*, and the wings of an *Eagle*.

The Four "Beasts" as Interpreted by Christian Theologians

Despite the obvious astrological implication of the four Beasts, most Bible commentators, ancient and modern, fail to acknowledge their astrological connection. Indeed, they go to extreme lengths to invent other associations. According to theologian William Barclay[4], about A.D. 170. Irenaeus an early Christian theologian held that the four Beasts represented four aspects of the work of Jesus Christ, which in turn were represented by the four Gospels: Matthew, Mark, Luke, and John. Barclay also states that this association was assumed by later theologians such as Athanasus, Victorius, and Augustine. However, they differed as to which evangelist—as they called the writers of the Gospels—was represented by which Beast.

Regrettably, on the basis of one man's inference, the association of the four Beasts with the Gospels has come to be taken for granted. For example, no fewer than thirty references to this association are made in *The Collected Works of C. G. Jung*.[5] The works of other less-renowned writers, Elisabeth Haich's *Sexual Energy and Yoga*[6] for instance, are permeated with this association as well. Yet it is difficult to see what significance one can draw from associating the four Beasts with the four Gospels. Far from casting more light on the matter, such an interpretation obscures the continuity of underlying psychic experience between various religious traditions—a continuum that both the Ezekiel and Revelation texts hint at.

It is noteworthy that the book of Ezekiel, in which these symbols first occur in the Bible, is historically placed at about 593. B.C.[7] By this time, the symbols of the Lion, the Bull, the Man, and the Eagle, taken together, were already well-established symbols of Babylonian astrology. This is corroborated by archeological findings. In a book, which discusses some of the high points of archeological discoveries, C. W. Ceram mentions the discovery of a winged lion among the highlights of the archeological excavations at the palace of King Assurnasirpal II (884–859 B.C.) at Nimrud (Mesopotamia). In his effort to place this discovery in perspective, he tells us:

Today we know the figures represented one of the four astral gods that were identified with the four cardinal points of the compass. According to the Assyr-

14 MEDITATIONS ON THE APOCALYPSE

ian tradition, *Marduk was shown as a winged bull, Nebo as a human being, Nergal as a winged lion, and Ninib as an eagle.*[8] [emphasis added]

These "astral gods," as Ceram calls them, were not associated with the four cardinal points of the compass. What they represented to the Babylonians is how we also refer to them—the four Fixed signs of the zodiac. Thus, we find at about 900 B.C. that symbols, which were later to play a part in both the Hebrew and Christian scripture, already were infused with astrological meaning. This is certainly not a case of a Christian or a Hebrew symbol being adopted into alien customs. Neither is it a case of the rehabilitation of the symbols by these later religions, but rather a show of common origin.

Other Layers of Knowledge in Revelation

Once we become wise to the astrological information in Revelation, we can access the other layers of information that constitute its message. This means that astrology is not the final resting place for our attention. It, however, makes it possible for us to get at the psychology and philosophy hidden by astrological and other symbolism.

The information provided in this book follows an organizational structure based on the various systems of knowledge used to encode the Revelation message. First, we have most of the first six chapters which can be regarded as an astrological overlay, dealing mainly with symbols occurring in the fourth and eleventh chapters of Revelation. Next, we have chapters six and seven, which qualify as psychological overlay, dealing with the psychic processes that "call the tune" to the expression of human life on earth. Third, chapters eight and nine qualify as the geographical overlay dealing with the principles embodied by the "seven Churches" in Asia—Ephesus, Smyrna, Pergamum, Sardis, Thyatira, Laodicea, and Philadelphia.

Next, we have what qualifies as a philosophical overlaying explaining the contents of the letters to the seven Churches found in the first three chapters of Revelation. Finally, we have the last two chapters which assist us in putting in place all the pieces of the jigsaw puzzle that constitutes Revelation. This section helps us to appreciate the overall structure of Revelation itself and how it connects to the overall Christian message.

Chapter 2

Astrological Symbolism in the Bible

Christian Opposition to Astrology

It is recorded that when the seventeenth-century astronomer, Dr. Halley, after whom Halley's Comet is named, remarked to Sir Isaac Newton, who is long recognized as the father of modern physics, that he did not believe in astrology, Newton rebuked him with the statement, "You have not studied the subject, sir; I have."[1]

We might say with some impunity that many Christians condemn astrology because they have not studied it, but the answer lies deeper than that. For the many Christians, who base their faith on the Bible, it is generally believed that astrology is condemned in it. However, in addition to misinformation Christians receive about astrology, they also are unaware, first, of the vein of astrological symbolism running through Judaism—Christianity's mother religion—and second, of the very rich astrological grounding on which Christianity itself was founded. These strong elements of astrology in Judaism and Christianity are confirmed by the evidence to be found in both the Old and New Testaments.

Astrological References in the Old Testament

In the Old Testament, in the many references to astrologers, star-gazers, and "dividing of the heavens," there is none that is critical of astrology as a discipline. Some of these references are often wrongly used by Christians to support their idea that astrology is condemned in the Bible. We must examine the full context of the more well-known biblical references to astrology in order to see them in a different light.

For example, let us look at Isaiah 47:13–14:

> *Thou art wearied in the multitude of thy counsels. Let now the astrologers, the stargazers, the monthly prognosticators,*

> *stand up, and save thee from these things that shall come upon thee.*
>
> *Behold, they shall be as stubble; the fire shall burn them; they shall not deliver themselves from the power of the flame: there shall not be a coal to warm at, nor fire to sit before it.*

When we examine the context within which this pronouncement is made, we will see that this is not a condemnation of astrology per se. The context of this pronouncement finds Isaiah prophesying about the "daughters of the Chaldeans." He criticizes their pursuit of pleasure—"thou that art given to pleasure, that dwellest carelessly"—and their misuse of knowledge—"Thy wisdom and thy knowledge, it hath perverted thee; and thou hast said in thine heart I am, and none else beside me" (47:8, 10). The condemnation, therefore, is not because the Chaldeans practiced astrology, but because of an overall approach to life that was inappropriate. In other words, to the extent that the Chaldeans used their "astrologers, stargazers, and monthly prognosticators" to support a decadent lifestyle, they were misusing astrology. It is to this misuse that the condemnation is directed.

In the book of Daniel, we find three instances where the powers of "the wisemen, the astrologers, the magicians, the soothsayers" were pitted against the powers of God as represented in the prophet Daniel. This group was sometimes referred to as "the astrologers, the magicians, and the Chaldeans." In two of these instances, the astrologers, the magicians, and the Chaldeans were called upon to give interpretations of King Nebuchadnezzar's dreams. In the other, they were called upon to decipher the writings which appeared on the wall of King Belshazzar's dining room.

In each instance, Daniel triumphed and proved that the power of prophecy is greater than powers achieved through learning. But this is not to say that astrology, along with the other divinatory practices were shown to be ineffectual. The truth of the matter is that the astrologers, magicians, and Chaldeans were being cast out of their own element. They were asked to produce results in an area other than that of their expertise. The exasperated Chaldeans showed this in their protests: "... There is not a man upon the earth that can show the king's matter; therefore there is no king, lord, or ruler, that asked such things of any magician, or astrologer, or Chaldean" (Daniel 2:10). Daniel himself conceded this: "... The secret which the king hath demanded cannot the wise men, the astrologers, the magicians, the soothsayers shew unto the king; But there is a God in heaven that revealeth secrets" (Daniel 2:27-28).

On a deeper level, zodiacal symbolism is found in the names and characteristics attributed to the twelve sons of Jacob—later to become the heads of the twelve tribes of Israel. The same has also been attributed to the twelve precious stones on the breastplate of the Hebrew high priest. Commenting on this relationship of Hebrew ceremonial life to zodiacal symbolism, Clement of Alexandria (A.D. 153–217)—recognized as one of the early fathers of the Christian—says:

> Now the high priest's robe is the symbol of the world of sense. The seven planets are represented by the five stones and the two carbuncles, for Saturn and the Moon ... The three hundred and sixty bells, suspended from the robe, is the space of a year, "the acceptable year of the Lord," proclaiming and resounding the stupendous manifestation of the Savior ...
>
> The twelve stones, set in four rows on the breast, describe for us the circle of the zodiac, in the four changes of the year.[2]

Thus, it should come as no surprise that mosaics representing the zodiac have been used to decorate certain synagogues. An entry in *The Interpreter's Dictionary of the Bible* states,

> Cosmic symbolism also penetrated Jewish worship in Palestine and elsewhere to an amazing degree in the third to sixth centuries A.D., as the synagogues which date to this period show. The zodiac, the four seasons, and Helios often occupy a central position in floor mosaics and appear in other ways in synagogue decorations.[3]

The practice of using astrological motifs was picked up by the early Christians, who modified the symbolism somewhat and substituted apostles for zodiacal signs. Even then, the zodiacal flavor remained. Remarking on this fact, Cardinal Jean Danielou, one of the contributors to the collective work, *The Crucible of Christianity*, wrote:

> The Christians brought the development of the zodiac-month-patriarchs equation to its culmination, transferring it from the floor to the dome, which was particularly suited to this subject.[4]

He then cited examples where this was evident.

Lest the early Christians be regarded as "copycats," adopting practices the significance of which they knew little, it should be pointed out that there is doctrinal precedence for this sympathetic regard for astrology. On this score, we gain some insight from the writings of Clement of Rome, another of the early "church fathers" and one who claimed to be third in the line of succession from Peter. Clement pointed out the allegorical relationship between the zodiac and Jesus and his apostles. He wrote: "There is only one prophet and we,

Figure 2.1 *Woodcut Depicting the Zodiac*

the twelve apostles, proclaim his word. It is he who is 'the acceptable year' and we, the apostles are the twelve months.'"[5]

Clement of Rome's association of Jesus and the apostles with the zodiac in no way represented a departure or an aberration from the underlying theological roots of Christianity. There is good precedence in the New Testament for the incorporation of astrological ideas into the expression of Christian beliefs.

Astrology in the New Testament

Setting aside for the moment the astrology–Revelation linkages being explored in this book, we can soon see that the Gospel of Matthew is rife with zodiacal/astrological symbolism. The most significant instance is the one already alluded to by Clement of Rome —the similarity of the relationship between Jesus and his twelve apostles to the zodiac and its twelve signs. The pattern of the relationship between Jesus and his apostles was one in which the twelve apostles each represented one of the zodiacal signs, with Jesus being the point of integration of all of these. Evidence for this connection is found in the meanings of the names of the apostles; each of these names shows affinities with the characteristics of the different zodiacal signs. A listing of the names of the original twelve apostles is found in the tenth chapter of Matthew, verses 2–4:

> *Now the names of the twelve apostles are these; the first Simon, who is called Peter, and Andrew his brother; James the son of Zebedee and John his brother;*
>
> *Philip and Bartholomew, Thomas and Matthew the publican; James the son of Alphaeus, and Lebbaes whose surname was Thaddaeus;*
>
> *Simon the Canaanite, and Judas Iscariot, who also betrayed him.*

The etymological meanings of most of the names can be obtained from Bible reference works such as Dr. Young's *Analytical Concordance to the Holy Bible* and the aforementioned *Interpreter's Dictionary of the Bible*. The insights such works provide can be supplemented with references to characteristics of some of the apostles as they are reported in the Gospels. Table 2-1 presents a list of the apostles' names and their meanings, together with the astrological signs they represent.

Some of the characteristics and events surrounding some of the apostles help in achieving their proper allocation on the zodiac. For example, the group of Peter, James, and John always accompanied Jesus. These three apostles represented the Fixed signs of the zodiac —one of the three groups into which the signs are arranged. The Fixed signs are Leo, Aquarius, Taurus, and Scorpio. Although Andrew relates to Leo, he was supplanted by Jesus himself for ceremonial reasons. Jesus was fulfilling his symbolic role as "lion of the tribe of Juda" (Revelation 5:5) and Son of God. The sign of Leo is symbolized by the lion and its "planetary ruler" is the sun.

Another aspect of the association of apostles and astrological signs is that it helps to explain the extreme care taken by the writers of the gospels to list the names of the apostles in a certain order. The names are given in pairs, but the true significance of their order lies in their arrangements in groups of four. This is done to reflect the signs according to their "Quality," a concept explained in Chapter Three. For example, let us look at the previously quoted second to fourth verses of the tenth chapter of Matthew.

> *Now the names of the twelve apostles are these; the first Simon, who is called Peter, and Andrew his brother; James the son of Zebedee and John his brother;*   10:2

Table 2-1. Apostles' Names and Their Meaning

Apostle	Meaning of Name	Zodiacal Sign
Simon Peter	Simon means "hearing" and Peter means "rock." To hear from rock, intuition	Aquarius, the Water Bearer
Andrew	Means "manly," strong	Leo, the Lion
James and John	No specific meanings in the names, but they were "sons of thunder" by Jesus. With Peter and Andrew, they completed the "four corners" of the zodiac	Taurus, the Bull Scorpio, the Eagle
Philip	"Lover of horses"	Sagittarius, the Centaur
Bartholomew[6]	"Furrowed, ready for seed"	Virgo, the Virgin
Thomas	Name means "twin"	Gemini, the Twins
Matthew	Name means "joined"	Pisces, the Joined Fishes
James, the son of Alphaeus	Alphaeus means "chief"	Aries, the Ram
Lebbaeus Thaddaeis	Name means "man of heart" and "breast nipple"	Cancer, the Crab
Simon the Canaanite	The term "Canaanite" does not refer to a place, but to the Aramaic term for "zealot, enthusiast"[7]	Libra, the Balances
Judas Iscariot	Name hard to place, but Judas was the money holder, the "business man"	Capricorn, the Goat

These four, Peter, Andrew, James, and John, represent the zodiacal signs of the Fixed Quality—Aquarius, Leo, Taurus, and Scorpio.

> *Philip and Bartholomew, Thomas and Matthew the publican*
> *...*
> 10:3

These four, Philip, Bartholomew, Thomas, and Matthew, represent the four Mutable signs of the zodiac—Sagittarius, Virgo, Gemini, and Pisces.

> *James the son of Alphaeus, and Lebbaeus whose surname was Thaddaeus;*
>
> *Simon the Canaanite, and Judas Iscariot, who also betrayed him*
> 10:3-4

These last four, James (son of Alphaeus), Lebbaeus Thaddaeus, Simon the Canaanite, and Judas Iscariot, represent the four Cardinal signs of Aries, Cancer, Libra, and Capricorn.

Before we resume our task of deciphering Revelation, we shall take a look at some of the technical factors behind astrology. This exercise will assist those of us who have not had a previous acquaintance with astrology. With this information we will be able to more easily follow along as we uncover the astrological information found in Revelation.

Chapter 3

Basic Concepts of Astrology

The Zodiac and the Twelve Signs

The zodiac and the twelve astrological signs are the most basic concepts in astrology. They are also the concepts most essential to an overall grasp of astrological symbolism. It is necessary that we are aware of the differences between the concepts of the *zodiac* and the *twelve astrological signs*. The zodiac is an *astronomical* concept, while the twelve signs into which it is divided is an *astrological* concept.

Although astronomy and astrology have a common historical origin in the study of the same heavenly phenomena, the difference between the two is that astronomy is concerned with probing the physical nature of the universe while astrology goes further by drawing inferences for human existence on earth from the observed movements and positions of planets and stars. In other words, astrology interprets the *movements* of the planets and the *positions* of the "fixed" stars in relation to these moving planets. The twelve signs get their names from the constellations of "fixed"—the stars are "fixed" in relation to the planets that orbit the sun—found in the zodiac belt. However, when astrologers refer to any of the signs, this reference generally does not correspond to the stars as such, but to a geometric grid superimposed on the zodiac belt, which divides it into twelve equal parts.

The zodiac is that area of the sky forming the background against which the sun is observed in apparent yearly motion. The effect of the earth's yearly motion around the sun is that the sun is seen against a background of stars that is always changing. This apparent path of the sun against the stars is called the *ecliptic*.

From any point of view on the earth, the zodiac encircles it. Thus, to have accurate points of reference on the ecliptic, degrees are used. The zodiac therefore measures 360 degrees, just as any circle, and its division into twelve equal segments, called *signs*, means that each sign is 30-degrees wide.

Basic Sign Characteristics

It is customary to name the signs, beginning with the first—Aries—in a counterclockwise manner. Therefore, we have Aries, Taurus, Gemini, Cancer, Leo, Virgo, Libra, Scorpio, Sagittarius, Capricorn, Aquarius, and Pisces. The signs are classified according to three different characteristics—Element, Quality, and Polarity.

The Elements. The Elements are identified as Fire, Earth, Air, and Water, and apply to the signs in sequence. We have Aries—Fire, Taurus—Earth, Gemini—Air, Cancer—Water, and so on as the cycle repeats itself over the signs. A complete listing is provided in the Table 3-1.

Table 3-1. Classification of the Signs According to Elements, Qualities, and Polarities

Elements:	Fire	Earth	Air	Water
Polarity:	Positive	Negative	Positive	Negative
Quality:				
Cardinal	Aries	Capricorn	Libra	Cancer
Fixed	Leo	Taurus	Aquarius	Scorpio
Mutable	Sagittarius	Virgo	Gemini	Pisces

The Qualities. The Qualities are three in number—Cardinal, Fixed, and Mutable. They apply to the signs beginning with Aries as Cardinal, Taurus as Fixed, and Gemini as Mutable, after which the cycle repeats itself until all twelve signs are assigned.

Polarity. The signs are also classified into alternating polarities of Male and Female, or Positive and Negative, or Active and Passive. The specific terminology is not all that important. The factor of Polarity is applied to the signs beginning with Aries as Positive and Taurus as Negative. The rest of the signs are alternatingly Positive and Negative. The result of this assignment is that the Fire and Air signs have a Positive expression while the Earth and Water signs have a Negative expression. Reading off from the table, we get the characteristics of the signs according to the criteria listed here.

Table 3-2. The Elements and Their Correspondence in Physics and Psychology

Element	Physics	Aspect of Being	Psychology
Fire	Igneous	Ego	Striving
Earth	Solid	Body	Consolidation
Air	Vapour	Mind	Curiosity
Water	Liquid	Emotions	Feeling

The Meaning of the Elements

The idea of the four Elements refers to the four states of consciousness normally expressed by man—four psychological modes of being. There is a parallel here with the concept of the four ordinary states of matter—igneous (Fire), solid (Earth), vapour (Air), and liquid (Water). The parallel is rather apt, for although we are dealing with something rather abstract, we can relate the Elements to four levels of human functioning—Fire is related to the ego, Earth to the body, Air to the mind, and Water to the emotions.

We can go one step further and relate the Elements to four functions that arise from these four levels of functioning. The ego can be related to striving, the body to consolidation or crystallization, the mind to thinking, and the emotions to feeling. Again, it must be stressed that the exact words do not matter that much. Rather, it is the psychological reality that is important. We shall see that these Elements come up time and again in Revelation.

The four Elements have been extensively utilized in the psychology of personality assessment although the psychologists themselves may not be aware of this. In C. G. Jung's descriptions of his "psychological types," we find his four basic types to be Thinking, Feeling, Sensing, and Intuitive. Thinking is related to the Air Element, Feeling to the Water Element, Sensing to the Earth Element, and Intuitive to the Fire Element. Jung divided his four basic types into the subclasses, Introverted and Extraverted. This division has overtones in the Positive and Negative polarities we encounter in astrology.[1] The information above is summarized in the Table 3-2.

The Meaning of the Qualities

In astrology, the three Qualities—Cardinal, Fixed, and Mutable—deal with the modes of expression of consciousness.

Table 3-3. The Qualities and Their Correspondence in Physics and Psychology

Quality	Physics	Psychology
Cardinal	Motion	Initiative, Dynamism
Fixed	Rest	Control, Stabilization
Mutable	Transformation	Adaptation, Volatility

Again, we can draw an example from physics. A body can be in motion, at rest, or in a state of chemical change—i.e., transformation. The idea of the Qualities describes how man perceives Reality and responds to it. As a Quality, Cardinal has to do with dynamism—initiative, Fixed with control—stabilization, and Mutable with volatility—adaptation. (See Table 3-3.)

The Meaning of the Polarities

The Polarities deal with the way one projects oneself onto the social environment. As previously stated, they can be related to what psychology calls introversion and extraversion. With the Positive, Masculine or Active polarity, one seeks to transform the environment; with the Negative, Feminine or Passive, one accepts and works within its structures.

The Interaction of Elements, Qualities, and Polarities

As we bring these concepts together, we get some of the psychological characteristics attributed to the astrological signs. The three Qualities multiplied by the four Elements gives us the twelve signs. Table 3.1 shows how the twelve signs are derived from a cross-classification of Elements and Qualities. The result is a unique combination for each sign.

Picture Symbols for the Twelve Signs

The characteristics by which the signs are most widely identified are those relating to certain picture symbols (see Figure 3-1). These symbols have been handed down from Babylonian times and their meanings have been embellished by a vast body of mythological literature, primarily Greek and Roman in origin. It has been sug-

Table 3-4. Characteristics of the Twelve Signs

Sign	Quality	Element	Polarity
Aries	Cardinal	Fire	Positive
Taurus	Fixed	Earth	Negative
Gemini	Mutable	Air	Positive
Cancer	Cardinal	Water	Negative
Leo	Fixed	Fire	Positive
Virgo	Mutable	Earth	Negative
Libra	Cardinal	Air	Positive
Scorpio	Fixed	Water	Negative
Sagittarius	Mutable	Fire	Positive
Capricorn	Cardinal	Earth	Negative
Aquarius	Fixed	Air	Positive
Pisces	Mutable	Water	Negative

gested that the symbols, most of which are in the form of animals, are the result of early man's attempt to see meaning in the designs that the stars appeared to form in the sky. However, the psychological power of these symbols to evoke associations attests to an origin that goes deeper than mere outlines of figures detected from a glance at the heavens. Table 3-5 contains a list of the symbols, together with the glyphs, that are used to represent the signs.

The Annual Cycle of Zodiacal Signs

The other piece of astrological data that is of general interest is the time of the year when the sun "enters" each of the twelve signs (see Table 3-6). These dates are approximate and exact dates may vary from year to year. Usually, anyone wishing to know exactly when the sun has entered, or is expected to enter a sign, can consult a log of accurate astronomical data called an *ephemeris*.

Geographical Factors Behind the Derivation of the Signs

The technical nature of the material to follow is such that, normally, it might be relegated to an appendix. In this instance, however, its inclusion in the text will help to facilitate an understanding of the signs as "real" factors, not just theoretical constructions.

Although astrological signs are usually thought to relate only to time of year, there are other factors concomitant with the seasons

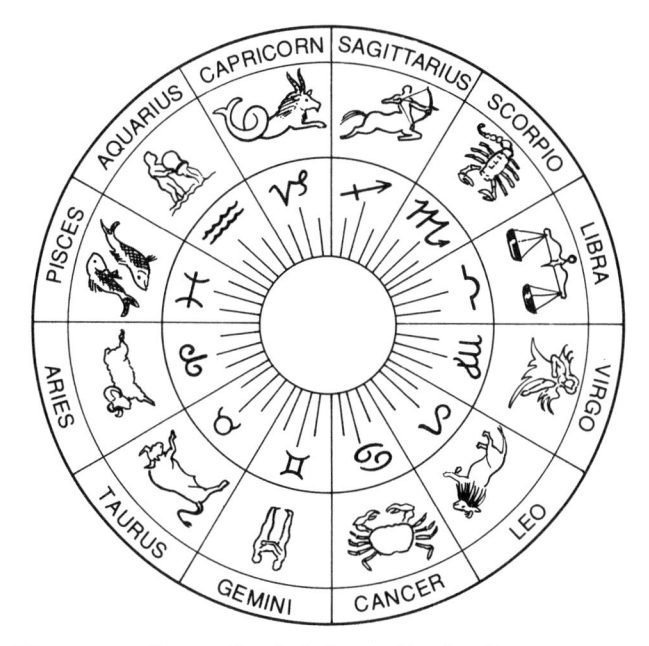

Figure 3.1 *Picture Symbols for the Twelve Signs*

that give distinctive differences to the signs. The relationship of earth to sun as the earth orbits around it is a dynamic one, not only from the perspective of the rotation of the earth and its orbital revolutions, but also because of the gyration or wobble that results from the tilt of the earth's axis. This wobble causes the earth to tilt different parts of its surface toward the sun through the course of its orbit. It is this tilting movement that lays the basis for the changes in the seasons, and therefore imparts a large measure of "reality" to the different signs.

Earth-Centered and Sun-Centered Views of the Earth–Sun Orbital Relationship

Just as two individuals observing an event from two different perspectives can each acquire a separate impression of what is going on, so it is that the earth–sun relationship can be conceptually experienced from two perspectives and represented by two different sets of data. The first view of the earth–sun relationship is a geocentric one, i.e., earth-centered, and the other heliocentric, i.e., sun-centered.

Geocentric means view obtained from the perspective of a position

28 MEDITATIONS ON THE APOCALYPSE

Table 3-5. The Picture Symbols and Glyphs of the Signs

Sign	Symbol	Glyph
Aries	The Ram	♈
Taurus	The Bull	♉
Gemini	The Twins	♊
Cancer	The Crab	♋
Leo	The Lion	♌
Virgo	The Virgin with Sheaf of Wheat	♍
Libra	The Balances	♎
Scorpio	The Eagle and Scorpion	♏
Sagittarius	The Centaur with Bow and Arrow	♐
Capricorn	The Sea Goat	♑
Aquarius	The Water Bearer	♒
Pisces	The Fishes	♓

on the earth. For example, when we talk about the sun being in this or that sign, or that the sun is at a certain point in its path on the ecliptic, we are viewing the earth–sun relationship geocentrically. Heliocentric, on the other hand, means that we are viewing things from the perspective of the sun as the reference point. When astrology is considered from a heliocentric perspective, we are able to take certain behaviors of the earth into consideration that would not be noticeable from a position on it.

To demonstrate these behavioral factors and show how they deter-

BASIC CONCEPTS OF ASTROLOGY

Table 3-6. Cycle of Zodiacal Signs

Season	Sign	Date
Spring (Equinox)	Aries	March 21st
	Taurus	April 20th
	Gemini	May 21st
Summer (Solstice)	Cancer	June 22nd
	Leo	July 23rd
	Virgo	August 24th
Fall (Equinox)	Libra	September 23rd
	Scorpio	October 24th
	Sagittarius	November 22nd
Winter (Solstice)	Capricorn	December 22nd
	Aquarius	January 20th
	Pisces	February 19th

mine the points of demarcation of the signs, it is necessary to introduce and define a few geographical and astronomical concepts.

The Celestial Sphere. This is the name given to the apparent dome of the sky. When extended in every direction, it gives the impression that the earth is enclosed in a sphere.

The Earth's Equator. This is the conceptual line going around the earth at its widest diameter. It divides the earth into two equal halves—the Northern and Southern Hemispheres.

The Ecliptic. This is the area of the sky defined by a changing background of "fixed" stars against which the sun appears to move throughout the course of the year. The ecliptic forms what may be called a "great circle." Astrologers divide the ecliptic into twelve sectors to form the zodiacal signs.

The Earth's Axis. This is the conceptual line running through the center of the earth connecting the two poles.

The Celestial Equator. This is the conceptual extension in every direction of the plane of the earth's equator onto the celestial sphere.

The Dynamic Relationship Between the Signs and Seasons

Throughout the course of the year several changes occur in the angular relationship between the plane of the earth's equator and the plane of the ecliptic. Any change that is observed in the angular relationship between these two great circles is also reflected in changes in the angle of intersection between the earth's axis and the plane of the ecliptic. This changing angular relationship determines the areas of the earth's surface where the direct rays of the sun fall, the direct rays being solar energy striking the earth's surface at a 90-degree angle.

Another result of this changing angular relationship between the ecliptic and the earth's equator is that the sun's elevation above the horizon varies over the course of the year. During periods of highest elevation in the Northern Hemisphere, the inclination of the plane of the earth's equator is such that the direct rays of the sun fall on the Tropic of Cancer, while during periods of lowest elevation, these direct rays fall on the Tropic of Capricorn—conversely, the periods of highest elevation in the Southern Hemisphere. For two periods during the year, direct rays fall on the equator, and these periods are coincidental with the plane of the equator being equal in inclination to that of the ecliptic.

The points of reference for the four seasons are also points of reference for the four Cardinal astrological signs. We might note that the seasonal reference point is a temporal concept while the zodiacal reference point is a spatial one.

> *The Spring Equinox and the Sign of Aries.* When the planes of the earth's equator and the ecliptic coincide, day and night are of equal length. This is the first day of spring, marked by the direct rays of the sun striking the earth at the region of the equator. It also marks the first point of the zodiac—zero degree of Aries. This coincidence of the earth's equator and ecliptic is called the Spring Equinox, which occurs annually about March 21st.

> *The Summer Solstice and the Sign of Cancer.* When the plane of the ecliptic is at an angle to the plane of the equator such that the direct rays of the sun strike the surface of the earth at the Tropic of Cancer, summer begins. This is also the point of maximum solar elevation in the Northern Hemisphere, giving us the longest period of daylight relative to

night. The beginning of summer marks the point on the zodiac of zero degree of Cancer and occurs about June 22nd.

The Fall Equinox and the Sign of Libra. After reaching the highest elevation in the Northern Hemisphere on June 22nd, the solar angle begins to decrease so that we arrive again at a point where the planes of the ecliptic and the equator coincide. Night and day are of equal length again. This is the point of zero degree of Libra, which occurs about September 23rd.

The Winter Solstice and the Sign of Capricorn. This is the point of lowest solar elevation in the Northern Hemisphere. The direct rays of the sun strike the earth's surface at the Tropic of Capricorn. It is the point of longest night relative to daylight in the Northern Hemisphere. It marks the beginning of winter and coincides with the sun being observed at zero degree of the sign of Capricorn. The date of this occurrence is about December 22nd.

Chapter 4

Representations of the Twelve Zodiacal Sign Energies in Revelation

The Four Beasts and the Fixed Sign Energies

We have already seen that the four Beasts occupy a central role in John's vision. They are found in attendance around the Throne that was occupied by the Lamb. In astrology, the four Fixed zodiacal signs also occupy a central role, being recognized as "the power signs of the zodiac." The energies of these four signs express themselves psychologically as the need for security (Taurus, the Bull), the need to express one's sexuality (Scorpio, the Eagle), the need to exercise personal power or will (Leo, the Lion), and the need to express one's individuality (Aquarius, the Water Bearer—represented by a human being). However, at a spiritual level, the energies of the Fixed signs are more finely tuned. Taurus energy will represent the capacity for contentment, Leo energy the capacity for will, Scorpio energy the capacity for transcendence, and Aquarius energy the capacity for expressing our humanity.

In Revelation, the energies of the Fixed signs are frequently singled out for special mention by John, who highlights the consequences that arise from their misuse. Sometimes he also shows the benefits that arise when the energies are properly applied.

The Result of Misuse of the Fixed Sign Energies

An indirect reference to the importance of the Fixed signs can be found in the lamentations of John concerning the lack of penitence by "the people of the earth" after they were subjected to the plagues released by the four angels at the sounding of the sixth trumpet:

> *And the rest of the men which were not killed by these plagues yet repented not of the works of their hands, that they should not worship devils, and idols of gold, and of silver, and brass,*

and stone, and of wood: which neither can see, nor hear, nor walk.

Neither repented they of their murders, nor of their *sorceries*, nor of their *fornication*, nor of their *thefts*.
Rev. 9:20–21

The "sins" enumerated here are not intended to be interpreted as specific deeds by an actual group of people. Rather, the sins and the events woven around them are to be regarded as conceptual structures through which deeper psychological truths can be presented.

Regarded in the light of astrology, the sins of *murder, sorcery, fornication*, and *theft* can be seen as terms for the results of the improper utilization of the energies of Leo, Aquarius, Scorpio, and Taurus, in that order. John's listing of these sins is really the enumeration of what the antithesis is, of the proper utilization of each of the Fixed sign energies.

Allocating the sins enumerated by John to the Fixed signs means that the misuse of Leo energy is "murder," of Aquarius energy "sorcery," of Scorpio energy "fornication," and of Taurus energy "theft." This scheme agrees with the descriptions astrologers give of negative expressions of the energies of Leo, Aquarius, Scorpio, and Taurus, respectively. In brief, the misuse of Leo energy may be expressed as bossiness, of Taurus energy as materialism, of Aquarius energy as subversiveness, and Scorpio energy as sexual preoccupation.

Now, let us turn our attention to the list of faults that results from a misuse of the energies of these signs as outlined by an astrological author.[1]

Faults of the Fixed Signs

Leo—"overbearing, too fixed in opinions, intolerant, autocratic, conceited, pompous, bombastic, sensual, snobbish, self appraising, patronizing"

Taurus—"too possessive, self-indulgent, stubborn, gets in a rut, stodgy, self-centered, grasping, resentful of contradiction, slavishly adherent to routine"

Aquarius—"perverse, eccentric, cranky, fanatically unconventional, touchy, rebellious, rudely tactless, lack of personal integrity and principle, too detached, erratic"

Scorpio—"brooding, resentment, jealousy, destructive, stubborn, secretive, suspicious, vindictive, capable of deliberate cruelty"

Psychological Processes That May Lead to These Faults

Leo—"the primitive urge for power Primary source of the power complex"

Taurus—"the primitive urge for organic relatedness, security, material sustenance"

Aquarius—"the primitive urge to identify oneself with the aims of the community. The impulse for reform and the establishment of human rights on the social and not individual basis."

Scorpio—"the primitive urge to identify oneself with one's source. Primarily in unconscious motive that is sought through the sexual function.... It is sex as a personal problem, the urge to be one, locked at the roots, with another human being."

Emphasis has been added to some of the above descriptions to underscore the similarity between these "faults" and the Revelation exposition of the sins of murder, sorcery, fornication, and theft. To understand the reason behind the assignment of these specific shortcomings to particular Fixed signs, we must turn to another astrological factor called the "Theme" of a sign.

The "Theme" of an astrological sign can be said to be a quality of consciousness, or a "preoccupation" with the consciousness that is unique to the sign. Theme could be said to be the default value of a sign, meaning that quality or facility of consciousness that requires the least effort to be brought into expression.

The "Themes" of the Fixed Signs

Table 4-1 presents the Themes of the four Fixed signs and shows the manner in which the Themes must be interpreted at a conscious level in order for the energy of the sign to find full expression.

Table 4-1. Themes of the Fixed Signs

Sign	Theme	Principle of Consciousness	Full Expression
Leo	"I will"	Self Expression	Creativity
Taurus	"I have"	Self Mastery	Stewardship
Aquarius	"I know"	Self Knowledge	Service
Scorpio	"I desire"	Self Transcendence	Resourcefulness

According to this table, Leo's Theme is "I will," and Leo energy, when fully expressed, gives one the capacity to demonstrate what the true meaning of will is. Its true expression, through the higher aspect of the Self, would result in creativity. But if Leo energy is expressed in such a manner that other individuals are prevented from expressing their own wills, and therefore prevented from being creative, then the individual expressing Leo energy inappropriately has in a sense "killed" them—amounting to psychic murder. Consequently, murder, in the sense that it is used in Revelation, is the misapplication of will.

For Taurus, the Theme is "I have," and the unconscious expression of its energy is the mastery of matter. The Theme of Taurus is fully expressed as stewardship or management. If Taurus energy is interpreted in the psyche to mean that matter is everything, the result will be bondage to materiality—instead of mastery—and insecurity with respect to money and material possessions. Such might lead to overaccumulation. In the world of Revelation, such overaccumulation is regarded as misappropriation and therefore theft. This subservience to materiality is also regarded as idolatry.

With respect to Aquarius energy, the Theme is "I know." This suggests that the energy of Aquarius is fully expressed in the utilization of intuition or wisdom. Aquarius energy belongs to that aspect of consciousness that tunes one in to mysteries not readily accessed through rational thought. This privilege must be properly reciprocated by the one so blessed using the energy at his disposal to inspire those who are not so attuned. If Aquarius energy is not used to serve but to create a sense of superiority and unconventionality, there is a subversion of understanding. Rather than serving the purpose of inspiration, the knowledge is used to obscure. Perhaps this is what John means by sorcery: the use of Higher knowledge for nonconstructive ends.

The Theme of Scorpio is "I desire," suggesting concentration and transcendence. The energy of Scorpio also can be expressed as the power of "libido" which, despite its sexual connotation, is really the capacity for sustained attention. Libido is the power that lies at the root of all manifestations of resourcefulness. When the power of concentration or libido is misused, the result is "fornication" or an ill-advised discharge of personal energy through an illicit union. The misapplication of this power may literally take the form of sexual promiscuity, but its most general misuse is in terms of placing attention in the wrong place. When fully expressed, the energy of Scorpio resolves itself in the impulse to transcend one's current situation and state of existence.

The Energies of the Four Mutable Signs as Featured in the Four Horsemen

The next group of signs, for which Revelation has provided an expose of the workings of their energies, are those of the Mutable category. They are Sagittarius, Virgo, Gemini, and Pisces. This expose is provided in Chapter Six of Revelation. Unfortunately, the popular interpretation of the four Horsemen usually misses the symbolism involved, leading individuals to see portents of tribulation where they should see psychological truths. Here is the reference to the Horsemen:

And I saw when the Lamb opened one of the seals, and I heard, as it were the noise of thunder, one of the four beasts saying, Come and see.

And I saw, and behold a white horse: *and he that sat on him had a bow; and a crown was given unto him: and he went forth conquering, and to conquer.*

And when he had opened the second *seal, I heard the* second *beast say, Come and see.*

And there went out another horse that was red: and power was given to him that sat thereon to take peace from the earth, and that they should kill one another; and there was given to him a great sword.

And when he had opened the third *seal, I heard the third beast say, Come and see. And I beheld, and lo a* black horse; *and he that sat on him had a pair of balances in his hand.*

And I heard a voice in the midst of the four beasts say, a measure of wheat for a penny, and three measures of barley for a penny; and see thou hurt not the oil and the wine.

And when he had opened the fourth *seal, I heard the voice of the* fourth *beast say, Come and see.*

And I looked, and behold a pale horse: *and his name that sat on him was Death, and Hell followed with him. And power was given unto them over the fourth part of the earth, to kill with sword, and with hunger, and with death and with the beasts of the earth.* Rev. 6:1–8

These symbols embody the characteristics of the signs of Sagittarius, Virgo, Gemini, and Pisces. However, to know which Horseman is aligned with which of these signs, we must pay careful attention to the manner in which each of the Horsemen is introduced and the different symbols used to accompany each Horseman.

First of all, each of the Horsemen is introduced by a different Beast, and these four Beasts, except for the first, are explicitly numbered two to four. This leaves us with the simple task of giving the number one to the first. The next step in interpreting the zodiacal affiliation of the Horsemen is to recall the order of the Beasts as they were first introduced, in the fourth chapter of Revelation, so that we can tell which is number one, two, three, and four.

When the Beasts were first introduced to us, number one was the *Lion* (Leo), number two was the *Calf* (Taurus), number three had a *Man's Face* (Aquarius), and number four was the *Eagle* (Scorpio). We can use this information to help determine which of the Horsemen represents which sign of the Mutable Quality.

The White Horse and Rider

The horse pointed out by the Beast representing Leo was *white* and its rider had a *bow* and a *crown*. The mission of this horseman was "to go forth to conquer." There are several symbols superimposed here.

The first is the horse, and the characteristic of it that is called upon here is its role as an *agency of mediation*. This is because a horse mediates between a person's mission and the place of discharge of that mission, in a manner of speaking. Therefore, the four Horsemen are appropriately representing the four Mutable signs, which are signs of mediation between the end goal of human striving —a spiritual orientation to life—and its antithesis, a self-centered materialism. Since this mediation between the spiritual and the material is accomplished at the level of ideas and utilizes our capacity for reasoning, the horse as a symbol can be seen to represent the faculty of the intellect.

White symbolizes primordiality rather than purity. For example, white light is primordial and only becomes visible light when broken up by a prism. When associated with a horse, white implies mediation at an advanced level. The functioning of the intellect indicated here is where one gains access to advanced knowledge. This is the process of spiritual discernment—a level of functioning where the intellect has gone beyond its known limits. By "spiritual discernment" we mean that level of understanding where we begin to understand how things fit together—where we are able to comprehend wholes, patterns, and principles.

This display of symbols representing Sagittarius is further strengthened by the bow and the crown. The bow is an instrument for extending the reach, and the crown is a symbol of dominion and rulership. The sum total of these symbols suggests a consciousness that is concerned with reaching out and expanding its own boundaries by conquering all that is perceived to be opposed to itself. This is the essence of the astrological sign of Sagittarius—the sign that is associated with higher learning, philosophy, religious fervour, law, and cultural exchanges.

The significance of this Horseman on the white horse being introduced by the Lion, the Beast that represents the sign of Leo, is that both of these signs belong to the Fire Element.

The Red Horse and Rider

The horse introduced by the second Beast, which represents Taurus, was *red*. Its rider was given a great sword, and power was given to him to kill with the sword and to take peace from the earth. The symbol of the red horse indicates that the mode of mediation between a spiritual orientation to life and self-centered materialism, in this instance, is *experience*. This is because red is the color of blood and of life in its most common expression. Such expressions as "of one blood," "blood is thicker than water," are generally used to express a certain commonality and kinship.

The symbol of the sword comes up quite frequently in Revelation, and its use here is similar to its use in the other instances where it occurs. The sword is an instrument for severing, and in this case, it is severing mankind from all the ties that bind it to the material and the ephemeral, and therefore the "false." The power of intellect, that is implied by the sword, is the power of logical, rational thinking borne out by experience. It is the representation of the analytical faculties as they are applied to practical situations.

As a symbol, the sword has another aspect too. It is an instrument with which one can "open up" mysteries so that one can know for oneself. The fact that the exposition of this Horseman was accompanied by the explanation that the sword was given to the rider that "they should kill one another" and "take peace from the earth" has led many to interpret this Horseman as a foreboding of war. It is rather naive for us to think that the expression should imply war since we cannot say that there was ever peace on the earth to begin with. Throughout all of recorded history, mankind has been at war with his neighbor. Insofar as the sword symbolizes our capacity for rational analysis, the only "peace" that it can take from the earth is complacency.

The sign of the zodiac represented by this Horseman is Virgo, credited astrologically with analyticalness, attention to detail, the healing properties of Nature, the maturing properties of time, and our capacity to reflect. It is fitting that this Horseman should be introduced by the Beast (the Bull) representing Taurus, since both of these are signs of the Earth Element.

The Black Horse and Rider

The horse pointed out by the Beast representing Aquarius was black, and its rider had a pair of balances in his hand. At the time when this horse made its appearance, a voice in the midst of the four Beasts—quite possibly the voice of the Lamb—said, "A measure of wheat for a penny, and three measures of barley for a penny; and see thou hurt not the oil and the wine."

The black horse indicates the opposite of what is implied by the white horse. We've seen earlier that the white horse represents the facility to discern patterns and principles as one of the modes in which the intellect functions. With the black horse, mediation takes place on a more practical level than spiritual discernment. The black horse symbolizes the juxtaposition of objects, the accumulation of facts, and fascination with the mundane.

The pair of balances carried by the Horseman on the black horse should not be confused with the balances that symbolize the energy of Libra. In this particular usage, the balances suggest the dynamic process that constitutes measurement—wavering, vacillation, determination of equivalents. We are therefore dealing with a change of order or a change of dimension. From the concrete reality of goods and commodities, we move to the more or less abstract domain of valuation or worth. These characteristics also sum up the manner in which the intellect functions in a questioning and speculative mode.

It is noted that the other Horsemen went about their ways without any announcements, but here, we have a voice announcing prices and suggesting caution with respect to particular commodities. This announcement suggests, in addition, awareness or bringing matters to the attention. The caution with respect to the oil and the wine suggests that the scope of the speculative mind is limited. Oil and wine represent the essences of other commodities, and symbolically speaking, they represent values. Given the skepticism and vacillation of the mind in its speculative mode, it cannot be regarded as a good judge of the more subtle domain of values.

The interpretation that fits the Horseman on the black horse sums up the basic characteristics of the sign of Gemini. In astrology, the energy of Gemini is said to express itself in the facilitation of communication and commerce. All the structures that support these functions are said to be of a Geminian character. In passing, we can say that it is appropriate that this sign should be announced by the Beast representing Aquarius (Man's face) which, with Gemini, are signs of the Air Element.

The Pale Horse and Rider, and Companion

The fourth Horseman is introduced by the Beast representing Scorpio. This horse is pale, and just as the black horse is the opposite of the white, this one is the opposite of the red. We are told the name of the rider of this horse—Death, and we are also told that Hell followed after him. Since we were not told the names of the previous riders, we have a dual symbol here, as we have the added feature of the symbols being augmented by names being given to the rider and his companion. The significance of these developments will be discussed shortly, as soon as we have dealt with our main symbol—the Horseman on the pale horse.

The pale horse signifies a method of intermediation between spirituality and ego-centered materialism that is characterized by the passive or mystical functioning of the mind—a mode where it no longer questions but witnesses and accepts. As a corollary, the description of this horse as pale implies that the life impulse has ceased. This contrasts with the red horse, the symbol for Virgo, which was used to symbolize the total involvement with life, with experiencing. Pale implies the opposite of experiencing, and in this case, it suggests the process of institutionalization. It is symbolizing a process that formalizes and settles an issue once and for all, at least that is what those who create institutions believe. The fact that the Horseman is named reinforces this theme of institutionalization. The name of Death does not imply physical death, but death of experiencing, or "ego death."

Hell, the companion who follows behind Death, seems to suggest a reinforcement to the process represented by the pale horse. It is a recurring theme in the Bible that we only gain life in its essence by consciously giving it up in its more ordinary manifestations. It is only then, it is said, that we find "True Life." By the same token, when we cling to life in its many ordinary expressions and refuse to die to the little or ego self, we become vulnerable to the real death, which is what Hell is here to symbolize. Hell, as it is used here, can be interpreted as the dispersion of one's essence such that there is an involuntary "loss of self," a process that may be accompanied by great fear.

THE TWELVE ZODIACAL SIGN ENERGIES   41

The pale horse with its rider, and their companion, together symbolize the sign of Pisces—the twelfth or last sign of the zodiac. Pisces represents the energy of dissolution, of withdrawal of the "I consciousness" and all factors that facilitate and reinforce this process. Therefore, Pisces represents the process of institutionalization. In terms of mental functioning, it is the mind that tries to give symbolic expression to that which is beyond the reach of rational analysis. It is thus the domain of the mystic, the poet, the musician, and sometimes the humorist.

Powers of the Horsemen

The powers attributed to the Horsemen are various modes of killing. This sounds ominous indeed, but only until we realize that the word "kill" is used symbolically. We shall take another look at Revelation 6:8 where the powers are set out.

> And power was given unto them over the fourth part of the earth, to kill with the sword, and with hunger, and with death, and with the beasts of the earth.

The interpretation of the various modes of killing must be made with the idea in mind that killing as used in this context is symbolic. The idea behind the use of the term "kill" is that of transformation—a process which involves "doing away with" that which is outmoded and outgrown. Thus, in the consciousness which characterizes most of earth life, a transformation that brings about a more spiritually inclined consciousness is a "death," and any agency that helps to bring this transformation about may be said to have "killed" the lower, ego-driven consciousness.

Revelation does not simply assume poetic license in its use of the term "kill" as the meaning of the word is applicable to pain that we may experience as an agency of transformation is working within our consciousness. Consequently, with the Horsemen, the means of killing are the ways or modes within which the mind must function to bring about growth.

Keeping in mind that the Horsemen represent the four Mutable astrological signs, each mode of killing also relates to the psychological expression of the energy of these signs.

> *To Kill with the Sword.* This should be interpreted as "to transform the consciousness by using the faculty of the rational mind." The mind as a faculty of discrimination sours the sweet taste of experiencing by converting sensations into

critical observations. To this extent, one is "killed" or becomes dead to the lower or unconscious self.

To Kill with Hunger. This should mean "to bring about transformation through a loss of satisfaction with one's present, mundane reality." The hunger implied here is the hunger for meaning, without which the search for something lasting may not be initiated. The hunger that transforms first creates "a hole inside" and one is forced to find ways of filling it, thereby facilitating transformation.

To Kill with Death. This should be interpreted as "to be transformed through the loss of self-importance." This death that transforms first asserts itself as a loss of effectiveness over the elements of one's life. It is awareness of this impotence that may lead an individual to strive for a more effective means of dealing with life, prompting a process of surrender to a Larger Power. The individual thus becomes more conscious of his or her functioning within a greater whole and realizes a larger measure of effectiveness as a result.

To Kill with the Beasts of the Earth. This should mean "to be transformed through the feelings of shame which may follow an acquaintance with the lower, or 'beastly' aspects to one's nature." Awareness of our beasts motivates us to try to shake them off. Since these beasts may remain rather close to us, the only defense may be the erection of laws and codes of conduct and the attempt to abide by them.

Themes of the Mutable Signs

The Themes for the Mutable signs are given in Table 4-2. They reinforce the interpretations given to the Horsemen as representing various mental faculties and modes of mental functioning.

Table 4-2. Themes of the Mutable Signs

Sign	Theme	Expression	Mode of Mental Functioning
Sagittarius	"I see"	Discernment	Ideals
Virgo	"I analyze"	Rationality	Experience
Gemini	"I think"	Deduction	Concepts
Pisces	"I believe"	Association	Symbols

The Energies of the Four Cardinal Signs as Featured in the "Two" Witnesses

The four Cardinal signs are the most difficult to locate in Revelation. The reason for this is that they are represented as the "two olive trees and the two candlesticks." Below is the reference in Revelation to the Witnesses.

> *And I will give power unto my two witnesses, and they shall prophesy a thousand two hundred and threescore days, clothed in sackcloth.*
>
> *These are the two olive trees, and the two candlesticks standing before the God of the earth.*
>
> *And if any man will hurt them, fire proceedeth out of their mouths, and devoureth their enemies: and if any man will hurt them, he must in this manner be killed.*
>
> *These have power to shut heaven, that it rain not in the days of their prophecy: and have power over waters to turn them to blood, and to smite the earth with all plagues, as often as they will.*
>
> *And when they shall have finished their testimony, the beast that ascendeth out of the bottomless pit shall make war against them, and shall overcome them, and kill them.*
>
> *And their dead bodies shall lie in the street of the great city, which spiritually is called Sodom and Egypt, where also our Lord was crucified.*
>
> *And they of the people and kindreds and tongues and nations shall see their dead bodies three days and a half, and shall not suffer their dead bodies to be put in graves.*
>
> *And they that dwell upon the earth shall rejoice over them, and make merry, and shall send gifts one to another; because these two prophets tormented them that dwelt on the earth.*
>
> *And after three days and a half the Spirit of life from God entered into them, and they stood upon their feet; and great fear fell upon them which saw them.*
>
> *And they heard a great voice from heaven saying Come up hither. And they ascended up to heaven in a cloud; and their enemies beheld them.*

> *And the same hour was there a great earthquake, and the tenth part of the city fell, and in the earthquake were slain of men seven thousand: and the remnant were affrighted, and gave glory to the God of heaven.* Rev. 11:3–13

Although the foregoing passage presents interesting material for analysis, it is necessary to limit the focus for the time being to the "two witnesses"—the two olive trees and the two candlesticks—and the powers attributed to them. These symbols were the subjects of an earlier vision by Zachariah in the Old Testament, that is worth reproducing here in part since it helps in the interpretation and understanding, at a psychological level, of these "two witnesses."

> *Then answered I, and said unto him, What are these two olive trees upon the right side of the candlestick and upon the left side thereof?*
>
> *And I answered again, and said unto him, What be these two olive branches which through the two golden pipes empty the golden oil out of themselves?*
>
> *And he answered me and said, Knowest thou not what these be? And I said, No, my lord.*
>
> *Then said he, These are the two anointed ones, that stand by the Lord of the whole earth.* Zachariah 4:11–14

Unlike the four Beasts and the four Horsemen, the Two Witnesses do not seem to embody individual characteristics as much as they embody general or universal principles. For this reason, it is difficult to identify immediately which of these Witnesses belongs to which sign. We do know that these Witnesses—the two olive trees and two candlesticks—represent the signs of Aries, Capricorn, Libra, and Cancer (counting clockwise from Aries). Our task now is to determine which signs are the olive trees and which are the candlesticks.

According to the Revelation and the Zachariah versions, both the two olive trees and two candlesticks, even though they represent four items, embody only two principles. The principle embodied by the olive trees is that of energy generation and circulation since, according to the Zachariah version, they produce oil which they spontaneously empty out of themselves into the candlesticks. The principle embodied by the candlesticks, on the other hand, is that of raising up or consecration of the energy.

It seems appropriate to associate the signs of Cancer and Capricorn with the act of consecration of energy, hence the two candlesticks. This association will also relate the candlesticks to the two solstices.

Aries and Libra, on the other hand, are more appropriate as generators of energy, hence the two olive trees. These latter signs also define the two equinoxes.

In this scheme of things, each pair of signs is a Witness: the Aries–Libra pair dealing with different degrees of awareness of Self, and the Cancer–Capricorn pair dealing with different degrees of definition of Self. Through the process of Self awareness, one produces energy. Psychologically speaking, the energy is the awareness itself—to raise up energy is to increase our capacity for conscious relationship with ourselves, our fellow man, and Nature. Through the process of Self definition, the energy is raised up in higher and higher expressions.

In Revelation the Two Witnesses are described as "standing before the God of the earth," while in Zachariah, they are said to "stand by the Lord of the whole earth." We can derive two levels of meaning from this description, both of which seem valid.

The first relates to the role of the *sun* as the identifiable source of life on earth: solar energy in the form of heat and light is the starting point for all food chains on the planet. Without the sun, all ecosystems on the earth would collapse. In this sense, the sun is the Lord, or God, of the earth, or "the power on which the destiny of the earth depends." To stand before the "God of the earth" could therefore be referring to the positions that Aries–Libra (equinoxes) and Cancer–Capricorn (solstices) occupy as points of reference and demarcation for the seasons.

The second level of meaning is psychological. It suggests that these Witnesses—Aries, Libra, Cancer, and Capricorn—when viewed as principles of our human psychic functioning, are engaged in the service of whatever it is that the destiny of the earth is supposed to be. Without getting lost in a discourse about the purpose behind the design of the universe and the destiny of the earth, we can still permit ourselves to say something about this special destiny in which the Cardinal sign energies play a part. We can infer what this destiny is by inquiring into what the "default condition" of the earth will be in the absence of the energy the sun provides. This condition is the state to which the earth will automatically return in the absence of conscious efforts to bring about a specific outcome—a state of maximum entropy, to borrow a term from physics, based on the engineering principle known as the "second law of thermodynamics." This theory postulates that a system, over time, will run down and become disorganized if there is no energy imported into it to maintain it.[2]

We can permit ourselves to say that any psychological posture that is dedicated to the circulation and consecration of energy serves the destiny of the earth and as such "stands before the God of the earth."

Powers of the Witnesses

The powers of the Witnesses are four in number, and they correspond to the characteristics of the signs of Aries, Libra, Cancer, and Capricorn. These powers are enumerated in Revelation 11:6. They are the:

- Power to kill their enemies with fire.
- Power to shut heaven so that it does not rain.
- Power to turn water into blood.
- Power to smite the earth with plagues.

The Power to Kill Their Enemies with Fire relates to the energy of Aries, the Fire sign of the Cardinal Quality. The idea of killing as it is used in this context is the same as in the description of the powers of the Horsemen. Therefore, this power is the power of transformation, and the idea of "fire" as the means of killing relates to the energy of Aries, which transforms inertia with enthusiasm.

The Power to Shut Heaven So That It Does Not Rain relates to the energy of Libra, an Air sign. In the way that it is used here, heaven relates to the earth's atmosphere, which condenses to form raindrops. The significance of this power for Libra is that rain is to the earth what peace is to Libra. Just as rain brings relief to a dry and hot earth, so does peace—the distilled essence of thought—bring relief to a mind in search of perfection, a mental state characterized by Libra. If we lack peace of mind, transformation is forced on us as we find it necessary to examine and rectify our consciences.

The Power to Turn Water into Blood suggests the energy of Cancer at work, since it is the Water sign of the Cardinal Quality. In astrology the Water signs symbolize the feeling and emotional aspects of our nature. The power to turn water into blood is a symbolic way of saying that the energy of Cancer turns what is commonplace (water) into that which is of value (blood), just as if one's body has undergone expansion. Turning water into blood is accomplished by converting feelings and sensations into deep concerns. The consequence is that one's body, which usually defines the limits of one's concerns, grows to include not just one individual physical being, but many, many more.

The Power to Smite the Earth with Plagues relates to the workings of the energy of Capricorn, the Earth sign of the Cardinal Quality. "Smiting the earth with plagues" suggests, psychologically, a process where we may experience a perpetual sense of crises and urgencies within the consciousness, propelling us to elevate our level of striving. This is the manner in which Capricorn energy operates, through the inner impulse, to hold one's own from what may appear to be external threats.

Themes of the Cardinal Signs

The Themes of the Cardinal signs help to shed more light on the powers of the Witnesses and their manner of working. In Table 4-3 below, the Themes are described in terms of how the energies of the signs are expressed. As a note of contrast with the Fixed signs, the relevant qualifier to the Themes centers around objective interpretations of their energies, while with the Mutable signs, the qualifications deal with the faculties through which they are expressed.

Table 4-3. Themes of the Cardinal Signs

Sign	Theme	Focus	Full Expression
Aries	"I am"	Ego	Perfection
Libra	"I balance"	Conscience	Peace
Cancer	"I feel"	Emotions	Belonging
Capricorn	"I use"	Ambition	Purpose

Chapter 5

The Problem of Duality as the Foundation of Revelation's Psychology of Transformation

Overview

Psychologically speaking, astrological signs symbolize mental "energies," which can be interpreted as thinking patterns and emotional drives. The zodiac is a symbolic framework representing various energies, some of which may be experienced as being contradictory one to the other from an ordinary human perspective—a perspective that regards the pursuit of happiness as the primary objective of life and that regards difficulties and hardships as failures and setbacks. The challenge before each of us is to conceptually acknowledge all of the zodiacal energies and arrive at a point of acceptance of life, both mentally and emotionally, where all these energies work in harmony.

It is this challenge of synthesis and acceptance that lies at the basis of our experience of duality—our individual struggles to come to terms mentally and emotionally with all that is perceived to be "not-self," or all that challenges our self-definition. Revelation's psychology of transformation begins with our human struggles with duality even though its writer does not speak in these terms. He speaks in terms of personalities and events, and in effect, invents a mythological drama that contains this psychology but in a concentrated form.

For John to have effected this reduction from psychological principles to a mythological drama, he needed a device to translate psychological processes into time–space events, into things we can ordinarily relate to. This same device now allows us to translate back—almost two millennia later—to the processes that lie at the back of Revelation's expositions.

We shall now look at how the problem of duality is approached and expressed in a temporal, action-oriented setting, and show how astrology provides the structure for its presentation in a systematic framework.

Figure 5.1 *A Dramatization of the Problem of Opposites*

The Duality Problem

In a more personal sense, the duality problem has to do with balancing and coming to terms in the consciousness with all conceptual pairs of opposites. At the heart of the problem is our perception of Reality as being of the self and not of the self. This is the basis of the many appearances of separateness and conflict that may dominate our consciousness. Astrology provides us with a frame of reference that can be used to organize a remedy for the problem. This frame of reference suggests to us ways in which conflicting energies can be made to work for the whole person rather than against it. The state wherein the consciousness is characterized by conflicting energies is aptly represented in the seventeenth century painting by Marolles (see Figure 5-1).

At the first level of synthesis of zodiacal energies, the twelve astrological signs become expressions of six principles only. Each of the six principles can be considered in two modes or phases: our subjective understanding of the principle, and its objective expression. Whereas our subjective understanding of each principle is based on personal biases, objective expression is based on how the principle is expressed in the absence of a personal bias. The twelve archetypal energies of the zodiac can be viewed as the result of these six principles, each expressing itself in these two modes.

To fully integrate the energy represented by each of the six principles into consciousness, an individual would have to solve all the conceivable conflicts that may arise in the application of the principle to himself and others. As each principle becomes integrated at a conscious level, we receive a "gift" in the language of Revelation. Conversely, failure to integrate any of the six principles into consciousness results in a "condemnation."

It is this psychological and zodiacal structure that gives rise to the praises enumerated in certain passages in Revelation, for example, in the eleventh verse of the fifth chapter. This same structure accounts for condemnations enumerated in the seventh and eighth verses of the twenty-first chapter.

Looking now at the praises, we find the following enumeration:

> *And I beheld, and I heard the voice of many angels round about the throne and the beasts and the elders: and the number of them was ten thousand times ten thousand, and thousands of thousands Saying with a loud voice, Worthy is the Lamb that was slain to receive power, and riches, and wisdom and strength, and honor, and glory, and blessing.*
> Rev. 5:11–12

The praises were sung to the "Lamb" because the Lamb symbolizes the fully integrated consciousness. It is the consciousness that has risen beyond the psychological conflicts that arise from duality. The idea behind the concept of the "Lamb that was slain" is the *primordial innocence* of the human soul, i.e., in its prior state, which is sacrificed for experiences in time–space, in earth life. Although this concept of the "Lamb that was slain" is thought to refer only to Jesus Christ, it also refers to a *type*. The "Lamb" is yet another way of representing the ideal toward which humanity must strive. Jesus Christ was also a tangible representation of that ideal. From the perspective of timelessness that Revelation has assumed, what is being presented to us is really a picture that represents a time–moment of human life. Therefore the ideal toward which humanity must strive exists simultaneously with our everyday reality. When the ideal as it exists at this moment is placed in a temporal context, the image that results is that of a Lamb that was slain. The showering of praises demonstrates that wholeness—fullness—is gained from this *ideal* taking a risk by incarnating itself in time–space.

Specifically, each of the praises showered on the Lamb is a state of being that arises in consciousness from having mastered the duality inherent in opposite zodiacal sign energies. Thus we can backtrack to show how the specific praises relate to the signs. Here, duality is expressed as pairs of opposite signs (see Table 5-1).

Table 5-1. The Relationship Between the Praises to the Lamb and the Signs of the Zodiac

Praises to the Lamb	Duality as Expressed by Opposite Zodiacal Signs
Power	Aries–Libra
Riches	Taurus–Scorpio
Wisdom	Gemini–Sagittarius
Strength	Cancer–Capricorn
Honor	Leo–Aquarius
Glory	Virgo–Pisces
Blessing	State Beyond Conflicts of Duality

Similarly, when we fail to master the conflicts inherent in duality the consequence is a "condemnation." Receiving a "condemnation" only means that we have failed to integrate the energies represented by particular zodiacal signs into consciousness. John enumerates "those" who will be condemned in the following manner:

> *He that overcometh shall inherit all things; and I will be his God, and he shall be my son. But the* fearful, *and* unbelieving, *and the* abominable, *and* murderers, *and* whoremongers, *and* sorcerers, *and* idolaters, *and* all liars, *shall have their part in the lake which burneth with fire and brimstone: which is the second death.* [emphasis added]   Rev. 21:7–8

These shortcomings are related to the zodiacal signs in Table 5-2.

The imputation of condemnations adheres to a different structure than the one used to allocate praises. The praises originate from

Table 5-2. The Results of Failure at Integrating the Energies of the Zodiac

Shortcomings	Signs or Polarity of Signs
Fearful	Aries–Libra
Unbelieving	Virgo–Pisces
Abominable	Cancer–Capricorn
Murderers	Leo
Whoremongers	Scorpio
Sorcerers	Aquarius
Idolaters	Taurus
All Liars	Gemini–Sagittarius

success at solving duality problems presented by opposing energies, while the condemnations result from unsolved conflicts and unassimilated energies. The condemnations that result from a failure to integrate the energies of the Fixed signs of Leo, Taurus, Aquarius, and Scorpio are listed individually.

The praises are seven in number, one for each pair of opposite signs, and an extra one for overall success at integration. By contrast, the condemnations are either eight in number—one for each of the four Fixed signs and one for each pair of Cardinal and Mutable signs—or six in number as in the following instance.

> *Blessed are they that do his commandments, that they may have right to the tree of Life, and may enter in through the gates into the city. For without are* dogs, *and* sorcerers, *and* whoremongers, *and* murderers, *and* idolaters, *and* whosoever loveth and maketh a lie.   Rev. 22:14-15

In this example, the shortcomings of the Fixed signs are enumerated separately, while the Mutable signs are lumped together as "whosoever loveth and maketh a lie," and the Cardinal signs as "dogs," meaning doers of "abominable" deeds—as in Revelation 21:7-8.

Beyond Duality: Entering the New Jerusalem

Success at integrating the energies represented by the zodiacal signs enables one to experience a shift in consciousness to a state that can be designated as being "beyond duality." John uses the imagery of going through the gates of "the city" to symbolize this state: "Blessed are they that do his commandments, that they may have right to the tree of life, and may enter in through the gates into the city." The "city" is elsewhere described as the "new Jerusalem."

In John's description of this city as he saw it, we get another example of the way he utilizes terms for objects and events to describe psychological processes. For example, his statement, "... and the street of the city was pure gold, as it were transparent glass" (21:21) is one way of describing an important aspect of what the state of consciousness that lies beyond duality is all about. To get more insight into what he is talking about here, we have to look at the various levels of the symbol he has employed. First, a city is a state of collective habitation. Therefore, it suggests a state of collective or cooperative existence, a state which would be attained by the individual when psychospiritual integration is attained and duality is mastered.

Next, a street of a city is a communications artery or a means of establishing contacts between individuals. If we now regard gold in the context of the prestige and preeminence in which it was held in John's time, the meaning we get from its use is that nothing is spared as far as establishing communication and contact between individuals is concerned. Furthermore, if we consider some of the uses of gold from our own time, we can see that gold is a metal of extremely high electrical conductivity, so much so that it is of utmost importance in electronics. Thus, a city with a street of pure gold would imply a state of collective existence where communication between its participants is of such conductivity and therefore simultaneity that the members of such a group could well be regarded as one person. At a practical level, a city with streets of pure gold represents a level of existence where many individuals live in telepathic and spiritual rapport with each other.

The above interpretation is reinforced by John saying that this "city" has twelve gates, "And the twelve gates were twelve pearls ..." (21:21). It should be noted that it is the pearl itself that constitutes a gate, not that the gates were made up of pearls. A *pearl* suggests a process of overcoming, of turning obstacles into opportunities. Thus, the pearl is used here to suggest that entrance to the "city" is controlled by process, nothing else. The twelve gates of pearls point to the processes by which the individual must overcome conflicting energies of the zodiac.

We shall now look at how the energies of the signs interact in their opposition and thus get an understanding of the principles they embody. In this way we can obtain a clearer understanding of the way in which blessings and condemnations were distributed.

The Six Psychological Principles at the Basis of the Twelve Zodiacal Signs

As previously stated, the twelve zodiacal signs may be considered as the embodiments of six principles in two aspects of their expression—interior and exterior or subjective and objective. Together, the six principles represent all phases, but not consecutive stages, of the process that leads to the full realization of the *Soul* or *Self*. Human consciousness grows through its familiarity with all these principles from both their interior and exterior aspects.

Table 5-3 presents this author's own scheme of the principles embodied by the six pairs of zodiacal signs and their expression in consciousness from their interior and exterior aspects, or subjective and objective. This scheme is a summary and paraphrase of the commonly accepted psychological characteristics of the zodiacal signs. In arriving at this scheme, the guiding principle was to capture the underlying psychological dynamic involved in opposite sign energies.

Table 5-3. The Six Psychological Principles Behind the Twelve Zodiacal Signs

Polarity	Principle of Consciousness	Interior and Exterior Aspects
Aries–Libra	Self Awareness	Being and Adjusting
Taurus–Scorpio	Self Expansion	Domination and Obligation
Gemini–Sagittarius	Self Exploration	Thinking and Understanding
Cancer–Capricorn	Self Definition	Belonging and Consecration
Leo–Aquarius	Self Expression	Will and Intuition
Virgo–Pisces	Self Assessment	Verification and Acceptance

The goal of psychospiritual integration is for an individual eventually to master all six principles. When one can relate to all six from the direction of their two poles, that person becomes blessed—a "Philadelphian." This undertaking, however, must not be thought of as a sequential one. The different tasks can be worked on simultaneously, and the fact that an individual may be more focused on integrating a particular principle into consciousness, does not rule out opportunities to work at integrating others at the same time.

Interpersonal relationships provide one of the chief means of assimilating the various principles. Different individuals possess various degrees of command at expressing these principles of consciousness. By one individual fully accepting another, he also accepts the principles to which that other person is giving expression in life. This is one avenue through which love figures in the picture. Because, by accepting another individual, we are able to look past whatever distortion that may result in that individual's struggle to give expression to a principle. Instead of focusing on the distortions, we are able to see the principle of consciousness itself as it seeks expression through the individual. This is spiritual love in its essence. It is the capacity to relate to a process from its own center. It is taking a conceptual walk in someone else's shoes.

It follows that whatever degree of success we may achieve from integrating all the psychological principles represented by the zodiac can usually be reflected in our attitudes toward others. The closer our consciousness approaches wholeness, the less we will regard to be not of the self. Consequently, mastery of the principles, or failure at mastery, can be thought of in attitudinal terms since in one way or the other, complete assimilation cannot take place outside of the context of human society.

Our approach at assimilating one of the six principles can be said to be reiterative, meaning that we normally begin with a subjective understanding of a principle then attempt to live it out in real life situations. Depending on what difficulties we may encounter in this venture, we will have to redefine our understanding of the principle we are living out. The sign that is opposite on the zodiacal wheel represents the adjustment that we might need to make before a complete understanding of one of the six principles is achieved.

It should become clearer after looking at Table 5-3 why the condemnations were allocated between the signs in the manner they were: Fear is the antithesis of Self awareness (Aries–Libra), unbelief of Self assessment (Virgo–Pisces), lying of Self exploration (Gemini–Sagittarius), murder of creativity (Leo), whoremongering of expansion through obligation (Scorpio), sorcery of intuition (Aquarius), and idolatry of domination (Taurus).

The Dynamic Interplay of the Six Psychological Principles Behind the Twelve Zodiacal Signs

In order to better illustrate the interdependence between the energies of opposite signs and the impossibility of fully expressing the energy of a sign without the incorporation of its opposite, the following scenarios are presented.

Aries–Libra: Polarity of Being and Accommodating (or Adjusting)

Principle of Consciousness: Self Awareness. The Aries–Libra polarity represents our attempts to express awareness of Self as a principle from two different perspectives, being and accommodating. The concept of being is expressed through spontaneity while that of accommodating is expressed through reflection. Another way of looking at this is to regard Aries as relating to being and Libra to becoming.

When we begin to express the energy of Self awareness from the Aries pole, we may begin to express such awareness by unbridled spontaneity. The actions that this subjective interpretation of Aries energy gives rise to take only personal needs and the most effective ways of fulfilling them into consideration. However, since there is an objective world of "others" to contend with, the subjective interpretation of the energy of Self awareness will prove to be deficient. If we act out Aries energy in this manner, we would eventually have to expand our definition of Self to incorporate more than our own physical and emotional being. When this reassessment is undertaken, we will discover that indeed, all is the Self. We will also learn that the satisfaction resulting from an act is greater, the greater the number of individuals whose needs are considered before action is undertaken.

With the Libra pole, awareness of Self is interpreted initially as the incorporation of as many possibilities as is feasible into the assessment of one's actions. In this sense, awareness of Self is initially expressed through the capacity for accommodation. Consequently, we express Libra energy by reflecting before acting so that we can ascertain the propriety of an action. This can lead to inertia and sterility in terms of what we bring into our personal interactions. Such sterility can be overcome when we come to grips with the implicit assumptions that lie at the basis of his accommodative gestures. We might find that our willingness to accommodate is motivated by the same assumptions that expressed themselves in Aries spontaneity, the primary one being the belief that we are somehow superior to others.

It is only when we express the energy of Libra from the starting point of equality with others, rather than superiority, that we can use the impulse of accommodation to properly interpret the principle of Self awareness. Only then will we have something to contribute to a personal relationship.

Taurus–Scorpio: Polarity of Domination and Obligation

Principle of Consciousness: Self Expansion. At the level of personal consciousness, we may experience the energy of the Taurus–Scorpio polarity as an impulse to expand. This may be felt either as the need to dominate through mastery of our surroundings or to undertake obligations through union.

The spontaneous release of energy at the Taurus pole is experienced by an individual as the need to acquire command and dominion over the environment, both physical and social. However, this impulse to dominate may result in the individual projecting importance on to material things and then trying to possess them. The inevitable consequence is that instead of adding to the stature of the Self, the Self becomes debilitated, since possessing and being possessed are in effect the same psychological reality.

When we place significance in possessing things, we are, in effect, vesting powers outside of ourselves with authority over our own inner state of contentment. It is only when this characteristic Taurus proclivity for dominance is balanced with the understanding that we are subjecting ourselves to that which we subject, that the expression of Taurus energy can lead to true Self expansion.

From the Scorpio pole, the impulse to expand the Self takes a more direct approach. The Scorpio impulse makes us want to merge directly with whatever we may want to add to our being. This impulse can also be experienced as a willingness to assume the obligations that go with a "larger" Self. However, this approach to expansion may result in an abandonment of the will to forces that we might consider to be congruent with expressions of a "larger" Self. Such an error can occur when we place interpretations on our experiences so that they conform to a given belief system. Under such circumstances, the intensity that characterizes the Scorpio energy may be applied to a wrong goal. The consequence may be a full acquaintance with partial aspects of the Self such that imbalances appear in the personality.

A practical example of this problem is the spiritual aspirant who wants to experience various forms of mystical experience and may practice austerities to bring these about. He may become so engrossed in his austerities that he may forget why he engaged in them in the first place, or worse, may be so "taken over" by the method utilized that he becomes blind to alternatives. In this case, he would become a fanatic.

When we approach the affairs of life in a Scorpio manner, we will have to balance the intensity that comes from full acquaintance with a partial aspect of the Self with Taurus practicality and propensity to exercise domination.

Gemini–Sagittarius: Polarity of Thinking and Understanding

Principle of Consciousness: Self Exploration. The principle of Self exploration finds expression in the Gemini–Sagittarius polarity as thinking and understanding. Behind the principle of Self exploration is the process of the Self becoming aware and familiar with all that does not appear to be of its own makeup. The activity of thinking is the direct result of the desire to know, while that of understanding stems from the desire to test what has been learned.

From the Gemini pole, we might embark upon the task of Self exploration by attempting to see what is unique in each thing and by attempting to communicate that knowledge. The result is that we see everything only in its own specific context. This means that we may acquire many pockets of knowledge without making any attempt to establish interconnectedness between them.

The consequence for anyone expressing the energy of Gemini in this manner is emotional fragmentation. Only when we acquire knowledge with the express purpose of giving us a better picture of the whole, is the principle of Self exploration served. An example of the misapplication of the Gemini quest for knowledge is the perpetual student syndrome, wherein one does not commit oneself to a particular philosophical view of life but is forever reading, searching, and exploring.

From the Sagittarius pole, we might approach the mission of Self exploration by initially erecting a belief system against which we compare all other systems of knowledge. This approach creates a centering effect for the person expressing the Sagittarius energy, enabling him to explore with confidence, the various reality structures he finds of interest. But here, when we approach Self exploration in the typical Sagittarius manner, we may neglect to see things from their own centers and in their own contexts. The Sagittarius propensity to draw connections from a point of center needs to be tempered with the Gemini proclivity for seeing things in their own contexts and in a way that is free of value judgments.

Cancer–Capricorn: Polarity of Belonging and Consecration

Principle of Consciousness: Self Definition. The Cancer–Capricorn polarity is an expression of the principle of Self definition through the impulse to belong or to consecrate one's being to a cause greater than oneself. The impulse to belong is expressed in an individual through feelings of shared heritage and the impulse to consecrate oneself through the desire to forge a common destiny.

If we experience and express Self definition from the Cancer perspective, we might begin by initially building a secure sense of Self by harboring around us only the familiar and the similar. The energy of the Cancer impulse expresses itself at a psychological level as the need to create circles of association around oneself. The danger in this approach at definition can lead to tighter and tighter circles until we discover that seeking definition through belonging and association often leads to exclusion, prejudice, and in the extreme, isolationism. The antidote is for us to learn definition by inclusion and function—the keynote of the Capricorn approach to Self definition.

When we approach from the Capricorn perspective, we might seek to express the principle of Self definition through inclusivity, or by ensuring that we have a part to play in some larger scheme. Through this approach, we may seek to consecrate the contents of our personal consciousness to collective endeavors through some compelling sense of purpose and desire to achieve. We might want to lay all our abilities at the service of the country or the state, making its objectives our objectives, its collective goals our personal goals. However, this impetus may lead to insecurity and blind ambition unless it is accompanied by the inner sense of personal integration and security that are characteristics of the Cancer pole. Only then can the Capricorn expression of Self definition become the signature of the Self.

Leo–Aquarius: Polarity of Will and Intuition

Principle of Consciousness: Self Expression. The energy of the Leo–Aquarius polarity is characterized by the impulse toward Self expression, either from the perspective of the creative faculty of will or from the faculty of intuition. When we utilize the Leo approach to Self expression, we attempt to make our mark on the cultural landscape as a testimony to the creativity of the Self. The urge to create, however, can lead to pride if, as we express Leo energy, we take the emanations of the Self as personal achievement. Creativity will then degenerate into elitism and Self expression into the urge to make personal impressions. Failure to recognize the Self as the source of all creative efforts can lead to a drying up of the flow of inspiration, leaving us stranded with only the little self of the personality to call upon instead.

The individual who experiences such a frustration of the creative process—through a drying-up of inspiration—might seek to express Leo energy by dominating others. At a psychological level, one who experiences a cut off of inspiration might derive some satisfaction from the power that comes from directing the efforts of others, whether by ethical or unethical means. In a strange way, someone acting in this manner regards power to manipulate the creative process of others as a substitute for a lack of contact with his own creative center. The way out for the one attempting to be creative is to return to the inspiration and guidance of the Higher Self by foregoing taking personal credit for the accomplishments of the Self.

From the Aquarius side of this polarity, Self expression is manifested in the individual as intuition. Intuition in this sense means the higher faculty that emerges from the marriage of mind, heart, and will—thinking, feeling, and willing. This kind of intuition functions as an integrative faculty, enabling one to receive understanding about life through direct knowing.

This intuition must be guided through productive channels, otherwise the one receiving the intuitive impress from the Self will hinder its efforts to make its mark in a temporal setting. If we are attuned to this creative input from the Self, but do not recognize our responsibility to become an emissary of the Self, then the result may be eccentricity—a false sense of superiority and a lack of cooperativeness. All these modes of being are certainly in contradiction to any authentic expression of the Self. The solution is for the one attuned to the Aquarius energy to learn from the Leo pole and conduct the energy through constructive channels. The responsibility lies with the one receiving inspiration to create a point of contact with humanity at large in order to share this.

Virgo–Pisces: Polarity of Verification and Acceptance

Principle of Consciousness: Self Assessment. The principle of Self assessment expresses itself from the Virgo pole as the verification impulse and from the Pisces pole as the acceptance impulse. The verification impulse is satisfied through the accumulation of experiences, while the acceptance impulse is satisfied through the need to believe.

The energy of the Virgo pole is dedicated to testing the mettle of the Self by taking it into all those areas of experience that may, at first glance, constitute a hazard to it. Through this exercise, causes are set into motion and the resulting effects are noted; thus the effectiveness and endurance of the Self is tested. The Self gains experiences that constitute food for its own growth through such maneuvers. However, if there is not an overall conscious plan to structure the experiencing, the Virgo impulse to experience can result in a confusion of means and ends. Recklessness and hedonism can result if the Virgo impulse is not guided by such a plan. This is where the opposite energy of the Pisces pole helps balance one. In expressing Virgo energy, we must also commit ourselves to utilizing the experiences gained, thereby building maturity.

Approaching from the Pisces pole, we might initially interpret the impulse of Self assessment as a need to affirm. The energy of Pisces also prompts one to acknowledge the flow of impressions that arise in the unconscious and flow into conscious awareness. This can lead to a fascination with the interphase of form and formlessness. Pisces energy can lead one to worship form as a reaction to the undertow of the formless that lurks just beneath the threshold of conscious awareness.

The Pisces impulse can thus prompt one into a mystical exploration of life just as easily as it can prompt one into a worship of institutions and the status quo. The Pisces impulse to affirm can result in the abandonment of one of the prerogatives of the Self, judgment. When this happens, our efforts to give expression to the Pisces impulse can become lost in the ocean of the formless. The solution is for the one expressing Pisces energy to affirm with some of the critical awareness of Virgo energy.

A Note on the Self

Many newcomers to Eastern philosophical thought may not at once capture the full significance of what the word Self means when spelled with a capital "S." The concept of the Self is as powerful in an Eastern context as the concept of Soul is to the West. They are different concepts however, and that is due in part to the overall differences in the ways East and West regard eternity or permanence.

In an Eastern context, eternity is conceived of in terms of something ongoing and changing—a process of transformation; while for the West, eternity is a state characterized by a lack of change. Everything stays as it is "for ever and ever."

Because the Eastern way of thinking views permanence as process, that which can endure permanence is seen as something that always grows, adjusts, improves itself. Reality, therefore, is understood in terms of recurring cycles. Consequently, that which endures must master cycles of change. Thus, if something has no endurance, it also has no permanence. And, if it has no permanence it has no identity, no Self.

The Self is seen in the East as something that stands above cycles, that resists the vicissitudes of life and is not tossed and buffeted to and from by such vicissitudes. It is free from domination by either adversity or prosperity. The Self is therefore independent of the human ego, which is energized by those very vicissitudes and draws its existence from adversity and prosperity. It is this ego to which the West attaches the label "self," spelled with a small "s."

There is no resemblance between the little self and the big Self—sometimes called the Higher Self. Actually, it is in the interest of the lower self, the ego, to lose its existence to the larger Self, to become subject to its standards and thereby gain permanence. The Western concept of Soul comes closest to the Eastern idea of the Self and regrettably, it often carries with it the idea of something that is already fully formed, that acts like an invisible double to the physical being.

Astrology gains its validity by recognizing the existence of an evolving Soul or Self and by recognizing that this entity can orchestrate events in time–space to foster its own experience and growth. The scenarios depicted earlier, showing how mastery of the six astrological principles is gained, are really a story of how the self or ego becomes acquainted with the existence of the Self or Soul. The Self or Soul has a vested interest in the accomplishment of the ego of such a feat, for it is only then that it can establish a beachhead for further activity and growth in a temporal, physical setting.

Chapter 6

Time, Space, and Process
The Utilization of Time and Numbers in Revelation as Metaphors for Psychospiritual Integration

The Year and the Zodiac

So far, we have seen how zodiacal symbolism provides the key to an understanding of some of the central concepts in Revelation. It is also possible to show how this same system of zodiacal symbolism has allowed the author of Revelation to represent certain states of consciousness relating to psychological and spiritual integration. These states of consciousness are discussed in terms of a drama of personalities, events, and durations of time. With this understanding, we can translate back from the events and personalities in the Revelation drama to processes dealing with psychospiritual integration. From this exercise, we obtain insights that might help us gain a perspective on our own transformational quest.

A key place to begin our task of uncovering the transformational psychology contained in Revelation is to show how space and time are related in it. There, time and space become interchangeable so that a discussion concerning a duration of time might also be discussing a certain psychological process. We are clued in to this time–space relationship from our discovery that the period of time it treats as a year is equivalent to the zodiacal wheel.

In Revelation, the year contains 360 days. The year is composed of twelve uniform months, each containing 30 days. This is comparable to the zodiacal wheel with its 360 degrees, broken down into twelve different signs of 30 degrees each. It is unlikely that the use of a 360-day year was due to ignorance on the part of John, since solar calendars assigning 365 days to the year had been in use in the Middle East for over a thousand years by that time. One can also find in the book of Jubilees, estimated to have been written about 105 B.C., a prescription for a 364-day year. S. J. De Vries writes:

It is fairly certain that in historical times the Israelites determined their year, not by the fluctuating agricultural and pastoral cycles, even though these natural phenomena must have influenced them deeply, but by observing the annual circuit of the stars and the sun. We have little evidence concerning the method they might have used for determining the completion of this circuit, but we do know that the new year began at one of the equinoxes, at the dividing point between winter and summer or between summer and winter.

He continues:

> A purely solar reckoning is employed in the calendar promoted by the sectarian book of Jubilees (circa 105 B.C.). Throughout this remarkable book ... a year of 364 days is prescribed, to be divided into four quarters, each of which contains thirteen weeks and three months of thirty or thirty-one days.[1]

It is also not likely that John was using the 360-day year for the sake of convenience. This becomes obvious when we look at the attempts made to express time in equivalents of years, months, and days.

When the year and the zodiacal wheel are made to coincide, units of time such as years, months, and days become equivalent to zodiacal revolutions, signs, and degrees respectively. This means that references to events that are hinged upon a specific duration of time can be interpreted in terms of spatial concepts, i.e., degrees of the zodiac. In such a scheme, where space and time are interchangeable, the facility is created to discuss complex processes that would otherwise be outside of our frame of reference. It must be emphasized, however, that in Revelation's use of this scheme, it is the idea of process that is pre-eminent, with time represented by the year, and space represented by the zodiac, acting merely as support structures.

The evidence for attributing this time–space framework to Revelation is available from several scenes and references dealing with the passing of time. The context from which the following is taken finds John being given a rod and commanded by an angel to measure the temple of God:

> *And there was given me a reed like unto a rod: and the angel stood, saying, Rise, and measure the temple of God; and the altar, and them that worship therein. But the court which is without the temple leave out, and measure it not; for it is given unto the Gentiles: and the holy city shall they tread under foot forty and two months. [emphasis added]*
>
> 11:1–2

This same period of forty-two months, though alotted in days, is mentioned again as that which is given to the Two Witnesses—we have already identified them as symbols for the Cardinal signs—to prophesy:

> *And I will give power unto my two witnesses, and they shall prophesy a thousand two hundred and threescore days.*
>
> Rev. 11:3

Both forty-two months and one thousand, two hundred and sixty days contain a factor of $3\frac{1}{2}$. They both represent $3\frac{1}{2}$ years. We find this factor of $3\frac{1}{2}$ being repeated in the length of time during which the bodies of the Witnesses would lie exposed after they were murdered.

> *And they of the people and kindreds and tongues and nations shall see their dead bodies* three days and a half, *and shall not suffer their dead bodies to be put in graves.* Rev. 11:9

The references to people, kindred, tongues, and nations show a widening circle of influence, indicating that we are not dealing with local events but processes involving localities (the people), communities (kindreds), races (tongues), and the human race (the nations).

The period of time mentioned as forty-two months is also repeated in a different setting. This time, it involves one of the most central dramas in Revelation:

> *And there appeared a great wonder in heaven; a woman clothed with the sun, and the moon under her feet, and upon her head a crown of twelve stars:*
>
> *And she being with child cried, travailing in birth, and pained to be delivered.*
>
> *And there appeared another wonder in heaven; behold a great red dragon, having seven heads and ten horns, and seven crowns upon his heads.*
>
> *And his tail drew the third part of the stars of heaven, and did cast them to the earth: and the dragon stood before the woman which was ready to be delivered, for to devour her child as soon as it was born.*
>
> *And she brought forth a man child, who was to rule all nations with a rod of iron: and her child was caught up unto God, and to his throne.*
>
> *And the woman fled into the wilderness, where she hath a place prepared of God, that they should feed her there* a thousand two hundred and threescore days. Rev. 12:1–6

As if to emphasize that we are not dealing with duration as much as with cycles and processes, the period of time during which the woman is protected and nourished is also referred to as a time and times, and half a time:

> *And to the woman were given two wings of a great eagle, that she might fly into the wilderness, into her place, where*

> *she is nourished for a time, and times, and half a time, from the face of the serpent.*   Rev. 12:14

There is yet another instance in Revelation where this period is used, this time given in months. It is the period of time allowed for the reign of the beast—not to be confused with the four Beasts "round about the throne."

> *And I stood upon the sand of the sea, and saw a beast rise up out of the sea, having seven heads and ten horns, and upon his horns ten crowns, and upon his heads the name of blasphemy.*
>
> *And the beast which I saw was like unto a leopard, and his feet were as the feet of a bear, and his mouth as the mouth of a lion: and the dragon gave him his power, and his seat, and great authority.*
>
> *And I saw one of his heads as it were wounded to death; and his deadly wound was healed: and all the world wondered after the beast.*
>
> *And they worshipped the dragon which gave power unto the beast, saying, Who is like unto the beast? Who is able to make war with him?*
>
> *And there was given unto him a mouth speaking great things and blasphemies; and power was given unto him to continue forty and two months.*   Rev. 13:1–5

Most interestingly, this period of time, whether expressed as duration or periodicity, is not confined to Revelation. It is referred to elsewhere in the New Testament book of James and the Old Testament book of Daniel. In James, the reference has factual overtones:

> *Elijah was a man subject to like passions as we are, and he prayed earnestly that it might not rain: and it rained not on the earth by the space of three years and six months.*
>   James 5:17

In Daniel, the reference was wrapped up with the symbology of Daniel's own visions:

> *And he shall speak great words against the most High, and shall wear out the saints of the most High, and think to change times and laws: and they shall be given into his hand until a time and times and the dividing of time.*   Daniel 7:25

The idea of process, rather than duration, shines through as the central idea behind these references to three years and a half, forty-two months, one thousand two hundred and sixty days, three days and a half, a time (one) times (two) and half a time, or a time, and times, and the dividing of time (half). The variety of contexts in which these references occur suggests that the cyclic quality of this period is used as a symbol for a particular process of some cosmic significance. However, to penetrate the mystery as to what this process is, we need to look at another zodiacal concept utilized in astrology. This is the decanate, a ten-degree segment of the zodiac that Revelation utilizes in its manipulations.

The Decanate Concept as the Building Block for Revelation's Time–Space Creations

In the letter to the church at Smyrna—one of "the seven churches that are in Asia"—at the beginning of the Revelation document, there is a particular piece of encouragement given to the Smyrnians. The church is told:

> *Fear none of those things which thou shalt suffer; behold the devil shall cast some of you into prison, that ye may be tried; and ye shall have tribulation ten days.* Rev. 2:10

This reference to tribulation for a ten-day period has completely defied commentators on Revelation. However, with the understanding that time and space have been used interchangeably, ten days can be translated as "ten units of space." In terms of the zodiacal framework we have been using, these amount to ten degrees of the zodiacal wheel. Thus, to have tribulation for ten days can be interpreted as "having to undertake the task of integrating all the energies represented by the ten-degree segments into the consciousness." Such a task can be regarded as "tribulation" in that it is extremely difficult to apply oneself to the task of becoming conscious in all aspects of life. Living consciously often involves breaking free from the conventional wisdom and social life of the day, an undertaking that is normally met with ridicule.

The ten-degree segment is the basic unit of space we are working with and that which becomes a symbol for one "unit" of experience. While experience is not usually divisible into individual units, we do know that specific life events do equip us with specific abilities to deal with future life contingencies. The astrological concept that relates to this ten days of tribulation is the *decanate*.

TIME, SPACE AND PROCESS 69

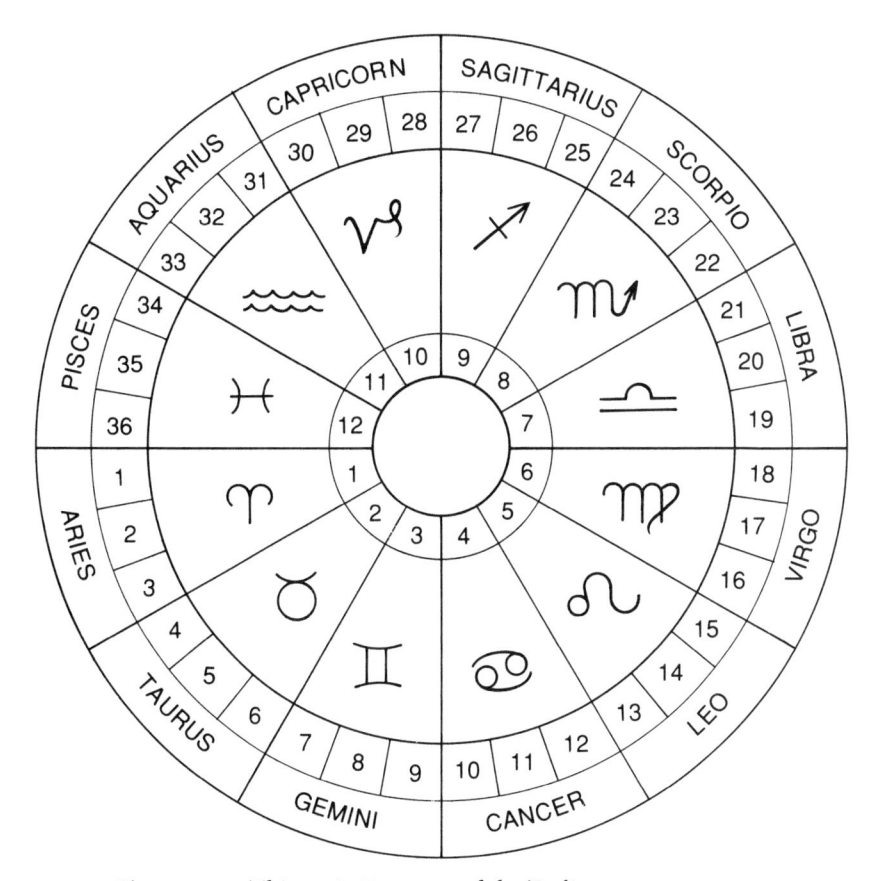

Figure 6.1 *Thirty-six Decantes of the Zodiac*

Each of the twelve astrological signs has three decanates, for a total of thirty-six on the zodiacal wheel (see Figure 6-1). The significance of the decanate is that it gives the "energy" of a sign three characteristic hues. The "energy" of the first decanate of a sign is said to be of the nature of the sign itself; the second decanate, of the nature of the sign ahead and of the same Element—going counter-clockwise; and the third, the nature of the sign preceding of the same Element.

An analogy that may facilitate an understanding of the decanate is to consider each sign as a sovereign state and the decanates as embassies of foreign states, with the exception of the first decanate. An embassy is technically regarded as the property of the state it represents even though it is ultimately subject to the jurisdiction of the host country. For example, the first decanate of Aries will be purely Aries, meaning Aries in both consciousness—or mentality—and expression. The second decanate will still be Aries in consciousness, but Leo in expression—Leo being the sign ahead and of the same Element, which in this case is Fire. The third decanate will be Aries in mentality, but Sagittarius in expression—Sagittarius being the preceding sign of the Fire Element.

The decanate concept is one that suggests relationship and synthesis. It is this concept that is at the basis of some of the other symbols in Revelation, which have themselves become important points of focus. We shall next consider how the decanate concept helps in understanding the meaning of the twenty-four Elders observed "round about the throne" with the four Beasts, and then show how the concept is used to construct other symbols relating to the dynamic in consciousness that leads to full psychospiritual integration and the opposite dynamic that subverts this process.

The Twenty-four Elders

The twenty-four Elders mentioned with the four Beasts help to complete the picture of the fully rounded consciousness. The Lamb symbolizes psychospiritual integration and Balance with respect to all the energies of the zodiac, represented here by the four Beasts and twenty-four Elders. Again, this is the arrangement as it is reported by John:

> *And immediately I was in the spirit: and, behold, a throne was set in heaven, and one sat on the throne. And he that sat was to look upon like a jasper and a sardine stone: and there was a rainbow round about the throne, in sight like unto an emerald. And round about the throne were four and twenty seats: and upon the seats I saw four and twenty elders sitting, clothed in white raiment; and they had on their heads crowns of gold.* Rev. 4:2–4

We have already seen that the four Beasts represent the four Fixed signs of the zodiac. The twenty-four Elders represent the decanates of the other eight signs belonging to the Cardinal and Mutable Qualities—i.e., eight times three.

The Elders represent the integration of our experiences, symbolized in this arrangement by their crowns of gold. The crowns symbolize achievement or spiritual realization in the synthesis and mastery of energies represented by the decanates of the Cardinal and Mutable signs. The Elders are therefore stand-ins for these signs

TIME, SPACE AND PROCESS 71

Figure 6.2 *The Twenty-Four "Elders" and the Four Beasts*

while the Fixed signs represent themselves in "heaven" where the throne was (see Figure 6-2).

The implication behind the four Beasts being in heaven is that they represent the energies of the Fixed signs. The four Fixed signs represent will (Leo), intuition as a higher level of intellectual functioning (Aquarius), contentment (Taurus), and transcendence (Scorpio). These energies are unfocused and therefore not manifest in the average human consciousness. Hence, they are in "heaven" as opposed to being on earth.

The four Horsemen and Two Witnesses are positioned on the earth to symbolize the energies of the Mutable and Cardinal signs. In order to get the message across that the energies that the Fixed signs represent are not yet fully integrated into our daily life, the writer of Revelation laments the lack of their proper expression by frequent reference to the results of their misuse—murder, idolatry, sorcery, and fornication.

The Number 1,260 as a Symbol for the Process of Psychospiritual Integration

The decanate idea will now enable us to show the zodiacal derivation of and the process implied by the period of time given as 1,260 days, forty-two months, or three years and a half. As was previously mentioned, the use of equivalent measures to express the same period of duration suggests that it is the process implied by the duration of time, rather than the passing of time itself, that is of importance. Furthermore, we have seen that this period of time can also be expressed spatially, as 1,260 degrees or three-and-a-half zodiacal wheel equivalents.

Within the context of Revelation, the number 1,260 implies the process of blending or synthesis using the decanate as the basic unit upon which the process operates. For a complete synthesis of the energies embodied in the zodiac, harmony must be established between every decanate and the thirty-five other decanates in the zodiac. In terms of behavior, when we are holding any one of these energies in our attention or our awareness—i.e., as a mental or emotional impulse—such an energy must not be expressed at the expense of any of the other energies. To represent the psychological process of combining energies the problem can be expressed in the following manner: *How can we gain mastery over thirty-six areas of awareness such that we can embody them all without conflict or animosity between them?* The solution is, for every one-on-one combination of these thirty-six areas of awareness, the opportunity and the capacity must be there to express the union in terms of each of the participants in the union.

As an example, if we are dealing with four objects, A, B, C, and D, and we want to combine them in pairs where the relative position of each one matters, the maximum expression of these unions, and therefore full synthesis, will be AB, AC, AD, BA, BC, BD, CA, CB, CD, DA, DB, and DC for a total of twelve combinations. Twelve, then, becomes the symbolic number representing the state of complete synthesis between four separate things.

The formal mathematical term for this relationship is that twelve is *the maximum number of ordered pairs* to be derived from four objects. Note that, in this example, the pairs AB and BA possess the same components, yet they are regarded as separate pairs when order of their arrangement is a consideration.

TIME, SPACE AND PROCESS 73

In terms of expressing and synthesizing energies, a concept that captures what is involved is that of *reciprocity*. An example from the musical scale will assist us to better understand how reciprocity relates to psychospiritual integration. When two musical notes are combined, a different effect is created depending on which note is played first. For example, the effect achieved by playing "re" after "do" is different from that achieved from playing "do" after "re." What makes their relationship different is the sequence of their expression in time.

Similarly, in order to achieve psychospiritual integration from the blending of the mental and emotional energies represented by the zodiac, it is necessary to have space–time reciprocity. Every combination, or blend of energies, must be expressed twice—first, spatially, i.e., as an idea or insight, and second, temporally, i.e., lived out at a practical level. Psychospiritual integration, therefore, involves much more than theoretical or cerebral learning: theory must be rounded out by a spiritual practice. Any approach used to reach psychospiritual integration that neglects practical application will lead to lopsided development.

Returning to the problem posed by the synthesis of the thirty-six decanates, it is necessary to use the mathematical formula for computing permutations to discover the maximum number of *ordered pairs* possible from thirty-six objects. In its general expression, this formula is given as $n!/(n-r)$, where "n" is the number of objects to be organized, "r" the desired relationship between the number of objects, which in our case is two since we are dealing with the relationship of pairing, and the expression "!" is used to signify the product of "n" and all consecutive numbers below it.

In solving our problem, $n = 36$, $r = 2$. These values are placed in the formula $n!/(n-r)!$:

$$36!/(36-2)! = 36!/34! = 36 \times 35 \times (34!)/(34!) = 36 \times 35$$

The result is 1,260.

The number 1,260 is symbolic of a state of consciousness that is fully comprehensive and reiterative. It represents full psychospiritual integration. In the context of the mathematical operation performed on 36 to arrive at it, 1,260 is symbolic of the consciousness which achieves spiritual realization by taking full advantage of the opportunities that earth life provides for experiencing space–time reciprocity. This spiritual realization is achieved by the individual living his or her insights, no matter how difficult this might be. It is this effort that is called "suffering" in the Smyrnian letter. As a matter of course, through the medium of earth–life experiences, the consciousness that is integrated in the psychospiritual sense also discovers the limits of the applicability of what it knows. Paradoxically, herein lies its completion.[2]

The Number 666 as Symbolic of Aborted Psychospiritual Integration

The opposite condition to the state of completion in time–space, characterized by a rounding out of theoretical with practical knowledge, also exists. This condition can also be numerically expressed; it is the number "666," described in Revelation as "the number of the beast." With regard to the significance of this number and its connection with the beast, John says:

> And he causeth all, both small and great, rich and poor, free and bond, to receive a mark in their right hand, or in their foreheads:
>
> And that no man may buy or sell, save he that had the mark, or the name of the beast, or the number of his name.
>
> Here is wisdom. Let him that hath understanding count the number of the beast: for it is the number of a man; and his number is Six hundred threescore and six. Rev. 13:16–18

Here, as in all other instances in Revelation where we encounter unusual characters, we need to look for the principle behind the characterization. By attributing a number to the "beast," the point is emphasized that the principle contained in its characterization does not belong to a person of history but can be possessed by everyone across the march of time. The "beast" is therefore a principle in consciousness.

Many attempts have been made to relate the number "666" to the sum of the letters in the names of well-known historical figures. This has been done by finding the numerical equivalents to the letters in the names and finding their sum. Such exercises miss the thrust of Revelation as a behind-the-scenes look at the factors that configure the psyche of man and thus presage human history. When John says that "666" is the number of a man, he is saying that it is a human characteristic. The Revised Standard Version confirms this interpretation. It says, "... for it is a human number" instead of "it is the number of a man" as is found in the King James Version.

We shall now demonstrate how this number also can be arrived at with the aid of a zodiacal framework. This framework begins with the decanate concept, the same one that was used to allow us to see the psychological reality behind the process symbolized by 1,260.

In contrast to the state of consciousness that is fully comprehensive and reiterative, a type of mastery can be produced by a short-circuiting of the process of psychospiritual integration of the thirty-six zodiacal energies. This is the type of mastery that is gained in the realm of pure theory. Here, application of the insight gained is neglected, and the consciousness so versed is lopsided. This state has its culmination in what may be called the linear mind—the mind dedicated solely to the mastery of technique rather than wisdom. We have here then, the consciousness of the fragmented genius, the individual whose mind—capacity for rational thought and analysis—has developed out of synchronization with his heart—capacity to feel. In terms of the zodiacal framework we are using, a short-circuit in the process of psychospiritual integration results from combining the energies of the thirty-six decanates, in pairs, without allowing for space–time reciprocity in their expressions.

In terms of mathematics, the operation that patterns this process is that where one is "sampling with replacement" for unique or novel combinations. This can be illustrated in the following manner: If we are seeking to make pairs out of four objects—A, B, C, and D—in such a manner that we are concerned with unique combinations, and therefore with novelty, the combinations that would satisfy us are AA, AB, AC, AD, BB, BC, BD, CC, CD, and DD, for a total of ten. No repeats are permitted, e.g., BA or CA, since we do not consider the order of arrangement important. The mathematical result from "sampling with replacement" for unique sets is called the *triangular number* of the number of things we are combining. Thus, with four objects, the solution could also have been derived by the following operation: $4 + 3 + 2 + 1 = 10$.

Applying the same principle to thirty-six gives us the sum of all the whole numbers from one to thirty-six. Thus:

$$36 + 35 + 34 + \text{etc} + 2 + 1$$

The result is "666," the number of the beast. We can also use the following formula for deriving the triangular number of a given number:

$$(n+1)/2 \times n$$

where "n" is the number to be operated on. When "n" is 36, the formula becomes:

$$(36+1)/2 \times 36 = 18.5 \times 36 = 666.$$

It occurred to me that a skeptical reader might consider the derivation of "666" contrived unless it could be shown that the Apostle John had the opportunity to become acquainted with the concept of triangular numbers. A year or so after I had first related the number of the beast—666—to the decanate concept, I stumbled upon a passage in one of the books of Clement of Alexandria that showed that he was acquainted with the concept of triangular numbers about a hundred years or so after the estimated time of the writing of Revelation. Clement, who lived from A.D. 153 to 217, not only showed that he had knowledge of the concept, he also revealed his dexterity at deriving mystical significance from it. In this book, he gives a discourse on, as he calls it, "The Mystical Meanings in the Proportions of Numbers, Geometric Ratios, and Music." He discusses the concept of triangular numbers, using the number 120 to illustrate his point. He shows that 120 is a triangular number of 15:

"The days of men shall be," it is said, "120 years." And the sum is made up of the numbers from one to fifteen added together.... On another principle, 120 is a triangular number...[5]

It does not seem unreasonable to expect that John, whose mystical insights were probably deeper than Clement's, could have been acquainted with triangular numbers and numerology just a hundred years previously.

To grasp the full psychological importance of the "beast" and its number, we must study its genesis and the context surrounding the part it plays in the overall Revelation drama. The genesis of the "beast" is to be found in the twelfth and thirteenth chapters of Revelation. Their contents are so important to the core message John has for us that we must digress from pursuing zodiacal associations for a while to undertake an in-depth analysis. This exercise will take place in the upcoming chapter. But first, we can take another look at the meaning of "666" from a totally different perspective.

The Similarity Between the Concept of Psychospiritual Integration and the Process of *Kundalini* Awakening

While we are on the subject of psychospiritual integration and synthesis of zodiacal energies, it must be mentioned that concepts do exist for expressing this idea of integration and synthesis at the physical–mental or neurological level of being. The engagement and operation of the process of psychospiritual integration is called *kundalini* in the tradition of the East. Basically, *kundalini* is described as a primordial energy common to all life, and is given as the source of manifestation of all living and nonliving things.[4] Its special significance for human beings is that it exists as a reserve of energy that lies dormant at the base of the spine. The energy becomes active with the proper spiritual observances. Upon activation, it is said to open up new faculties of perception, which may include mystical experiences, spiritual insights, and psychic abilities.

In the colorful language of the East, *kundalini* is described as a sleeping serpent coiled three-and-a-half times around the lower pole of the spinal axis. It is said that when the "serpent" awakens, it uncoils itself and makes its ascent to the brain through a passageway in the center of the spinal column. Upon reaching the brain, it produces illumination. The idea of a serpent is, of course, metaphorical. If we make allowances for differences in conceptualizations and terminologies, we see that the *kundalini* concept bears a great deal more than a passing resemblance to the process in Revelation that is represented by a duration of time with a periodicity of three-and-a-half.

Let us consider the basic difference in the ways transformation is viewed in the East and the West. Eastern concepts are expressed in terms of spatial adjustments, that is, of shifting from one state of nature to another. For example, the adjustments that are required to facilitate the transformational process are symbolically viewed in terms of the uncoiling of the *kundalini* serpent and its ascent to the brain. This imagery suggests a reorganization of one's perception of the universe—a reorganization that can be compared to the writhing of a serpent in its movements.

In the Western view, as typified by Revelation, transformation is presented in terms of temporal adjustments or endurance. Thus, time is the central feature in this system as it is assumed that time and change are inseparable. When Revelation talks about 1,260 days, or 42 months, or $3\frac{1}{2}$ years, or "a time and times and half a time," it is touching bases with the East where instead of duration, adjustment is the point of focus. The idea of "666," when viewed in this context, suggests an incomplete awakening of this *kundalini* energy such that it is functioning just enough to cause pride, and perhaps genius, but not enough for full psychospiritual synthesis and surrender to the will of God.

Chapter 7

Revelation's Perspective on the Forces that Define the Psyche of Man

Overview

In Chapter Six, we saw how the author of Revelation built structures around the concept of time that represent psychological processes. To illustrate this approach, several passages from the twelfth chapter were reproduced without an in-depth analysis of their contents. Here, we shall look into the characterizations and compelling dramas that are used to represent the processes we've described as full psychospiritual synthesis—integration—and incomplete synthesis. These portrayals are found in the twelfth chapter and brought to their zenith in the thirteenth.

Basically, what John is presenting to us in these two chapters are the inner workings of the ego-driven human psyche. Due to the difficulty of expressing these dynamic processes in human terms, what he presents appears both bizarre and frightening, but there is still a sense of order and structure underlying it all. It is the same sense of structure that we get from studying mythology—that category of literature that offers more or less personified and dramatized explanations of cosmological processes.

Two Conflicting Dynamics of Consciousness: The Woman in Labor and the Dragon

John begins the twelfth chapter with the announcement, "There appeared a great wonder in heaven," then proceeds to describe this wonder:

> ... a woman clothed with the sun and the moon under her feet, and upon her head a crown of twelve stars,
>
> And she being with child cried, travailing in birth, and pained to be delivered.   Rev. 12:1–2

He leaves this wonder to describe another that arose independently of the first. He says, "And there appeared another wonder in heaven." This time, he describes a "great red dragon" that was antagonistic to the woman and the child she was bearing.

> ... and behold a great red dragon, having seven heads and ten horns, and seven crowns upon his heads.
> And his tail drew the third part of the stars of heaven, and did cast them to the earth: and the dragon stood before the woman which was ready to be delivered, for to devour her child as soon as it was born. Rev. 12:3–4

Here, the two wonders are brought together as the dragon is shown standing before the woman with the express purpose of devouring her yet unborn child.

We must leave the narrative for now, first to get a grip on these two great wonders, and second, to discover why the purposes of the woman in labor and the dragon are in conflict.

The woman with child represents the ongoing process of synthesis in the psyche, and she of herself represents "Nature" or "Matter." She is the psyche that has had its focus narrowed by the density of matter, but she is using this "limitation" to great advantage. She also represents the meeting place of different realities. These different realities are symbolically represented as the sun, moon, and stars.

Looking psychologically at the realities that the woman represents, we have the forces of life (the sun clothing her), feeling (the moon under her feet), and mental faculties (the stars in her crown) being blended to arrive at a new reality, the child. The child she is carrying in her womb is therefore a symbol of the product of the synthesis of the various realities coming to a point of meeting in the woman.

We are told later that this child, after it was born, was a man-child, and that its destiny was to rule the nations with a rod of iron. Because of the attributes given to the child, some parts of this drama of the woman and child have been treated as history by conventional Christian theology. Some have claimed that this is "the Incarnation" and that John is here giving a portrayal of the birth of Jesus. Sure enough, some of the attributes of this child are also the attributes of Jesus Christ, and in a sense, we do have a "replay" here. Nevertheless, this replay does not concern a historical figure, but what we may call "Christ Consciousness." Christ Consciousness is the outcome of our human efforts to discern spiritual principles and live our lives by them—an exercise that represents spiritual striving. Since the child represents the product of our spiritual striving, it also symbolizes the outcome of the spiritualization and redemption of matter.

Despite his stated destiny of ruling the nations with a rod of iron, we are told that this male child "was caught up unto God, and to his throne." Why, we must wonder. The reason is that the child's life was in jeopardy. As a newborn, it is helpless to defend itself from external threats. At a psychological level, this defensive strategy for rescuing the child relates to the outcome of our daily efforts at giving birth to our spiritual nature, to Christ Consciousness. Just as the child was caught up to God, our efforts at arriving at a synthesis or reconciliation of our earthly and spiritual natures may seem at times not to have any noticeable result. But this is on account of the results of our efforts being hidden from view—these results accumulate at an unconscious level.

As for the dragon, John later calls it "that old serpent, called the Devil, and Satan." This description should not lull us into a false sense of recognition, for what we are dealing with here is a process. The dragon is described as having seven heads and ten horns, with seven crowns upon its heads. These heads symbolize centers of will, and the crowns upon them symbolize their sovereignty or independence of functioning. Having several autonomous decision-making centers, the dragon is therefore the very epitome of disorganization, of centrifugal or dispersive forces. These draw our attention away from doing our share in fulfilling our spiritual calling.

Thus, we can now see why the dragon wanted to devour the Christ-Consciousness child. It was not out just to destroy it, but to annex it, to gobble it up, to assimilate it. We can draw an analogy here—as unpleasant as it may be—with the practices of certain primitive peoples where the victor in battle eats the heart of the man he has conquered. This is done with the belief that he is ingesting the courage of his worthy, though vanquished, opponent.

The psychological reality that is symbolized by the dragon is the human sense of "I-ness," or the "ego." The ego is our sense of "I-separate-from-everything-else." This sense of self is the complete opposite of Christ Consciousness as symbolized by the child that was caught up to God. With a sense of self characterized by this Child, we do not feel that our individual lives are ends unto themselves. Just as the newborn was caught up to God, we consecrate the proceeds of our spiritual efforts back to the whole of life. However, with a sense of self characterized by the dragon, there is a desire to consume immediately the product of our individual efforts —the chief characteristic of the ego-bound consciousness of the Self.

A sense of Self as a separate and autonomous entity is not consistent with an inclusive and holistic view of life. This sense of Self is therefore a threat to Christ Consciousness as represented in this Revelation drama as a Child. This is why the dragon—alias the ego—was expelled from heaven. This suggests that in order to protect the Christ Consciousness that is being generated in us from our earthly strivings, the ego has to be separated from our deepest reality and our truest sense of Self. The result is that ordinarily, we do not have consciousness of our true Self. That part of ourselves that we ordinarily experience as our identity is limited to the realm of matter and conscious experience in order to allow our separative tendencies to play themselves out and become exhausted.

The Battle in Heaven

John gives some detail of the battle in heaven in which the dragon was overthrown. He says:

> *And there was war in heaven: Michael and his angels fought against the dragon; and the dragon fought and his angels,*
>
> *And prevailed not; neither was their place found any more in heaven.*
>
> *And the great dragon was cast out, that old serpent, called the Devil, and Satan, which deceiveth the whole world: he was cast out into the earth, and his angels were cast out with him.* Rev. 12:7–9

The meaning behind the name "Michael"—the leader of the victorious host of angels—presents us with a clue that allows us to arrive at a psychological understanding of the process represented by the war in heaven. According to Young's *Analytical Concordance to the Holy Bible*, the name "Michael" means "Who is equal to God?" The name is the expression of a question and as such does not have a "meaning" in the sense of explaining the unfamiliar in terms of the familiar. The name "Michael" is the embodiment of awe, wonder, admiration of the majesty and incomprehensibleness of God. It symbolizes the process of unknowing. Michael and his angels overthrew the dragon because the characteristics represented by Michael are destructive to the ego and its attributes.

When the dragon was cast out, certain pronouncements were made that supply additional clues we can use to deepen our understanding of the processes at work. As we take up John's narrative again, we shall see how the foregoing interpretations are reinforced. He says:

> *And I heard a loud voice saying in heaven, Now is come salvation, and strength, and the kingdom of our God, and*

> *the power of his Christ: for the accuser of our brethren is cast down, which accused them before our God day and night.*
>
> *And they overcame him by the blood of the Lamb, and by the word of their testimony; and they loved not their lives unto the death.*
>
> *Therefore rejoice, ye heavens, and ye that dwell in them. Woe to the inhabiters of the earth and of the sea! for the devil is come down unto you, having great wrath, because he knoweth that he hath but a short time.* Rev. 12:10–12

The overthrow of the dragon from heaven signifies an incompatibility between a separative sense of identity and Christ Consciousness. A separative sense of self tends to utilize the gains made possible from spiritual striving to further augment separateness. At a personal level, this means that we may tend to become inflated by our spiritual progress unless we regard such progress as the collective property of humanity. For example, if we've gained wisdom as a result of spiritual disciplines and spiritual inquiry, ego inflation may tempt us to demand special status from others. We may regard such progress only as the product of our efforts and ignore the role of Grace.

When our full spiritual identity is hidden from our separative sense of self, spiritual growth continues without interruption. This is what is implied by the statement "now is come salvation, and strength, and the kingdom of our God, and the power of his Christ." In other words, the impetus for spiritual striving is born out of the absence of a feeling sense of our spiritual nature. Until we've outgrown our separative impulse, this disconnectedness will continue.

To call the dragon "the accuser of our brethren," and to say that it "accused them before our God day and night" is to say that the false sense of self leads to feelings of inadequacy and unworthiness. While we experience life from the perspective of the egoic self, we feel disconnected and inadequate. In turn, these feelings of disconnectedness and inadequacy are what motivate our striving and activities. When the dragon (the ego) accuses us before God, it exposes our insufficiency of being. The only antidote for the dragon (the ego) is the blood of the Lamb (humility), which was used by the saints to overcome the dragon.

The announcement also says that the saints were able to overcome the dragon by the "word of their testimony" and because they "loved not their lives unto the death." First, the "word of their testimony" is the conscious expression of their convictions. The message for us here is that *we can always be victorious over the dragon when we live by the truth that we have realized.* Second, to say that they "loved not their lives unto the death" is to say that they did not use their energies to pursue those activities which in themselves hasten death. In other words, they possessed true will. This quality allows us to use our energies for the good of the whole being, not just part of it.

As we review the defense of the saints against the dragon, or Satan, or the Devil, which are epithets for a self-seeking sense of identity, we understand the efficacy of this defense. Humility—the awareness that our life is not an end unto itself, sincerity—living according to our convictions, and will—the ability to organize personal powers for the good of the whole being are, in combination, the only true antidote for an ego-bound perspective on life.

Persecution of the Woman by the Dragon

To pick up the narrative after the dragon was cast out, John tells us that the dragon "persecuted the woman which brought forth the man child":

> *And when the dragon saw that he was cast unto the earth, he persecuted the woman which brought forth the man child.*
>
> *And to the woman were given two wings of a great eagle, that she might fly into the wilderness, into her place, where she is nourished for a time, and times, and half a time, from the face of the serpent.*
>
> *And the serpent cast out of his mouth water as a flood after the woman, that he might cause her to be carried away of the flood.*
>
> *And the earth helped the woman, and the earth opened her mouth, and swallowed up the flood which the dragon cast out of his mouth.*
>
> *And the dragon was wroth with the woman, and went to make war with the remnant of her seed, which keep the commandments of God, and have the testimony of Jesus Christ.*
>
> Rev. 12:13–17

The idea of the dragon being filled with wrath "because he knoweth that he hath but a short time" means that when our sense of self is experienced only in the material, earthly sphere, that sense of self is restricted to the duration of life in the body. The ego, therefore, exists only as long as the body lives. Consequently, a sense of self dominated by egoic consciousness plays itself out with great intensity. The dragon persecutes the woman in the sense that the process of trying to distil Christ Consciousness from life experiences may be accompanied by a tremendous sense of alienation and hopelessness. If this leads to discouragement, the dragon wins.

The "two wings of the eagle" that are given to the woman so that she could "fly into the wilderness" are suggestive of the energy reserves we can tap into by persevering and being resolute in times of difficulty. The "two wings" represent the power to transcend time–space limitations by enabling us to stay with an endeavour longer and to go deeper. These energies are symbolized in the astrological sign of Scorpio, symbolized by the eagle. These "two wings" also refer to the activation in the body of forces that lift the consciousness of the entire body, making it receptive to a spiritual approach to life. In a sense, this is a mental bypass operation: the mind cannot interfere with it. The wilderness where the woman took refuge is suggestive of the unconscious where the work of transformation of consciousness continues unobserved by the conscious mind.

We have already seen that the nourishment of the woman for "a time and times and half a time" refers to the process of achieving complete psychospiritual synthesis. We can now also say that being nourished for "a time and times and half a time" implies the education of the body with the ideals of the Spirit. Thus educated, the body is able to express spiritual principles as naturally as any instinctual impulse.

Since the dragon cannot divert unto itself the proceeds of our spiritual effort, it wants to subvert the process. The water that it spews out after the woman is symbolic of the feeling and attachment principle. In a psychological sense, when we are engaged in the process of extracting Christ Consciousness from the experiences of life, our sensitivity becomes more finely tuned. Consequently, we might become subject to an exaggeration of the feeling principle and be overwhelmed by feelings of alienation and discouragement. These are the times when we feel the temptation to seek refuge in conformity with the crowd.

However, this is where the earth, matter, density, comes in. On one hand, our earthly environment narrows the focus of the egoic sense of self, restricting our sphere of perception. On the other hand, this narrowing of the perceptual field presents an opportunity to harness the attention so that we can rise above collective desires and social mores. The idea behind the earth swallowing the water spewed out by the dragon is suggestive of some of the compensations available to us from being involved in earth life—compensations such as the need to assume responsibility or care for ourselves and others.

The Beast from the Sea

As we move into the thirteenth chapter, another character is added to the mythological drama. This time, it is a beast, which we shall identify as *beast number one* since there is another one to come with an equally significant role to play. John says:

> *And I stand upon the sand of the sea and saw a beast rise up out of the sea, having seven heads and ten horns, and upon his horns ten crowns, and upon his heads, the name of blasphemy.*
>
> *And the beast that I saw was like unto a leopard, and his feet were as the feet of a bear, and his mouth as the mouth of a lion: and the dragon gave him his power, and his seat, and great authority.* Rev. 13:1–2

Beast number one is a composite of attributes of several animals. It has a leopard's coat, a bear's feet, and a lion's mouth. The leopard's appearance is appropriately chosen to represent the appearance of this beast because the leopard's most characteristic features—spotted coat, stealth, and swiftness—are suggestive of the psychological attributes of discontinuity and volatility.

This beast is also given a lion's mouth because, first, a lion is symbolic of power and strength, and second, the mouth is symbolic of speech and articulation. The roar of the lion sends fear into man and beast alike; it is symbolic of the authority and the power that the lion carries. There is nothing out of place with a lion having a lion's mouth, but with this composite beast, the lion's mouth is the only thing belonging to a lion. With only the mouth of a lion, what we have here is pride, claims that cannot be validated or substantiated. In another word, it represents "bombast."

As for the feet of a bear, these represent tenacity. Bear's feet are used for mauling and are a bear's foremost weapon. Also, in biblical imagery, bears are used to portray anger and wrath, particularly if their cubs are interfered with. As part of the composite beast, bear's feet are a powerful symbol for the idea of enforcing claims of possession.

When we combine the attributes of these symbols used to represent *beast number one*, we get something that is always shifting (its leopard aspects), given to pride and bravado (lion's mouth), and clinging and destructive simultaneously (bear's feet). Together, these represent the "false emotional center" in man. This "false emotional center" predisposes us to attachments and identification. This false center then becomes the recipient of various powers, symbolized here by the dragon giving *beast number one* "its power, its seat, and great authority." This is to say that the false sense of self, the ego, is the force that energizes and gives apparent authenticity to the feelings of personal identity that characterize this false emotional nature. Power represents energy, impetus; seat represents identity; and great authority represents deep conviction.

In psychological terms, the description of *beast number one* and the source of its power is commenting on our predisposition to feel we have identity on the basis of our sense of possessiveness and ownership. It is as if the consciousness is saying, "I possess things; I have power over others; therefore I am." But identity in its true sense is not established or proven by identification and attachment. These attest to the lack of true identity because true identity is not hinged on external props.

The characteristics of *beast number one* supply us with some of the attributes of the false emotional center in us, which it represents. As we examine these characteristics, we find several oddities. The beast has seven heads and only one mouth! These seven heads represent seven independent centers of will—just like the dragon, all uncoordinated. The beast has ten horns with crowns upon them. It is odd that it is the horns that have the crowns and not the heads. The horns represent instruments for goring and probing. The crowns on them symbolize the authority that they carry. At a psychological level, the ten horns represent the five physical senses in their outer and inner levels.

The false emotional center in us functions on the basis of subjective experience. Usually, the desire nature—our sense of neediness or lack which further leads us to form a view of the world colored by what we expect to extract from it—supplies the subjective coloring that is given to an outer experience. The five physical senses of hearing, sight, taste, smell, and touch are all duplicated at the subjective level. For example, in the emotional desire nature, the sense of hearing is replicated as unspoken words—as thoughts. Sight exists there as the ability to visualize and form objects of attachment. The sense of taste exists as longing. As for the physical sense of smell, its emotional counterpart exists as the tendency to prejudge. Finally, touch in the domain of the emotional represents sensuousness.

As John continues his description of the beast, he says:

> *And I saw one of his heads as it were wounded to death; and his deadly wound was healed; and all the world wondered after the beast.*
>
> *And they worshipped the dragon which gave power unto*

> *the beast and they worshipped the beast saying, Who is like unto the beast? Who is able to make war with him?*
>
> *And there was given unto him a mouth speaking great things and blasphemies; and power was given unto him to continue forty and two months.*
>
> *And he opened his mouth in blasphemy against God, to blaspheme his name, and his tabernacle, and them that dwell in heaven.* Rev. 13:3–6

A careful reading of this description will show that John is not describing from a visual standpoint, but from a mental one. His "seeing" relates to the mental impressions that he is receiving. One of these impressions is that one of the heads of this beast was wounded to death, but that this wound was healed.

Recalling that these heads, as mentioned previously, refer to centers of will, it would mean that if one were wounded to death it would have lost its autonomy and would now be functioning for the good of the whole being. But John tells us that this wound was healed. In other words, the conversion of this center was only temporary: it then reverted to its previous functioning, and with more power. From having thrown in its lot with the whole being, it acquired more power than it had previously. We learn also that this head was wounded by a sword (13:14). John also hints at the type of interpretation we should seek. After describing this beast and its behavior, he intimates:

> *If any man have an ear, let him hear. He that leadeth into captivity shall go into captivity: he that killeth with the sword must be killed with the sword. Here is the patience and the faith of the saints.* Rev. 13:9–10

The statement, "If any man have an ear, let him hear" is suggesting that what he is divulging is esoteric information. The statement alerts us to the fact that an interpretation is required that is not obvious from a surface reading of scriptures. Because of this alert, we must read "He that leadeth into captivity shall go into captivity" and "He that killeth with the sword must be killed with the sword" to mean that he is talking about the *Law of Karma*.

We are now better equipped to add to our explanation of the head receiving a deadly wound by a sword and surviving it. The seven heads of the beast, which represent centers of will in a person, are all organized in a way that fits our individual *karma*. The *Law of Karma* has many levels of interpretation. The first level is fairly simple: We reap the consequences of all our deeds. At a higher level of interpretation, we can say that "All tendencies to a separative existence must be rectified at the deepest level of being through the realization that these tendencies and the actions they lead to are self-defeating." The "saints" know this and that is the secret of their endurance.

The head of this beast that was "wounded to death" refers to one of the centers of will coming to a realization of the self-defeating nature of a separative tendency. Psychologically speaking, being "wounded to death" also refers to a glimpse of Truth that might invade our consciousness from time to time. There is nothing wrong with glimpses of Truth per se. The problem arises when we do not wait for the whole picture to unfold. The metaphor of the head surviving the deadly wound means that a glimpse of Truth, rather than leading one to further assimilation into the totality of existence, can cause one to revert back to separativeness.[1] This second state is even more damaging than the first.

Now, the center of will, that was almost converted but balked, acts in the consciousness to inflate one's image of oneself so that one feels that one is a messenger of God. One feels that one is a visionary, far-sighted, has the good of humanity in mind, and is in a better position than others to speak on its behalf. There can hardly be anything more dangerous than a false emotional center armed with the conviction of the visionary.

John says that people wondered after the beast. They worshipped the dragon that gave the beast power, and they also worshipped the beast. This underlies the fact that the false emotional center and the separative sense of self, which gives rise to it, are often made the objects of veneration by individuals. Thus the only authority such individuals need to do absolutely anything is to "feel" that they should do it.

The Beast from the Earth

The scene now changes to present us with yet another character: another beast, but one which arose from the earth. For the sake of identification, we shall call this one *beast number two*.

> *And I beheld another beast coming up out of the earth; and he had two horns like a lamb, and he spake as a dragon.*
>
> *And he exerciseth all the power of the first beast before him, and causeth the earth and them which dwell therein to worship the first beast, whose deadly wound was healed.*

And he doeth great wonders, so that he maketh fire come down from heaven on the earth in the sight of men.

And deceiveth them that dwell on the earth by the means of those miracles which he had power to do in the sight of the beast. Rev. 13:11–14

What we have in *beast number two* is a faculty born of the material nature. This is what it means for this beast to have arisen from the earth. The origin of this beast compares with that of the dragon that came down from heaven, representing the Fire Element, and the beast that arose from the sea, representing the Water Element. In these three characters—these three principles—we have three of the four Elements of Fire, Water, Earth, and Air. We shall encounter the fourth, the Air Element, later on.

Beast number two looks harmless enough with its two horns of a lamb, yet it speaks like a dragon, meaning that it expresses itself with pride and bravado. It is a composite of the first beast and the dragon: we were earlier told that the dragon gave the first beast its power and we are now informed that the second beast has all the powers of the first. This succession of power is equivalent to a coalition. What it amounts to, psychologically speaking, is the ego energizing the emotional nature, and now the emotional nature feeding into a third faculty. But what is this faculty that the second beast represents?

To discover this we must take a further look at the activities of the second beast: It caused people "to worship the first beast, whose deadly wound was healed." This means that the principle the second beast represents causes people to regard the principle the first beast represents as the outermost limits of striving. "To worship the first beast" is to limit one's perspective to whatever it is the first beast represents.

A pattern has developed and should be pointed out at this juncture. We saw that people were caused to worship the first beast upon the appearance of the second, and we also saw that upon the appearance of the first beast, people worshipped the dragon who gave him power. The pattern is one of drawing energy downward rather than upward.[2] It is a mentality that is the opposite of the evolution and growth of consciousness. The second beast is the intellectual nature, or more accurately, the mental apparatus that is matter bound, that cannot see beyond "an incomplete vision of the Real" which the first beast represents.

Looking at the dragon, the beast from the sea, and the beast from the earth together, we have first, a sense of independent existence (dragon) bolstering a sense of false identity as represented by the emotions (the beast from the sea), and the two together feeding into the intellect (beast from the earth). We can also say that *beast number two* represents the ambitions since this is how the intellect that is bounded by form most characteristically expresses itself. The intellect in man is that which is dedicated to the worship of individual differences; it is that which emphasizes categorizations and downplays interconnectedness.

The rest of the description of how this beast functions can now be more clearly understood. We are told that he brought fire down from heaven in the sight of men. Bringing fire down from heaven deals with speeding up progress on earth, with the acceleration of evolution on earth. But the phrase "in the sight of men" indicates that bringing fire down from heaven—and the progress for which this is a metaphor—occurs in appearance only. Progress occurs only in the estimation of man.

Also, *beast number two* did miracles that were performed in the sight of the first beast. Miracles are happenings that take place outside of natural law, or at least outside of what is thought to be natural law. So this beast, this false intellectual center, is pushing back the frontiers of knowledge. It is extending man's concept of what is or is not possible. It is therefore performing "miracles"!

To say that the miracles are done in the sight of the beast, meaning *beast number one*, is to say that in terms of what *beast number one* represents, that is, the false emotional center, the activities of the materialistic intellect are miracles. In a general sense, we have a mentality here that tells man how separate, how individual, how perfected he is. It endows him with a sense of accomplishment.

The Image Made to the Beast from the Sea and the Mark of the Beast

Beast number two did not stop at miracles. We are told that he commanded the people with particular instructions,

> ... *saying to them that dwell on the earth, that they should make an image to the beast, which had the wound by a sword and did live.*
>
> *And he had power to give life unto the image of the beast, that the image of the beast should both speak, and cause that as many as would not worship the image of the beast should be killed.*
>
> *And he causeth all, both small and great, rich and poor, free*

and bond, to receive a mark in their right hand or in their foreheads:

And that no man might buy or sell, save he that had the mark, or the name of the beast, or the number of his name.
Rev. 13:14–17

After this narration of the activities of *beast number one*, John says:

Here is wisdom. Let him that hath understanding count the number of the beast: for it is the number of a man; and his number is Six hundred threescore and six. Rev. 13:18

We have already seen what the number 666 implies astrologically and psychologically,[3] and in a sense, we have come almost full circle. To complete the circle, we must see what the image of the first beast is and what is meant by receiving its mark and other indications of identification and allegiance.

Those who dwell on the earth were asked to make an image to *beast number one*. By way of interpretation, "them that dwell on the earth" means those whose consciousness is restricted to only the material, instinctual realm. To make an image to *beast number one* is to accept a symbol that honors this beast—the false emotional center. The image is given life by the second beast, so that the image has its own power to command allegiance.

The image in honor of the first beast represents the Air Element alluded to earlier. The dragon came from heaven (Fire), the first beast came from the sea (Water), the second beast came from the earth (Earth), and the image came from the mind (Air).

As we place this coalition of the dragon, the two beasts, and the image of the first beast into a psychological context, we uncover the process through which the human ego validates itself. The first beast, which represents the emotional nature, receives homage from the second beast, which represents the materialistic intellect. The second beast creates an image to the first beast and animates it. The animated image then solicits allegiance on behalf of the first beast. In other words, the animated image functions as an extension of the first beast. It reflects back to the first beast how important the first beast is. Therefore, the image is one's sense of self-worth seen from an egoic perspective.

In terms of something that functions in real life to validate the egoic self and adds to its prestige, money serves this function perfectly. There are even terms in our language to express the powers of money—"money speaks," "money makes the world go 'round." The implication here is that money is vested by the matter-bound mind of man with tremendous powers to circumscribe an individual's value to society, to measure one's worth.[4] However, only those "who dwell on the earth" and those who receive the mark of the beast give so much authority to money.

Those who did not worship the image of the beast were caused to be killed. This does not refer to being killed in a literal sense. The explanation lies at a psychological level. It means that those who do not measure themselves by money are deemed to be of no value and are therefore "cutoff" from the mainstream of society.

The idea of worshipping the image of the beast is equivalent to having received its mark on the right hand or on the forehead, or to have the name or the number of the name. Those who did not receive the mark could not buy or sell; they could not enter into exchanges of energies with those who had the mark. Those with the mark and those without it could not have mutually beneficial interactions because there was no point of contact for such to take place.

The mark of the beast—remembering that it is a way of indicating that one worships or belongs to what amounts to a cult of success—is a level of identification, like a brand. Having the mark on the hand relates to the activities one engages in, and having it on the forehead points to the thinking pattern and the way of life. In a broader sense, we can say that the mark on the hand relates to the job or the life pursuit or the career, and on the forehead to the education and the values. When our life pursuits, education, and values are taken up with little or no consideration for spiritual enrichment, but only with regard to achieving status and success, then we bear the mark.

In addition to the mark, one can also have the name or the number of the name. To have the name is to be driven, not so much by money, but by pride. It is full emotional and sympathetic identification with the false emotional center. The number of the name, of which much was said earlier, relates to mental identification.

The mark, the name, and the number of the name are three ways that one can serve the lower nature. These are the lust of the flesh (the mark), the lust of the eyes (the name), and the pride of life (number of the name). This is how John, the same John who is credited with writing the book of Revelation, expressed it:

> *For all that is of the world, the lust of the flesh, and the lust of the eyes, and the pride of life, is not of the Father, but is of the world.* I John 2:16

To recap, if one is not driven by need, or by greed, or by pride, one cannot become part of the mainstream of society according to

Revelation and the exhortation above from John. The different ways of serving the lower nature must be placed in perspective with what the first beast represents—a false understanding of who we are and a false approach to assessing our Self worth.

The following chart is provided as a means of clarifiying the convergent forces that define the psyche. Shown are the apocalyptic symbol, its astrological element, and the human counterpart.

Table 7-1. The Coalition of Forces that Define the Psyche of Man

Symbol	Astrological Element	Human Counterpart
The Dragon that was cast from "Heaven"	Fire	The Ego, False sense of Self
The Beast that came up from the Sea	Water	The attachment principle, false emotional nature
The Beast that came from the Earth	Earth	The Materialistic intellect, misdirected ambition
The Image made to the Beast from the Sea	Air	False sense of value, epitomized by love of money

The Alternative to the Mark of the Beast

We shall conclude this phase of our analysis on a note of contrast. John gives us an insight into what the alternative is to having the mark of the beast. We find this insight in the fourteenth chapter. He says:

Here is the patience of the saints: here are they that keep the commandments of God, and the faith of Jesus.

And I heard a voice from heaven saying unto me, Write, Blessed are the dead which die in the Lord from henceforth; Yea, saith the Spirit, that they may rest from their labours; and their works do follow them. Rev. 14:12–13

The term, "patience of the saints" is a way of speaking about the secret of the saints' powers of endurance. This endurance is expressed by the saints in their striving. They strive out of the desire to express Christ Consciousness—the "faith of Jesus"—and not out of a desire for earthly recognition and rewards. They kept the commandments of God, meaning that they strove to become living embodiments of higher principles. When one lives in this manner, one does not see the physical life as the beginning and end of existence, but as a medium within which one can objectify the makeup of one's consciousness and deal with weaknesses as they show up.

When such a person departs this life, that individual "dies in the Lord," which is to say that consciousness is on an ascending arc—one has established the foundation for further growth. In contrast, a consciousness on a descending arc is one where unlearning must occur before further growth can take place. Whatever principles one has been able to embody mark the extent to which one has contributed to the Work—the spiritualization of matter and the spiritualization of the body. This is what is suggested by the statement that "their deeds do follow them." This is in a sense a truism, for the deeds that follow one onto the spiritual realm have to do with the extent to which one has contributed to making one's existence permanent through one's labors at embodying spiritual principles in the mind and body.

This is in total contrast to the whole thrust of the dragon, *beast number one, beast number two,* and *the image to beast number one.* In all those instances, the premise of life is: "Make only what is tangible the objective of striving, and realize the proceeds of such striving while you can."

Chapter 8

Seven Churches, Seven Cities, Seven Planets:
Factors Connecting the Seven Churches to the Zodiac

Overview

The most conclusive case for an astrological interpretation of Revelation is to be found in the first three chapters covering the section containing the letters to "The Seven Churches in Asia." There is some poetic irony in the fact that this is the section of Revelation that students of the Bible feel most comfortable with, not realizing that within it are cues directing one closer to the underlying nature of the Revelation document.

On the surface, it appears as if the letters to the Seven Churches just provide the rationale for the rest of Revelation. This sense is conveyed by the very first words that were spoken to John by the one who appeared to him as "the son of Man." John is told:

> ... What thou seest write in a book, and send it unto the seven churches which are in Asia; unto Ephesus, and unto Smyrna, and unto Pergamos, and unto Thyatira, and unto Sardis, and unto Philadelphia, and unto Laodicea.   1:11

From this instruction, it is clear that the contents of the entire book of Revelation were to be sent to each of the Churches. However, individualized instructions were dictated to these Seven Churches within a somewhat standardized format. Each letter possesses the following: (a) an address whereby the sender, Christ, identifies himself by a set of attributes, (b) a salutation, which acknowledges the chief characteristics of the Church being addressed, (c) a rebuke, in which the shortcomings of the Church are identified, (d) a warning, wherein the Church is told the consequences of not rectifying those shortcomings, and lastly (e) a promise, telling the Church of the rewards that are possible for it, should it conduct itself with propriety.

Hiding behind this apparently straightforward scheme of addressing seven ordinary churches is a structure that has to do with the twelve zodiacal signs and their energies. This means that the section of Revelation dealing with the seven letters to the Seven Churches is no less symbolic than the rest of it. Just as zodiacal symbolism provides the key to an understanding of the portion regarded as apocalyptic, so it also unlocks the symbology of this portion to bring it to life.

The consequence of the astrological nature of the letters is that the specific instructions to the Seven Churches should be read and regarded with the relevance and urgency of a personal and social psychology. For indeed, this is exactly what the intention behind their presentation is.

The Cities of the Seven Churches as the Relevant Points of Focus for the Seven Letters

In order to properly interpret and understand the letters to the Seven Churches, we must evaluate them from two focal points. The first relates to the cities to which the letters were sent, and the second to the contents of the letters themselves. From the way in which the Revelation material is conveyed, one might infer that it is the church in one of the seven cities that is the point of focus for the instructions. However, such an assumption breaks down when any attempt is made to determine why these seven churches in particular were chosen to be recipients of the letters.

The first incongruity that confronts the questioner is that the churches presented as "the Seven Churches that are in Asia" do not exhaust the number of Christian congregations or "churches" that circumstantial evidence indicates should have existed in Asia at that time. In a very valiant effort to come to grips with the incongruities surrounding the Seven Churches and the seven letters, a theological professor by the name of Sir William Ramsay published a book in 1904 addressing these issues.[1] He saw the Seven Churches as embodying a particular principle that he attempted to unearth. He did not explore the astrological factor, but nevertheless, has left us with an extremely rich legacy of information on the seven cities where the churches were.

On the matter of what principle the Seven Churches embodied, and whether the churches addressed were the only ones in Asia, Ramsay observed:

Another important point to observe is that the Seven Cities were not selected simply because they were situated on the circular route above described[2] nor yet because they were the most important cities on that route. The messenger must necessarily pass through Hierapolis, Tralleis and Magnesia on his circular journey; *all those cities were indubitably the seats of Churches at that time*;

yet none of the three found a place among the representative cities, although Tralleis and Magnesia were more important and wealthy than Philadelphia or Thyatira. What then was the principle of selection?[3] [emphasis added]

Ramsay's main concern was to discover what else the cities had in common besides sharing the same geographical region. He went on to outline the hypothesis that the cities were distribution points in a church communication network. He further postulated that the seven cities were the best points on a particular geographical circuit to function as centers of communication within the seven districts served by the seven cities. This hypothesis, although it recognizes the churches' representative function, falls short of explaining what they really represented.[4]

Ramsay also was alerted to the symbolic use of the word "church" and recognized the letters to the Seven Churches as addresses to the cities themselves. In commenting on John's use of the term "church," Ramsay remarked:

> He assumes always that the Church is, in a sense, the city. The local Church does not live apart from the locality and the population, amid which it had a merely temporary abode.[5]

This theme was further developed in his examination of the individual letters to the church at Sardis. He said:

> The Church of Sardis is not merely in the city of Sardis, *it is in a sense the city*; ... the Church here is addressed, apparently with the set purpose of suggesting that the fortunes of ancient Sardis had been its own fortunes.[6] [emphasis added]

Astrological Factors Connecting the Seven Cities

It is one thing to realize that the cities were the true points of focus and another to explain satisfactorily why this is the case. These particular cities were addressed because their geography and cultural heritage combined to make each a representation of one of seven psychological principles. The seven psychological principles that the cities represented are based on the energies of the twelve astrological signs in their relationship of opposition on the zodiacal wheel. This means that each city represented, not one sign, but a pair of signs occupying opposite sides on the zodiacal wheel.

Of the seven cities to which the letters were directed, six of them had astrological connections. The six are Ephesus, Smyrna, Pergamum, Thyatira, Sardis, and Laodicea. The city of Philadelphia lay outside of this zodiacal scheme, and its inclusion with the other six was intended to serve as a point of contrast for the others in order to demonstrate how consciousness functions when it is freed from the psychological conflicts generated by duality or pairs of opposites.

Specifically, the cities relate to astrological polarities in the manner of Table 8-1:

Table 8-1. The Relationship Between the Seven Cities and the Twelve Signs of the Zodiac

The Seven Cities of the Seven Churches	Zodiacal Polarities
Ephesus	Cancer–Capricorn
Smyrna	Virgo–Pisces
Pergamum	Gemini–Sagittarius
Thyatira	Aries–Libra
Sardis	Leo–Aquarius
Laodicea	Taurus–Scorpio
Philadelphia	Beyond Zodiacal Influence

General Outline of Available Evidence to Support the Affinities of Cities and Zodiacal Signs

The evidence in support of this scheme can be gleaned from various sources. Published historical and archeological reports on the seven cities provide a good deal of the information allowing us to tie the cities to the zodiacal signs. The historical and archeological information provide the material from which we can clearly establish the links between the cities and pairs of astrological signs. The information is useful in two ways.

First, historical descriptions of the cultural life of these cities provide us with a sense of the dominant psychological and sociological influences during the general period when Revelation was written. This information is useful in enabling us to establish an informal correlation between the psychological and sociological ambiance prevailing in each city with the psychological factors of the astrological polarity assigned to it.

Second, archeological findings provide us with a sense of the mythological heritage of a city by supplying information on the deities of Greek and Anatolian—early Turkish—mythic origins that figured prominently in the religious worship of a city and that usually functioned as its guardian.[7] It is possible to show affinities between these deities worshipped or honored in the cities and the planetary rulers of the astrological signs that comprise a zodiacal polarity.

There are a few obstacles that, though they eventually may be overcome, initially stand in the way of achieving a matching of zodiacal signs and cities. These occur because most of the studies that were conducted on these ancient cities were usually done from the perspective of the traditionally accepted academic disciplines only. Consequently, most of the information supportive of the zodiacal case is either misinterpreted, downplayed, or ignored entirely.

One of these obstacles is where a ruling deity was associated with more than one city, as for example, Cybele in Sardis and Smyrna. Another is where several deities were worshipped in one city, for example, Zeus, Aesclepius, Dionysus, and Athena in Pergamum (as Ramsay's book reports). In the case where a deity was associated with more than one city, that obstacle is overcome by realizing that different aspects of a deity were abstracted from the other attributes and worshipped at particular places. Sometimes, these aspects were quite diverse, as the worship of Cybele as the Fates in Smyrna, and as a pair of lions in Sardis, demonstrates. Where apparently more deities than are required to form an astrological relationship were connected to a place, we find that more prominence was given at that city to those deities that figured more directly in the astrological qualities of the signs the city represented.

The relationship between cities and signs goes much deeper than casual comparisons of the psychological ambiances of the cities—as portrayed in the deities worshipped there—and astrological energies of the signs. To fully appreciate the extent of this connection, it is necessary to introduce and explore yet another astrological variable—that of the planets and their relationships with the signs. This additional astrological information is necessary because the planetary rulers of the astrological signs provide the strongest links with the cities of the Seven Churches through affinities with the ruling deities found in each city.

The Relationship Between "Ruling Planets" of Astrological Signs and the Seven Cities

In astrological language, each of the twelve signs is said to be "ruled" by one of the planets in the solar system. For purposes of analysis, the sun and moon are included in the scheme of rulership, and astrologers, in order to facilitate astrological discussion, refer to them as "planets." The traditional system of planetary rulership was established for the planets that are observable from the earth with the unaided eye. These include Saturn, Jupiter, Mars, Venus, Mercury, and the two Lights—the sun and the moon.

In this traditional system, each planet was assigned to the rulership of two signs each, and each Light to one sign only. This covered the twelve signs—i.e., two each for Saturn, Jupiter, Mars, Venus, Mercury, and one each for the sun and moon. The later planets to be discovered, Uranus (in 1781), Neptune (in 1846), and Pluto (in 1930), were incorporated into this scheme of rulership and are regarded as higher octaves—in a psychological sense—of some of the more ancient ones.

The concept of planetary rulership means that the given planet is a particular focalizer of the energy of the sign that it rules. The basic idea behind these rulerships is that the effect of a planet varies from sign to sign and that its energies are most clearly defined and focused (i.e., the strongest) in the sign of its rulership.

For each of the six cities that can be linked to an astrological polarity, there are two planets represented—one for each of the signs in the polarity. The planets were represented in their deified, mythological form in the ancient cities, as for example, Zeus for Jupiter, Apollo for the sun, or Aesclepius (alias Hermes) for Mercury. In Table 8-2, the planets associated with pairs of signs are given. This framework sets up a point of reference against which we can later examine the ruling deities of the cities for astrological associations.

Table 8-2. The Relationships Between Signs and Planets

Zodiacal Polarities	Ruling Planets
Aries–Libra	Mars–Venus
Taurus–Scorpio	Venus–Mars
Gemini–Sagittarius	Mercury–Jupiter
Cancer–Capricorn	Moon–Saturn
Leo–Aquarius	Sun–Saturn
Virgo–Pisces	Mercury–Jupiter

From knowing the astrological signs that are associated with each city and from knowing which planets rule the signs involved, we are alerted as to what sort of planetary representation to expect in the cities. The information presented in Table 8-3 is important in this regard.

Table 8-3. The Seven Cities and Their Planetary Influences

Cities With Astrological and Planetary Affiliations	Planetary Influences
Ephesus	Moon–Saturn
Smyrna	Mercury–Jupiter
Pergamum	Mercury–Jupiter
Thyatira	Mars–Venus
Sardis	Sun–Saturn
Laodicea	Venus–Mars
Philadelphia	No Planetary Connection

The idea of planetary influences is used in the psychological sense rather than the physical one—not that a planet physically affected a place, but that the environment of that place was permeated with emotion-evoking symbols and rituals found there in honor of a planetary deity. In this sense, it can be seen how an astrological idea or principle was given embodiment.

The schematic diagram in Figure 8-1 has been constructed in order to facilitate a conceptual overview of the connective chain linking the Seven Churches to astrological signs and principles.

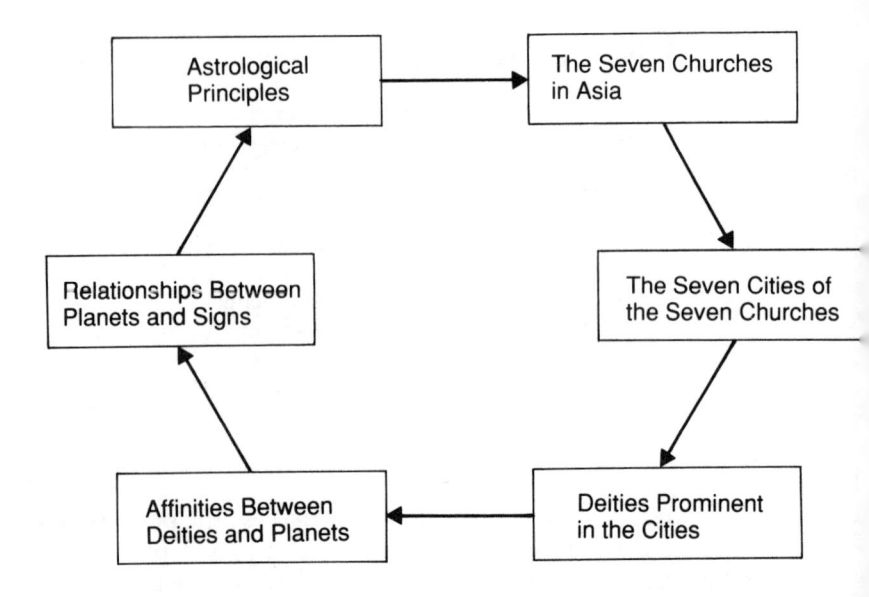

Figure 8.1 *Relationship between Astrological Signs, Planets, Cities, and Churches*

Chapter 9

The Principles Linking Specific Cities to Specific Zodiacal Signs

Introduction

As the evidence is presented to show that these early cities were living symbols of astrological principles, we will look at each city one by one to attempt to capture its salient features—the things for which it was best known—and examine these against the principles embodied by the zodiacal signs associated with each city.

The City of Ephesus: Embodiment of the Cancer–Capricorn Principle

Ephesus was, in a sense, the most well-known of the seven cities. This can be attributed to the fact that is mentioned in the New Testament and that the church there was a recipient of one of Paul's epistles—i.e., Ephesians. This city, whose history goes back over a thousand years before the birth of Christ, was at the time of the writing of the Revelation letters, a living embodiment of the archetypal qualities of The Great Mother.

The characteristics of the Church at Ephesus that are being addressed in the Revelation letter are those that, from the astrological point of view, belong to the signs Cancer and Capricorn and their respective planetary rulers, the Moon and Saturn. Most of these characteristics are detectable from the cultural history and religious disposition of Ephesus, of which the single most pervasive influence was the worship of the goddess Artemis. The temple of Artemis, which stood out as the focal point of the religious and cultural life of the city, earned recognition as one of the seven wonders of the ancient world.

Artemis dominated the life of the Ephesians to such an extent that she was at the center of the commercial crafts. Many craftsmen were engaged in making silver replicas and shrines for devotees (Acts 19:24–41). The physical representation of Artemis was in the form of a female figure, clothed, but displaying sac-like protuberances

Figure 9.1 *The Ephesian Artemis*

from her entire chest area that have the likeness of breasts or eggs (Figure 9.1). One source describes her in the following manner:

Artemis (the Roman Diana) of Ephesus, the Mother Goddess shown with many breasts—some scholars have interpreted them as the ova of the sacred bee which can be seen adorning the figure".[1]

Behind this physical representation of Artemis were ideas that are as universal as they are timeless. She was just the local crystallization of the ubiquitous Great Mother, Mother Goddess, Moon Goddess, and more. Mythologists differ somewhat on the genealogy of Artemis, but in terms of the characteristics she embodied, there is close agreement. Robert Graves, in his two-volume work entitled

The Greek Myths,[2] says that Artemis was Apollo's sister, while Edith Hamilton in her book *Mythology*,[3] says that she was a moon-goddess and sister of Helios, the sun-god. Artemis is described by Graves as "protectress of little children, and of all suckling animals," and by another source as "Mistress of Beasts, Lady of All Wild Things," and "A Lion unto Women." This latter source, *A Dictionary of Greek and Roman Mythology*,[4] further states that one of her titles was "Eileithyia," meaning "who is come to aid women in childbirth."

All these characteristics of Artemis—Great Mother, Protectress of little children, Guardian of pregnant women, Moon Goddess, and so on—when superimposed one upon the other, create a composite of the attributes of Cancer. This sign has always been a symbol of "the Great Mother." All our institutions and customs that nurture and give sustenance, together with the human feeling response generally, are expressions of Cancer as an astrological archetype. It can also be said that this archetype imprints itself on all situations where there is voluntary bonding, as for example, within organizations that take on characteristics of a family—goodwill organizations, churches, and so on.

It is interesting to note that the Motherhood theme of Ephesus was carried over into Christian times and has persisted to the present day through the legend that Mary, the mother of Jesus, retired, died, and was buried there. Whether or not this actually happened, there is a shrine in the vicinity of ancient Ephesus where a small chapel houses a sanctuary, altar, and a statue to Mary.

With respect to the opposite sign, Capricorn, its characteristics were also expressed through the Ephesian goddess in one of her symbols—the bee. This symbol was represented on coins used in Ephesus, and as Ramsay tells us, there seems to have been some type of struggle for dominance between it and a more personal representation of Artemis. The outcome of this struggle was determined by whichever influence—Western or Asiatic—was the more dominant. Ramsay reports that the conquest of Ephesus by Alexander the Great in 335 B.C. led to a growth of the Greek spirit that began to reflect itself in a change in the coinage. He states:

The bee, the sacred insect and the symbol of the Great Goddess, had hitherto always been the principal type of Ephesian coin. Now, about 295 B.C. a purely Greek type, the head of the Greek Artemis, the Virgin "Queen and Huntress chaste and fair" was substituted for the bee on the silver coins, while the less honorable copper coinage retained the old hieratic types.[5]

He also points out that another change took place about A.D. 196 when Ephesus was captured by Antiochus the Great and entered a phase where the Asiatic spirit was again being fostered, resulting in a return of the bee as the characteristic type on the silver coinage.

The significance of the bee as a symbol, as opposed to a more personalized representation of the spirit of Ephesus, has to do with the fact that the bee portrayed this spirit in a much more abstract, and therefore direct way, than other symbols.[6] Whatever the bee represented to the Ephesians, it was important enough for them to have patterned the ceremonial life after it. Ramsay remarks,

> In the Ephesian ceremonial, the life of the bee was the model; the Great Goddess was queenbee, the mother of her people, and her image was in outline not unlike the bee ... her priestesses were called Melissai (working-bee) and a body of priests attached to the Temple was called Essenes (the drones).[7]

He further credits the Ephesians with a good understanding of the life history of the bee, of which the Greek naturalists were apparently in error—regarding the queen-bee as male and therefore king of the hive.

The bee, as a hard worker and organizer, given to formality and protocol, can be said to epitomize the qualities that astrological analysis attributes to the sign of Capricorn. The human psychological attributes epitomized by this sign and its ruler, Saturn, are the impulse to succeed (ambition) and a refined sense of duty. When these two attributes are brought together, the result is self-definition and evaluation—two of the building blocks of maturity. However, until we get to the point where we are mature enough to learn by reflection, the Saturnian and Capricornian facets to our nature (i.e., ambition and sense of duty) ensure that we involve ourselves in life.

Actually, what may happen is that we may be forced to undertake activities through a restriction of our field of awareness. The consequence is that actions are undertaken, the true results of which we may not comprehend or appreciate at the time of acting. It is quite difficult to find a better representation of the workings of the Cosmic Plan in exacting compliance out of humanity, with or without our consent, than through the example of the bee.

The City of Smyrna: Embodiment of the Virgo–Pisces Principle

The origin of Smyrna as a city also dates back to over one thousand years before Christ. The city was founded initially as a Greek colony but was soon captured by Ionian Greeks and made into an Ionian colony. At about 600 B.C., the city was captured by the Lydians under King Alyattes and destroyed. The city that existed at the time of the Revelation letter was refounded by Lysimachus according to a plan that was given to Alexander the Great in a dream. Legend has it that during this dream, the goddess of Smyrna, Nemesis, appeared to him and revealed the plan. This event was commemorated on coins of Smyrna depicting the dream in which the plan was communicated to Alexander by Nemesis, who appeared as two figures.[8]

Smyrna portrayed the astrological polarity of Virgo–Pisces. As such, it was an embodiment of the process of psychological synthesis of the conflicts that exist between Virgo characteristics and Pisces characteristics. Generally speaking, the Virgo side of this polarity deals with experience in the practical aspects of life while the Pisces side deals more with experiences of the mystical and transcendental sphere. There is ample evidence to substantiate this connection of Smyrna to zodiacal motifs.

First-century Smyrna was famous for a large public theatre, which was reputed to have been the largest in Asia. The city was also acclaimed for being the birthplace of the great epic poet Homer who was said to have been born and brought up beside the sacred river Meles. Ramsay remarks that Homer appears more frequently than any other figure on the coinage of the city. Both the theatrical connection and, through Homer, the poetic association, links Smyrna to the sign of Pisces which in astrological analysis expresses its energy through the poet, musician, dramatist, and the idealist.

The patron goddess of Smyrna was Cybele, also known as the Sipylene Mother. However, the form in which she was worshipped was in the nature of Nemesis. Ramsay says that in Smyrna alone of all the Greek cities, Nemesis was regarded not as a single figure but as a pair. This adaptation of Nemesis to conform to the characteristics of the Fates of Greek mythology had the effect of linking Smyrna ever more strongly to the Virgo–Pisces polarity. This becomes more evident upon an examination of the characteristics of the Fates.

In tracking the "cult" of Nemesis that existed at Smyrna, Jack Lindsay, in a book entitled *Helen of Troy—Woman and Goddess*,[9] wrote:

Especially in later phases the cult showed a strong syncretizing trend; Nemesis took over the attribution of others, most of all in Smyrna and Alexandria, and the conflation with Fate and Fortune (Tyche) gave her the Wheel of the City—Tyche.

The adaptation of Nemesis to fit a localized psychological need went even further, as Lindsay tells us:

> Nemesis and Artemis shared the epithet Oupis, which may be linked with *opizesthai*—to look on or watch with awe and dread. Artemis is the Watcher over women in travail; and in literature Oupis is extended for Nemesis to mean the Watcher over human life ... At Smyrna too she was associated with an Aiolic form of Dionysos, Breseus (Briseus). She had strong links with the underworld.[10]

This blending of characteristics heaped upon Nemesis, characteristics which astrology attributes to Pisces, on one hand, and to Virgo on the other. The concept of "Watcher" over human life associates her with the idea of "reward and punishment," or to use the Hindu concept, *karma*. The idea of *karma* is that every action has its equal and opposite reaction and that no causative agent in the Universe can avoid the actions it has set into motion.

In astrological analysis, this idea is given its most succinct expression through the energies of the signs of Virgo and Pisces. Virgo is associated with the physical conditions of one's existence—the body, health, and the activities undertaken to sustain the body, such as remunerative work. Pisces is associated with the unconscious and all that is contained there; thus Lindsay's remark that Nemesis was associated with the underworld cements this connection.

Robert Graves associates Nemesis with Tyche, Zeus' daughter:

> ... to whom he has given power to decide what the fortune of this or that mortal shall be. On some she heaps gifts from a horn of plenty (i.e., cornucopiae), others she deprives of all they have. Tyche is altogether irresponsible in her rewards, and runs about juggling with a ball to exemplify the uncertainty of chance: sometimes up, sometimes down. But if it ever happens that a man whom she has favoured, boasts of his abundant riches and neither sacrifices a part of them to the gods, nor alleviates the poverty of his fellow-citizens, then the ancient goddess Nemesis steps in to humiliate him. Nemesis whose home is at Attic Rhammus, carries an apple bough in one hand, and a wheel in the other.[11]

The apple bough and wheel are important symbols from the astrological point of view since they are further links with the signs. The wheel symbolizes the concept of *karma*, which was already discussed, and as for the sheaf of wheat that is part of the Virgo symbology.

How the apple bough became transformed into the sheaf of wheat is hard to tell, but the fact that this transformation took place is attested to by another source. In the book *Man and His Gods:*

An Encyclopedia of the World's Religions, Tyche or Chance is described as having become a city-goddess in the public life of Hellenistic and Roman times. It describes a famous bronze statue by Eutychides depicting the Tyche of Antioch seated on a rock representing the Mother's mountain throne, with a sheaf of wheat in her hand symbolizing prosperity, and a battlemented crown on her head for the protection of the city.[12]

The relationship between Nemesis and Tyche is further clarified there in this way:

Tyche (fortune), like Dice and Aedos (personifications of Natural Law, or Justice, and Shame), was an artificial deity invented by the early philosophers; whereas Nemesis ("due enactment") had been the Nymph-goddess of Death-in-Life whom they now redefined as a mortal control of Tyche. That Nemesis's wheel was originally the solar year is suggested by the name of her Latin counterpart, Fortuna (from *vortumma*, "she who turns the year about"). When the wheel had turned half circle, the sacred King, raised to the summit of his fortune, was fated to die—the Achaeon stags on her crown announce this—but when it came full circle, he revenged himself on the rival who had supplanted him.[13]

The wheel of Nemesis, and the importance of its half and full turns suggests a relationship to the zodiacal wheel where Virgo represents a half-turn—i.e., the sixth sign, and also concludes the first half of the solar year which begins on or about March 21st and reaches half point on or about September 23rd—and Pisces the full turn—the twelfth and final sign. The retributive facets of Nemesis' character, i.e., in her role as Tyche, fit the concept of *karma* as it applies to Virgo and Pisces. Pisces deals with the seeds of *karma*—unconscious, desire forces—and Virgo deals with the outcome in terms of physical experience.

As a final thread of connection, Nemesis in one of her roles is linked with one of the mythological attributes of Mercury. This is quite evident from one of the passages from Lindsay:

In inscriptions as well as in literature Nemesis became a watcher over tombs, an avenger, especially of violent death; and at times like the Erinyes[14] she could herself bring death about. But all developments making her into a figure embodying modern ideas of Nemesis (i.e., vengeance) are late. In late art she was given attributes like those of Etruscan Erinyes; wings, short chiton, sword. She further appeared as soul guide with the *caduceus of Hermes*, and even as judge of the dead.[15] [emphasis added]

The link with Mercury through the symbol of the caduceus of Hermes seems to complete the Virgo side of the association through Mercury's close association with Virgo as its ruling planet.

The City of Pergamum: Embodiment of the Gemini–Sagittarius Principle

The more significant phases of Pergamum's history was the third century before Christ when it became, under Eumenes II (197–159 B.C.) the capital of the Attalids and "the finest flower of Hellenic Civilization."[16] Pergamum, as a city, had impressed upon it the imprint of the Gemini–Sagittarius astrological axis through the learning, culture, and religious faiths for which it was famous. Culturally, education was very important in the city of Pergamum. One writer describes it as having little or no commerce, but as distinguished for its learning, refinement, and science, especially medicine.[17]

That learning was high priority in Pergamum can be attested to by the fact of the city's having had, at one time, a library second in size of collection only to Alexandria. This library was said to have housed 200,000 volumes, a large number even by modern standards. It is said that the library was eventually transferred to Alexandria as a gift from Anthony to Cleopatra.

The learning theme, and therefore the Gemini–Sagittarius character of Pergamum is even further enhanced by the etymological linkage of the word "Pergamum" to the word "parchment," which has its roots in the word "pergamena."[18] This similarity is cited to reinforce the legend that parchment was invented in Pergamum when the Egyptians had cut off the supply of papyrus to Pergamum in retaliation for the attempt of the king of Pergamum, Eumenes, to lure a famed librarian by the name of Aristophanes away from Alexandria to work there.

The emphases on learning, culture, and religion, for which Pergamum was renowned, are also those factors that characterize the expressions of the signs of Gemini and Sagittarius. These signs are related to the mind in its practical and general philosophical applications. The sign of Gemini symbolizes the rational mind and associative thinking. As a consequence, all support structures that are conducive to and facilitate the formulation of associations can be said to be of a Geminian character. Basic general education, and the communication of information generally, fall into this category.

The sign of Sagittarius deals with the mind in its capacity for inductive reasoning—the process of reasoning from particulars to general principles. This type of mentality gives rise to one of the key props of any civilization—law-making, and with it, the need for law enforcement through various organizations and levels of government. The energy of Sagittarius is also related to systems of thought that endeavour to place human life in a larger context. Through this function it is connected to organized religion, systems of philosophical thought, and higher education—meaning education that is connected with more than the practical needs of life.

Pergamum was famous for the religions that flourished there. It was the center of worship of Zeus and Aesclepius, although other deities were represented there in a lesser capacity, e.g., Athena and Dionysos. The prominence of Zeus and Aesclepius is evidenced by the temple of Zeus–Aesclepius, which was one of the more important places of Pergamenian life. *The deities of Zeus and Aesclepius are synonymous with Jupiter and Mercury.*[19]

Aesclepius, however, had a stronger representation than Zeus. Aesclepius was known as "the Pergamene god"[20] and was credited with powers of healing. His symbol in Pergamum was "a dignified human figure similar in type to Zeus supporting his right hand on a staff round which a serpent twined." He was the nucleus of a "religious cult" centered around the shrine of Aesclepius. At one time, this shrine was known as the most remarkable health center in the ancient world. This health center, or Aesclepieum as it is referred to by *The Interpreter's Dictionary of the Bible*, was part of a complex that included a library and cult center for the deified Roman emperors, an open-air theatre, and a temple dedicated to Zeus–Aesclepius. The center was housed in a "rosette shaped" building and was connected by tunnel to sacred wells and pools in the center of the courtyard. It is said that cures were effected through the physical means of baths and mudpacks, diet and exercise, as well as psychotherapeutic techniques such as dream analysis, isolation, and faith healing.[21]

The Zeus side of Pergamum's religious heritage was also well represented:

> The most spectacular aspect of this remarkable city was the upper terrace of the citadel with its sacred and royal buildings. Of these, the most remarkable was a great altar of Zeus which jutted out near the top of the mountain. A famous frieze around the base of the altar depicts gods of Greece in victorious combat against the giants of earth symbolizing the triumph of civilization over barbarism.[22]

The serpent-entwined staff of Aesclepius has come down to the present day as a serpent-entwined sword. This symbol, known as the caduceus, is a widespread symbol of the healing arts and sciences in the Western World. The caduceus is the mythological staff of Hermes[23] who, of course, became Mercury of the Romans. The equivalence of Aesclepius the healer, and Hermes the messenger are expressed in the characteristics of Mercury as an astrological symbol.

There are two major astrological facets of Mercury, learning and healing, and these are represented in its astrological rulership of Gemini and Virgo. In a sense, it is the health facet of Mercury that more aptly represents Virgo. Nevertheless, it is not a contradiction to have the healing side of Mercury in the form of Aesclepius representing Gemini since the thinking and homeostatic processes in humans—which are responsible for health—are inseparable.

There is a common bias to regard mentality as the only mythological attribute of Mercury, ignoring the healing side. Such a bias is evidenced even in *The Acts of the Apostles* in the New Testament. On this occasion, a healing had taken place, and the healer, Paul, had conferred upon him the title "Mercurius." The writer of "The Acts," however, implied that the name was conferred upon Paul because of his role as a communicator—"because he was the chief speaker":

> *And there sat a certain man at Lystra, impotent in his feet, being a cripple from his mother's womb, who never had walked:*
>
> *The same heard Paul speak: who steadfastly beholding him, and perceiving that he had faith to be healed,*
>
> *Said with a loud voice, Stand upright on thy feet. And he leaped and walked.*
>
> *And when the people saw what Paul had done, they lifted up their voices, saying in the speech of Lycaonia, The gods are come down to us in the likeness of men.*
>
> *And they called Barnabas, Jupiter; and Paul, Mercurius, because, he was the chief speaker.* Acts 14:8–12

The Geminian character was imprinted even on the topography of Pergamum. The following description, taken from Ramsay, relates to the area surrounding the city.

The rock ... as it were plants its foot upon a great valley; and its summit looks over the southern mountains which bound in the valley, until the distant lofty peaks south of the Guild of Smyrna, and especially the beautiful *twin peaks* now called the *Two Brothers* close in the outlook.[24] [emphasis added]

The Two Brothers, of course, recall The Twins, Castor and Pollox, who are said to epitomize, psychologically, the characteristics of the Gemini disposition. According to one mythologist, Castor and

Pollox alternatingly spent half their time on earth and half in heaven in order to share each other's fate. Edith Hamilton says: "They were especially honored in Rome, where they were worshipped as 'The great Twin Brethren to whom all Dorians pray'."[25]

The City of Thyatira: Embodiment of the Aries–Libra Principle

Thyatira was founded by Seleucus I as a military outpost to guard one of the approaches to his empire. The city was situated in the mouth of a long valley that served as a natural communications artery. Ramsay says that in ancient times one of the chief routes of Asia Minor traversed it and that in Roman times, the Imperial Post-Road took that course. Not having any natural fortifications, the city had to depend on the "spirit of its soldier-citizens"[26] for its defense. Thyatira, then, was a city always ready for combat, but only in the capacity of defense.

In 190 B.C., the city fell to the Romans and became first, part of the kingdom of Pergamum, then later of the Province of Asia. Thyatira prospered under the peaceful conditions of Roman rule and flourished as a center of manufacturing and marketing. According to Ramsay, more trade guilds were known in Thyatira than in any other Asian city. He cites inscriptions referring to such occupational types as wool workers, linen workers, tanners, bakers, slave dealers, and bronze smiths.

Thyatira was a cosmopolitan city. The Thyatirans attempted to represent this characteristic of their city in the deity they regarded as its ruler, named Helios Tyrimnaios Pythios Apollo. He possessed a combination of varied characteristics. Ramsay describes him from his image found on coins as "a standing figure, wearing only a cloak (chalmys) fastened with a brooch round his neck, carrying a battle axe over one shoulder, and holding forth in his right hand a laurel branch." Very little, however, is known of this deity and more than likely, he was created to serve local needs. As his battle-ax and laurel branch (peace symbol) would suggest, he was the embodiment of two extremes—war and peace.

To capture and present what Thyatira portrayed in more universalized symbols, we have to turn to the deities Hephaestus and Pallas Athena who were also well represented there and displayed on the coinage. In describing such coins, Ramsay says,

The divine Smith, Hephaestus, dressed as a workman, is here seated at an anvil (represented only by a small pillar), holding in his left hand a pair of forceps, and giving the finishing blow with his hammer to a helmet, for which the goddess of war, Pallas Athena is holding out her hand.[27]

In terms of astrological connections, the city possessed the more outstanding features of the signs of Aries and Libra. Despite this connection, the ruling planets of these signs, Mars and Venus, are not fully represented by the deities Hephaestus and Pallas Athena. However, the presence of Hephaestus and Pallas Athena in Thyatira, as opposed to purer representations in the forms of Mars and Venus, tends to further confirm that what was seeking representation there was not pure male–female archetypes as traditionally understood, but male and female psychological and biological principles at an advanced stage of transmutation.

Hephaestus was known as the divine smith and artisan and was regarded as patron of the crafts, while Pallas Athena was the warrior goddess and protectress. This is a reversal of traditional roles in which warfare and physical prowess were regarded solely as male prerogatives and relegated to Mars, while artistry and proficiency in the arts and crafts were regarded as feminine expressions and ascribed to Venus. In terms of the true expressions of Mars and Venus, their stand-ins in Thyatira are closer to representing these than conventional notions do.

The traditional astrological notions attribute to Mars such characteristics as aggression, power, impulsiveness, masculinity, and more, while in terms of its (his) mythological roots, these were secondary characteristics. This is recognized by some sources as can be seen in the following description:

It seems that the first great god of the Romans was Mars. In later times he is familiar as the war-god. But earlier he was equally involved with agriculture.[28]

Hephaestus restores some of this earlier peaceful disposition. Edith Hamilton says of him: "The God of Fire, sometimes said to be the son of Zeus and Hera, sometimes of Hera alone, who bore him in retaliation for Zeus's having brought forth Athena." She adds, "His wife is one of the three Graces in the Iliad, called Aglaia in Hesiod; in the Odyssey she is Aphrodite"—i.e., Venus.

This relationship is important from the point of view that Venus is the ruler of Libra and represents the energy with which a disposition characteristic of Mars and Aries must become reconciled. Of Hephaestus' disposition she writes,

He was a kindly and peace-loving god, popular on earth as in heaven. With Athena, he was important in the life of the city. The two were the patrons of handicrafts, the arts which alone with agriculture are the support of civilization; he was the protector of the smiths as she was the weaver.[29]

The process of transmutation of pure types is further felt in the way that Pallas Athena's character developed from that of a ruthless warrior to a refined patron of the arts. Again, turning to Edith Hamilton, we find the following description:

> She was the daughter of Zeus alone. No mother bore her. Full-grown and in full armor, she sprang from his head. In the earliest account of her, the *Iliad*, she is a fierce and ruthless battle-goddess, but elsewhere she is warlike only to defend the State and the home from outside enemies. She was pre-eminently the Goddess of the City, the protector of civilized life, of handicrafts and agriculture; the inventor of the bridle, who tamed horses for men to use. She was Zeus's favorite child. He trusted her to carry the awful aegis, his buckler, and his devastating weapon, the thunderbolt. The word oftenest used to describe her is "gray-eyed," or, as it is sometimes translated, "flashing-eyed." Of the three virgin goddesses she was the chief and was called the Maiden, parthenos, and her temple the Parthenon. In later poetry, she is the embodiment of wisdom, reason, purity. Athens was her special city; the olive created by her was her tree; the owl her bird.[30]

The final note to be struck in support of the notion of Thyatira as a city of synthesis of the Aries–Libra polarity originates from one of the activities conducted there. In Acts (16:14), Paul mentions a woman from Thyatira named Lydia who was a seller of purple. According to varying sources, this purple was either obtained from a variety of Mediterranean mollusks (of the Gastropoda class) or from a variety of plants—madder-root, which grows abundantly in the region. The former view is held by *The Interpreter's Dictionary of the Bible* and the latter by Ramsay. However, both agree that this "purple" included a range of colors in the red-purple range, and as Ramsay points out,

> It is well known that the ancient names of colours were used with great laxity and freedom; and the name purple, being established and fashionable, was used for several colours which to us seem essentially diverse from one another.[31]

Ramsay insists, therefore, that the color that was really meant was Turkey-red, a bright red obtained from the madder-root.

Although by itself, this additional intelligence about Thyatira may not seem significant, when viewed in the context of the Aries–Libra astrological signs with which we have associated it, the astrological link is reinforced. Astrology associates the color red with the sign of Aries, but since Thyatira was the embodiment of a blend of Aries and another sign, Libra, the range of colors from red to purple that could have been meant seems to symbolically reflect this.

The City of Sardis: Embodiment of the Leo–Aquarius Principle

From what is known of Sardis, one particular characteristic stands out as a recurring feature. It, more than any other of the seven cities, enjoyed the status of a ruling city. This is one of the features of Sardis that helps to cement the link that it had with the astrological polarity of Leo–Aquarius.

Sardis was located some fifty miles east of Ephesus on a northern spur of Mt. Tmolus. The site of the city overlooked the broad and fertile plane of the Hermus. The history of Sardis goes back to over one thousand years before Christ. It was captured in 334 B.C. by Alexander the Great who left a garrison in the acropolis. Under the Seleucid Dynasty, Sardis continued as an administrative center. Between 189 and 133 B.C., it came under the Romans and was placed under Pergamene rule. It became the center of a *conventus iuridicus*—a provincial capital in a federation comprising a large number of Lydian cities.

Religion in Sardis centered around the worship of Cybele, a deity that was some variant of the Mother Goddess theme. However, the Cybele that was worshipped here was particularly suited to local conditions and was a proper representative for Leo–Aquarius characteristics. Cybele was represented in Sardis by a pair of lions. The lion was also represented on coins of Sardis. Commenting on this, Ramsay says:

> The lion, as type of the oldest Lydian coins, was certainly adopted, because it was the favorite animal and the symbol of the Sardian goddess. The Anatolian goddess, when envisaged in the form of Cybele, was regularly associated with a pair of lions or a single lion.[32]

The symbol of the lion is used to represent the sign of Leo. The characteristics of Leo, for which the lion is considered to be a fit embodiment, are courage, propensity to dominate, and self-expression. These aspects formed part of the heritage of Sardis. In his description of the changes in status early Sardis underwent, Ramsay says:

> As the capital of the great kingdom of Lydia, Sardis had a history marked by frequent wars. In it the whole policy of a warlike kingdom was focussed. The master of Sardis was the master of Lydia. Thus in early centuries Sardis stood forth pre-eminently in the view of the Greek cities as the Oriental enemy on whose action their fate depended. They were most of them involved in war with Sardis, and fell one by one beneath its power. *It was the great, the wealthy, the impregnable city against which none could strive and prevail.* In the immemoral [sic] contest between Asia and Europe, it represented Asia, and the Greek colonies of the coast-lands stood for Europe. Sardis was the

one great enemy of the Ionian cities; it learned from them, taught them, and conquered them all in succession. Among an impressionable people like the Greeks, such a reputation lived long; and Sardis was to their mind fully justified in inscribing on its coins the proud title, "Sardis the First Metropolis of Asia, and of Lydia, and of Hellenism." The Hellenism which found its metropolis in Sardis was not the ancient Greek spirit, but the new form which the Greek spirit had taken in its attempt to conquer Asia, profoundly modifying Asia, and itself profoundly modified in the process. Hellenism in this sense was not a racial fact, but a general type of aspiration and aims, *implying a certain freedom in development of the individual consciousness* and in social and political organisation.[33] [emphasis added]

In this description of the spirit of Sardis, Ramsay has touched upon all those attributes that characterize the expression of Leo, and one particularly important Aquarian attribute—the quest for freedom. These attributes are highlighted by the underlined portions of the excerpt. When it is remembered that Ramsay was not writing from an astrological perspective, his descriptions lend striking validity to the astrological interpretation.

Ramsay expresses his loss for a theme that would unify the abundance of insights available in his description of the religion of Sardis. He says:

The Sardian religion was the fullest expression of the character and spirit of the city; but it has not yet been properly understood. The coins show several remarkable scenes of a religious kind, evidently of purely local origin and different from subjects otherwise known in hieratic mythology; but they remain unexplained and unintelligible. The explanation of them, if it could be discovered, would probably illuminate the peculiar character of the local religion; but in the meantime, although abundant archeological details might be described, *no unifying idea can be detected*, which might show how the Sardians had modified, and put their own individual character into, the general Anatolian religious forms.[34] [emphasis added]

He again laments the lack of a focus in the following excerpt:

But the specialized character of the Sardian goddess Cybele, the qualities and attributes which she gathered from local conditions and from the ideas and manners of the population, are unknown, and can hardly even be guessed at for lack of evidence. To the Greek mind the Sardian Cybele seemed more like the Maiden Proserpine than the Mother Demeter; and the coins of the city often show scenes from the myth of Proserpine. For example, the reverse of [one] coin ... shows the familiar scene of Pluto carrying off Proserpine on his four-horse car.[35]

The unifying idea in the religious symbology of Sardis is, of course, the astrological one, as we have seen in the preponderance of themes representative of Leo. As for the Aquarius side, the aspect of Sardis that represented those characteristics is embodied in legend and another aspect of Cybele, that found expression there—that of Kora Proserpine (or the Maiden Persephone).

One particular legend that characterizes Aquarius is that associated with the curative properties of certain hot springs not far from Mt. Tmolus. As Ramsay tells us:

> Healing power was everywhere attributed to the local embodiment of the divine idea, but in Sardis it was with exceptional emphasis magnified into the power of restoring life to the dead. It was, doubtless, associated specifically with certain hot springs, situated about two miles from Sardis in the front hills of Tmolus, which are still much used and famous for their curative effect. As the hot springs are the plain manifestation of the divine subterranean power, the god of the underworld plays a considerable part in the religious legend of the district. He appeared to claim and carry off as his bride the patron goddess of the city, in the form of Kora-Persephone, as she was gathering the golden flowers, the flower of Zeus, in the meadows near the springs; the games celebrated in her honour were called Chrysanthia; and it may be confidently inferred that crowns of the flowers called by the name were worn by her worshippers.[36]

The concept of healing waters points to the astrological symbol for Aquarius, that of "The Water Bearer." With respect to the myth of Persephone, this is another psychological aspect of the sign of Aquarius. However this link is indirect—through the astrological attributes of Uranus, one of the planetary rulers of Aquarius. The qualities that are attributed to Uranus are all found here in the goddess Proserpine.

In Greek mythology, Proserpine was abducted by Pluto and taken to his underworld abode (Hades). Proserpine's mother, Demeter, bereaved and angry, wreaked vengeance upon the earth until Zeus, the chief of the gods, sent a message to Pluto to return Proserpine. Pluto, however, had taken the precaution of having Proserpine eat some pomegranate seeds before her departure. This ensured her return to him in Hades where she spent half the year with him, returning to her mother to spend the other half. Proserpine was also known as the "Bringer of destruction," an allusion perhaps to the destruction caused by her bereaved mother, Demeter, when she was abducted.

The psychological factor portrayed by Proserpine is that of the repressed side of the human psyche, or of the unconscious. This side usually asserts itself spontaneously and may leave destruction in its wake. But this is only destruction from the perspective of the personality that is unwilling to be integrated into the larger Self. It is this reality of sudden upheavals—that may lead to a confrontation with the unconscious—that mankind collectively projects onto the planet Uranus, co-ruler of Aquarius.

The City of Laodicea: Embodiment of the Taurus–Scorpio Principle

The city of Laodicea, whether we consider it from the historical and cultural aspects, or from its religious heritage, was a very close characterization of the Taurus–Scorpio axis. The city was founded by the Seleucids under Antiochus II, presumably about 250 B.C.—Antiochus was the son of Seleucus I, founder of the dynasty—and named after his wife Laodice.

Laodicea displayed, quite openly, the astrological characteristics of Taurus and Scorpio. Astrologically speaking, Taurus represents the psychological impulse to accumulate. It is said to "rule" resources, valuables, and values. In the generic sense, it is the principle of increase, of virility, which taken to its logical conclusion, also includes the longing for immortality.

Scorpio, its opposite sign, represents the fulfilment of the desires generated by the Taurus impulse. Scorpio therefore represents resourcefulness, the germinative seed—the life force in concentrated form, the sex organs, and the sex act itself.

The Taurus side of Laodicea found expression in its wealth and its reputation as a great commercial and financial center. This is attested to by reports that in 51 B.C. Cicero brought orders with him to be cashed at Laodicea as the city was a center of banking and exchange.[37]

As for the Scorpio side, this was expressed through the themes of resourcefulness, transmutation and reproduction, and rejuvenation. The resourcefulness of Laodicea is brought out by a historical incident of A.D. 60. During that year, Laodicea suffered a devastating earthquake, but being so rich and independent, it refused any help from the Roman government and the citizens rebuilt the city out of their own resources. In reporting this incident, Tacitus wrote:

In the Asian province one of its famous cities, Laodicea, was destroyed by an earthquake in this year, and rebuilt from its own resources without any subvention from Rome.[38]

In terms of the reproduction and transmutation theme mentioned above, we learn that Laodicea was famous for a type of wool, glossy black in color and soft in texture, produced by a secret system of crossbreeding sheep. Here, the sex and reproduction functions were controlled and directed toward a specific end.

The other theme with which we can link Laodicea with the sign of Scorpio is that of rejuvenation, as expressed by the chemical and medical research carried on there. Ramsay says that Laodicea possessed a school of medicine that practiced the art of healing with heterogeneous compounds based on the teaching of one Herophilos (330–250 B.C.), who held that compound diseases required compound medicines. Ramsay also related that the names of leading physicians of the school at the time of Augustus could be found on Laodicean coins.

Generally speaking, medical chemistry may be said to be concerned with unlocking the secrets of Nature and, as such, is consistent with the energy Scorpio. Every process that works beneath the surface—with no conscious guidance—is in an astrological sense, the energy of Scorpio at work.

In terms of a coherent religious structure, very little information is directly available on Laodicea. Of fragments there are many, and they are what we must follow to enable us to develop a composite of the religious heritage of this city. Ramsay mentions that the ruling deity was a local variation of Zeus represented by a human figure holding an *eagle* in his right hand. The eagle, it must be remembered, is the higher expression of the sign of Scorpio. Rather than the general Zeus attributes, it is the attribute of the eagle that sought expression in Laodicea, just as the lions were that aspect of Cybele that sought expression in Sardis.

Two other deities were associated with Laodicea, the functions of whom, and the manner of whose worship were unclear to Ramsay, among others. Ramsay, for instance, mentions the Carian god, Men, and a Semitic god Aseis, whom he says the Laodicean god was sometimes called. Commenting on Men, he says, "Between Laodicea and the 'Gate of Phrygia' lay a famous temple, the home of the Phrygian god Men Karou, the Carian Men. This was the original god of the valley."[39] Other sources give the name of this god as Men Carou.[40]

Of Aseis, Ramsay writes:

The Laodicean god was sometimes called Aseis, perhaps a Semitic word meaning "powerful." If that be so, it would imply that a body of settlers from Syria were brought into the new city at its foundation, and that they had imparted an element of their own character to the god who was worshipped in common by the citizens generally.[41]

What Ramsay and others have separately presented are relics of an ancient Phrygian mystery religion built up around the worship of Mithra (or Mithras). This was a religion of Indo-Iranian origin.

Due to the secrecy surrounding its practices, very little is known apart from what can be deduced from the temples and sculptures it has left. Mithraic temples themselves formed a significant part of the rites performed by the religion. These temples are described as generally small, vaulted, underground caverns, consisting of a central corridor and flanked on either side by platforms with raised benches on which initiates could sit and watch the ceremonies conducted.

The most important object and focus of attention in the hall of worship was the depiction of a scene where Mithra was in the act of slaying a bull. This representation was either in painting, sculpture, or moulded in stucco. Mithra himself is represented as a youth wearing a Phrygian cap on his head and a cape over his shoulders as he performs the sacrificial act, which according to some descriptions, he does not do too willingly. He presses the bull down with a bent knee while he thrusts his knife into its throat. He is flanked by two male attendants—called "dadophors"—each of whom holds a torch, one pointing down, the other up.

The representations of the sacrificial act usually show a dog and a snake, among other things, with the former waiting eagerly and the latter licking the bull's blood. The explanation accompanying one text's reproduction of a Mithraic painting demonstrates the riddle that it presents for modern scholarship:

> The central mystery of Mithraism—the slaying of the bull—eludes final explanation. The most that can be said is that it certainly had to do with the burgeoning of new vegetative life: the snake which licks the bull's blood probably symbolizes the earth which will be fertilized by the blood, and the bull's tail sometimes ends in ears of corn.[42]

What cannot be reconstructed solely from Mithraic relics can be inferred from similar cults that possessed similar motifs to Mithraism. C. G. Jung, in the following excerpt, shows the close relationship between the cults of Mithra, Men, and Attis-Cybele:

> Once again we meet the motif of the Dioscuri: mortal and immortal, the setting and rising sun. The Mithraic bull-sacrifice is often represented as flanked by the two dadophors, Cautes and Cautopates, one with a raised and the other with a lowered torch. They form a pair of brothers whose characters are revealed by the symbolic position of the torches . . . . One would stand for death, and the other for life. There are certain points of resemblance between the Mithraic sacrifice (where the bull in the centre is flanked on either side by dadophors) and the Christian sacrifice of the lamb (or ram). The crucified is traditionally flanked by two thieves, one of whom ascends to paradise while the other descends to hell.[43] The Semitic gods were often flanked by two *paredroi*; for instance, the Baal of Edessa was accompanied by Aziz and Monimos (Baal being astrologically interpreted as the sun, and Aziz and Monimos as Mars and Mercury).

> As Cumont[44] observes, Cautes and Cautopates sometimes carry in their hands the head of a bull and of a scorpion respectively. Taurus and Scorpio are equinoctial signs,[45] and this is a clear indication that the sacrifice was primarily connected with the sun cycle: the rising sun that sacrifices itself at the summer

solstice, and the setting sun. Since it was not easy to represent sunrise and sunset in the sacrificial drama this idea had to be shown outside it.[46]

From the above, we get several pieces of information that bring Laodicea's religious heritage into clearer focus. We can safely surmise that the Laodicean god Ramsay calls Aseis is the dadophor of Baal, Aziz mentioned by Jung. The Semitic origin fits Ramsay's speculations, and the fact that Aziz is a representation of Mars also satisfies Ramsay's suggestion that the god's name means "powerful." This, too, satisfies the astrological picture of Mars as the planetary ruler of Scorpio, one of the signs that was being represented there.

The Taurus side of these mysteries is represented by the sacrifice of the bull—the symbol of Taurus. One needs no additional evidence to authenticate the representation of these two signs than the symbolism of the dadophors, Cautes and Cautopates who represented mortality and immortality, death and rebirth, fecundity and transmutation. As some representations of the dadophors show them, one carries the head of a bull and the other the head of a scorpion, signifying Taurus and Scorpio—in Scorpio's lower expression.

The City of Philadelphia: Embodiment of the Consciousness Beyond Duality

The city of Philadelphia was selected to belong to the seven because it possessed the characteristics that would allow it to represent the state of human consciousness beyond duality, or beyond conflicts normally generated by attempts to come to grips with pairs of opposites. It is therefore not surprising that the major influences that gave rise to the founding of Philadelphia, and to the particular philosophical flavors of life there, were those that can be considered as the highest of which mankind is capable.

From its very founding, Philadelphia became a monument to the working of the Divine Spirit in man. It was founded to commemorate the loyalty and devotion of Attalus II to his brother Eumenes II, King of Pergamum. Attalus earned himself the epithet, "Philadelphus," meaning "lover of his brother." The name Philadelphia has come down to us to mean "city of brotherly love."

Philadelphia was founded between 159 and 138 B.C. in a district which, Ramsay says, came into the possession of the Pergamene King, Eumenes at a treaty in 189 B.C. Geographically, it was situated on high ground and was the juncture of trade routes leading to Mysia, Lydia, and Phrygia—a location that gave Philadelphia the title of "gateway to the East." Philadelphia was linked by road with Rome, Troas, Pergamum, and Sardis.

Unlike the cities that relate to astrological signs and polarities, Philadelphia has to be evaluated not against some accumulated body of knowledge or by a mythological heritage, but by the quality of the hope that it held out for the human race. The city was a monument to the process of interphase, of mediation. It was symbolic of the process that assimilates one into a new society, be it terrestrial or celestial. Consequently, the city represented a holding pattern where one neither belongs wholly to the new or the old. In addition, Philadelphia was the most recent of the seven cities and could therefore symbolize new ground and the uncertainty that comes with all new ventures.

Since the understanding of Philadelphia does not require any special knowledge such as the knowledge of astrology and mythology that are the prerequisites for the understanding of the other six, Ramsay was able to capture the essence of this city much more than of the others. He calls Philadelphia a "missionary" city because of its role as a center for the diffusion of Greek language and letters in a peaceful land by peaceful means. He says:

> Philadelphia was founded more for consolidating and regulating and educating the central region subject to the Pergamenian Kings. The intent of its founder was to make it a centre of the Graeco-Asiatic civilisation and a means of spreading the Greek language and manners in the eastern parts of Lydia and in Phrygia. It was a missionary city from the beginning, founded to promote a certain unity of spirit, customs and loyalty within the realm, the apostle of Hellenism in the Oriental land. It was a successful teacher. Before A.D. 19, the Lydian tongue had ceased to be spoken in Lydia, and Greek was the only language in the country.[47]

In terms of human consciousness and functioning, the state of being that would represent an existence "beyond duality" is frequently referred to as *enlightenment*. This is not *enlightenment* in the general use of the word, but in the specific sense of a level of consciousness that is the consummation of personal striving. It is the state where a person ceases to "be of the world" though in it—meaning that the mode and quality of perception are not constrained by a material reality though actions may be so constrained.

Other concepts that can be used to describe this state are the Jungian terms "Individualized" man or "Modern" man. The characteristics Jung selected to distinguish the "Modern" man from among men can also be used to distinguish Philadelphia as a city among cities. Of this "Modern" man Jung says:

> The modern man is a newly formed human being; a modern problem who has just arisen and whose answer lies in the future.... I must say that the

man we call modern, the man who is aware of the immediate present, is by no means the average man. He is rather the man who stands upon a peak, or at the very edge of the world, the abyss of the future before him, above him the heavens, and below him the whole of mankind with a history that disappears in primeval mists. The modern man—or, let us say again, the man of the immediate present—is rarely met with. There are few who live up to the name, for they must be conscious to a superlative degree. Since to be wholly of the present means to be fully conscious of one's existence as a man, it requires the most intensive and extensive consciousness, with a minimum of unconsciousness. It must be clearly understood that the mere fact of living in the present does not make a man modern, for in that case everyone at present alive would be so. He alone is modern who is fully conscious of the present.

The man whom we can with justice call "modern" is solitary. He is so of necessity and at all times, for every step towards a fuller consciousness of the present removes him further from his original "participation mystique" with the mass of men—from submersion in a common unconsciousness. Every step forward means an act of tearing himself loose from that all-embracing, pristine unconsciousness which claims the bulk of mankind almost entirely. Even in our civilization the people who form, psychologically speaking, the lowest stratum, live almost as unconsciously as primitive races. Those of the succeeding stratum manifest a level of consciousness which corresponds to the beginning of human culture, while those of the highest stratum have a consciousness capable of keeping step with the life of the last few centuries. Only the man who is modern in our meaning of the term really lives in the present; he alone has a present-day consciousness, and he alone finds that the ways of life which correspond to earlier levels pall upon him. The values and strivings of those past worlds no longer interest him save from the historical standpoint. Thus he has to become "unhistorical" in the deepest sense and has estranged himself from the mass of men who live entirely within the bounds of tradition. Indeed, he is completely modern only when he has come to the very edge of the world, leaving behind him all that has been discarded and outgrown, and acknowledging that he stands before a void out of which all things may grow.[48]

The outstanding features of Jung's "Modern" man are that, (1) he is at the cutting edge of growth, (2) history commands no hold over him, and (3) everything about his life is "unsettled" as he strives to live in the "immediate present." These are all characteristics that can be applied to the city of Philadelphia, or rather, to the consciousness of which Philadelphia was only an outward, symbolic expression.

Philadelphia, as the most recent of the seven cities, symbolized the end stage of a progression. The city, therefore, had "less" history than the rest. Its founding had a much clearer beginning and was infused with a much higher purpose than any of the others. Also, in terms of being unsettled, the city underwent a period of unsettlement in the first century that was long remembered and associated with Philadelphia for some time to come.

One particular event that seemed to have disrupted life in Philadelphia in John's time was an unusually severe earthquake in A.D. 17 that devastated twelve cities in the great Lydian Valley, including Sardis and Philadelphia. The effect of this earthquake on Philadelphia was prolonged as the city lived in continuing terror from the frequent shocks that were experienced for a long time afterward. During this period, many of the inhabitants remained outside the city, living in huts and booths while those who remained within had to resort to whatever method possible to secure the walls and the houses against the recurring shocks.[49]

Much of what took place in Philadelphia in the ensuing period seems to add to the significance of the place as a symbol for the end state of the progression of human consciousness. After the disaster, Philadelphia received considerable assistance from Emperor Tiberius and, to show its appreciation, took part with other cities in erecting a monument in Rome as a commemoration of their gratitude.

Ramsay speculates that it may have been in response to the kindness shown by Emperor on that occasion that Philadelphia assumed the name NeoKaisereia. The evidence given is that the name is found on coins and in epigraphy during the ensuing period. This new name, however, fell into disuse about A.D. 42–50 after it was used solely, then jointly with the old. Appraising the situation, Ramsay says,

Philadelphia was the only one of the Seven Cities that voluntarily substituted a new name for its original name: the other six were too proud of their ancient fame to sacrifice their name, though Sardis took the epithet Caesareia for a short time after A.D. 17.[50]

Later, according to Ramsay, Philadelphia again experimented with a new name, this time during the rule of Vespasian, A.D. 70–79. It called itself Flavia, and this name was used jointly with the original throughout the second and third centuries.

In summing up the factors that distinguished Philadelphia from other cities, Ramsay emphasized the following: (a) it was a missionary city, (b) its people lived always in dread of disasters, (c) the people went out of the city to dwell, and (d) it took a new name from the "Imperial god."

Although Ramsay was likely looking for factors that tie the city of Philadelphia to the contents of the Revelation letter, these factors could also be applied to the individual who has experienced *enlightenment*. This state ushers in a phase of life where (a) one becomes an emissary of a new way of being upon the earth ("missionary"); (b) one may experience many difficulties such that life at the personal level may be regarded as difficult; (c) one might feel an outcast even in his native culture ("leaves the city"); and (d) one lives life with the consciousness that his or her personal life is not an end unto itself, but an aspect of a Greater Life ("takes a new name").

Chapter 10

The Pattern of the Letters

When the churches are seen to represent the six astrological polarities, and their resolution—i.e., Philadelphia—the specific instructions directed to them through the letters take on a more general meaning. In this light, the letters become instructions for us all.

Revelation's approach of addressing a certain dynamic in conscious, which the church represents, is not to be taken to mean that the message directed at a church relates only to individuals whose astrological birth signs coincide with either of the two signs the church represents. The whole idea of astrology is that the psychological aspects attributed to the signs are possessed by everyone, with particular factors having various degrees of prominence in the expression of consciousness. The association of an individual with one of the twelve signs, through birth, is only a small part of the picture.

The instructions given in the letters are written in such a way that we can derive directions as to how to go about tackling the problems that conflicting energies create in our consciousness. For purposes of decoding the information contained in the letters, we must examine the information along structural lines. The structural pattern of each of the letters is basically the same, with departures from the standard format being the exception. In terms of structure, the letters consist of:

- An introduction;
- An address, which may contain praises and criticisms;
- A warning, which may include a call to repentance; and
- A final encouragement and promise.

The contents of the letters with respect to the above structural components can be schematicized as in Table 10-1.

In the introduction, Christ declares himself in such a way as to establish the authority for what is to follow. The introduction begins with the words, "This is he that . . ." etc., etc. What this introduction is doing is to prompt the individual to conceive of the solution to

128   MEDITATIONS ON THE APOCALYPSE

Table 10-1.   The Letters and Their Structural Components

Church	Introduction	Praise	Rebuke	Warning	Repent	Promise
Ephesus	Yes	Yes	Yes	Yes	Yes	Yes
Smyrna	Yes	Yes	No*	No	No	Yes
Pergamum	Yes	Yes	Yes	Yes	Yes	Yes
Thyatira	Yes	Yes	Yes	No	Yes	Yes
Sardis	Yes	No	Yes	Yes	Yes	Yes
Laodicea	Yes	No	Yes	Yes	Yes	Yes
Philadelphia	Yes	Yes	No	No	No	Yes

* A warning or a call for repentance is unnecessary in Smyrna's case since suffering cannot now be averted.

the problem posed by a particular conflict of opposites. This way, the individual gets some idea of how he would target for a solution to the psychological task confronting him.

The address or acknowledgment may identify some strong point of a church and may balance this with some form of criticism. It begins with the words: "I know thy works...," after which follow certain words of praise. The criticism may begin with "Nevertheless, I have something against thee." This criticism is really a rebuke against taking the easy way out. As can be seen in the table, not all the churches received praises or rebukes in the addresses directed to them.

Another structural component of the letters is the warning. This usually takes the form of a call to repentance coupled with a threat. The exception to the call to repentance and threat is the case where it is too late for the destiny of a church to be changed, as is the case with Smyrna. In the context of the astrological meanings that have been given to the churches, the lack of a threat or a call to repentance for Smyrna represents a psychological condition of inevitability.

Finally, the letters end with a promise that awaits the church that overcomes. This is usually combined with a statement that encourages the church not to lose what it has already gained, but rather to maximize them.

The overall result is a series of instructions for the churches that, in effect, create a composite picture of Christ. This composite shows Christ as that psychological point of integration (or synthesis) where all conflicting zodiacal energies exist in harmony. Furthermore, by matching the affirmations in Christ's introductions of Himself with the promises he extended to the churches, we can see that each

Table 10-2. The Relationship Between the Introductions and Promises

Church	Christ's Introduction	Promise to Church
Ephesus	Holds seven stars in right hand; walks in midst of the seven golden candlesticks.	To eat of the tree of life in midst of the paradise of God.
Smyrna	The first and the last; was dead yet liveth.	Not be hurt by the second death.
Pergamum	Has sharp sword with two edges.	Eat of hidden manna; given a white stone with name written in it.
Thyatira	Son of God; eyes like flame of fire; feet of fine brass.	Power over nations to rule with a rod of iron; be given the morning star.
Sardis	Has seven spirits of God and the seven stars.	Clothed in white; will not blot out name from the Book of Life; will confess one before the Father.
Laodicea	The amen, the faithful and true witness, beginning of the creation of God.	To sit with Christ on His throne.
Philadelphia	He that is true, holy; has key of David, opens and no man shuts and shuts and no man opens.	Will make a pillar in the temple of God and will have no need to go out; will write his new name upon him.

promise is a natural outgrowth of the affirmation in each introduction (see Table 10-2). In a way, the introduction provides a point of contact with the Christ Reality, which also serves as a homing device to take one to the psychological reality implied by the promise.

Chapter 11

The Ephesus Letter:
Instructions on Integrating Cancer–Capricorn Energy

The Letter

King James Version

Unto the angel of the church of Ephesus write; These things saith he that holdeth the seven stars in his right hand, who walketh in the midst of the seven golden candlesticks;

I know thy works, and thy labour, and thy patience, and how thou canst not bear them which are evil: and thou hast tried them which say they are apostles, and are not, and hast found them liars:

And hast borne, and hast patience, and for my name's sake hast labored, and hast not fainted.

Nevertheless I have somewhat against thee, because thou hast left thy first love.

Remember therefore from whence thou art fallen, and repent, and do the first works; or else I will come unto thee quickly, and will remove the candlestick out of his place, except thou repent.

But this thou hast, that thou hatest the deeds of the Nicolaitans, which I also hate.

He that hath an ear, let him hear what the Spirit saith unto the churches; To him that overcometh will I grant to eat of the tree of life, which is in the midst of the paradise of God.

Revised Standard Version

To the angel of the church in Ephesus write: "The words of him who holds the seven stars in his right hand, who walks among the seven golden lampstands.

I know your works, your toil and your patient endurance, and how you cannot bear evil men but have tested those *who call themselves apostles but are not, and found them to be false; I know you are enduring patiently and bearing up for my name's sake and you have not grown weary. But I have this against you, that you have abandoned the love you had at first. Remember then from what you have fallen, repent and do the works you did at first. If not, I will come to you and remove your lampstand from its place, unless you repent. Yet this you have, you hate the works of the Nicolaitans, which I also hate. He who has an ear, let him hear what the Spirit says to the churches.*

To him who conquers I will grant to eat of the tree of life which is in the paradise of God." Rev. 2:1–7

Interpretation

Introduction

In this letter, Christ introduces himself as "he that holdeth the seven stars in his right hand and walketh in the midst of the seven golden candlesticks." The reason for this introduction can be obtained from a consideration of the deeper meaning of the energies at work in the Cancer–Capricorn polarity which Ephesus represents.

The seven stars are interpreted in Revelation 1:20 as "the angels of the seven churches" and the seven candlesticks as "the seven churches." However, an angel is not a reality that the ordinary human consciousness can relate to, and therefore, further explanations must be found as to what the stars represent. The stars represent seven principles to be distilled from all the conflicts and experiences of life, and whether these are represented by particular heavenly bodies, be they planets or stars proper, is not really the issue. As for the seven candlesticks, these imply means of raising energies.

As objects, stars and candlesticks are very apart in terms of brilliance and proximity. The sum of these as symbols seems to suggest the diversity existing between the principles the churches ought to strive to embody and what they actually accomplish. When Christ introduces himself as he that holds the seven stars in his right hand, he is emphasizing that he has gained mastery over the principles of life represented by the seven stars. The individual is therefore challenged to strive for the same mastery. It is also significant that the right hand is specified. There is a wealth of references to the right hand of God and of Christ in the New Testament. In this context, the right hand is used to imply an operating principle, or cause, as opposed to effect or consequence, which would be symbolized by the left hand.

In terms of the energies of Cancer and Capricorn, the stars are related more closely to the Capricorn side of this astrological polarity, while the candlesticks relate more closely to Cancer. The energy of Capricorn marks the psychological point in life where a person attempts to make his mark on the social environment. At this point, he becomes susceptible to the material rewards, recognition, and accolades that society offers. This energy can be misused by individuals if they do not continually query the meaning behind all impulses to act. Lack of caution in this respect can result in blind ambition and a loss of understanding and appreciation for all the mysteries, subtleties, and paradoxes of life.

As for the candlesticks and the Cancer side of the polarity, which they represent, these are not in the same league with the stars. They are, however, made of gold, which implies that they represent the best of earth. The gold signifies purity and sincerity of endeavour in the consecration.

Despite the differences of size and significance between a candlestick and a star, one principle is common to them, and that is the principle of illumination. One is light of earth and the other is light of "heaven." The candlesticks relate to beginnings while the stars relate to consummations. Just as the candlesticks deal with the act of consecration, the energy of Cancer, which they symbolize, deals with the consecration of human experience—the feeling principle. Irrespective of what events and encounters a human being may have experienced, it is still up to the individual to decide how these are to be accepted. This is essentially what the candlesticks symbolize.[1]

As a point of contrast, it can be said that while the feeling principle which Cancer represents has to do with receiving, the consummative principle of Capricorn energy has to do with giving. This is not to say that one is superior to the other, for it is with the experience of being able to receive that one can know what it means to give and be able to give what is of value to others.

The space or distance that separates stars and candlesticks is an awesome space when viewed from a physical perspective. For Christ to hold the stars in his right hand and to walk in the midst of the seven candlesticks must imply that he is that Reality which relates stars and candlesticks, meaning that he is the bridge between Divine principles and human aspirations. With Christ, Cancer and Capricorn as principles are unified, and consequently, so are receiving and giving,[2] consecration and consummation. Furthermore, by holding the stars in the right hand and walking in the midst of the seven candlesticks simultaneously, Christ is himself, acting as the synthesis of earth and heaven.

The concept of walking in the midst of the seven candlesticks is meaningless if we do not understand the underlying symbolism. In the Revised Standard Version, this is translated as walking "between" the seven lampstands. And indeed, if the only level of interpretation applied is the materialistic one, then it does not make sense for Christ to be walking in the "midst" of the candlesticks; He must walk "between" them. However, the candlesticks are symbolic of something else. Christ is speaking of Himself as a principle. So it makes perfectly good sense, in this context, for Him to walk "in the midst of" or through the candlesticks.

The candlesticks can be said to symbolize what is known in some Eastern religious traditions as *chakras*. These *chakras* are described as areas of interphase between the physical body of man and the divine principles as they operate in man. The areas of the body where the *chakras* are located are also the areas where seven major endocrine glands are found. These *chakras*, however, are not of the physical body, but of the "energy" body. The Sanskrit names for each of these *chakras* and the general locations of the body where they are found are given in Table 11-1.[3]

Table 11-1. The Seven Chakras

Order	Sanskrit Name	Locality	Endocrine Gland
I	Muladhara	Coccyx	Gonads/Ovaries
II	Svadvishthana	Groin	Cells of Leydig (Male) Hilar Cells (Female)
III	Manipura	Navel	Adrenals
IV	Anahata	Heart	Thymus
V	Vishuddha	Throat	Thyroid
VI	Ajna	Forehead	Pineal
VII	Sahasrara	Top of Head	Pituitary

If the seven golden candlesticks are thought of in this manner, the idea of Christ walking through them would relate to the energy moving through the *chakras*. The idea behind the *chakras* is that life energy is refined in its expression as it moves up the order. At the lowest level, the expression is in terms of survival, while at the highest level, it is in terms of giving life. At this stage, the individual becomes fully obedient to the Will of God.

Address

In this address, the church is commended for its labor, its patience, its aversion to them that are evil, and its trial of those who falsely claim to be apostles.

By commending Ephesus for its works, and so on, Christ is really addressing the archetypal energies of Cancer–Capricorn in their highest expressions. The picture that is painted of the ideal expressions of these energies is one of industriousness, perseverance, bearing, and a natural repulsion of evil. The meaning of evil in this context is failure to be true to one's deeper essence, or *true self*. Both Cancer and Capricorn are signs of activity, and with Aries and Libra (Thyatira), they comprise the four Cardinal signs of the zodiac. If there is a sin related to the Cardinal signs, it has to do with doing things more to one's own wishes rather than shirking responsibilities. In the case of Ephesus, it is apparent that its detest of evil itself is a natural outgrowth of the energy of Cancer–Capricorn being expressed at the archetypal level, i.e., work, labor, patience. In other words, its natural expressions are antithetical to evil.

As for trying those who claim to be apostles and finding them liars, this relates to the fact that, for individual consciousness, a zodiacal polarity presents a dilemma for the individual to transcend. For Cancer–Capricorn, the dilemma is that of carving out the right pathway between dependency and ambition. Basically, these two signs deal with the individual as a messenger, or more accurately, a transformer of energies over time and space.

We transform energy over time when we are able to focus our past experiences, and over space when we are able to gain a sense of purpose. Because of this role of transforming energy over time and space, these signs deal with the organic growth process in the individual, including the emotional aspects.

To the extent that the individual must respond to two contrasting emotional drives, his maturity in taking a satisfactory course between them is constantly tested. This maturity on which one is tested relates to both the internal and external spheres. Internally, maturity takes the form of self-definition, and relates more to the Cancer pole and to the energies of its planetary "ruler," the Moon. Externally, maturity is expressed in terms of making an impact on the external environment. Capricorn and its planetary "ruler" Saturn epitomize all the factors that conspire to get the individual to give his energy to the world.[4]

Specifically, the tests, which these energies set for those who claim to be apostles, can be called *the independence test*, attributable to Cancer, and *the test of ambition*, attributable to Capricorn. Together, these measure the ability and sincerity of the individual who would aspire to be a messenger of Christ.

The test which originates from Cancer, the independence test, stems from the complexity of the Cancer energy itself. Cancer is symbolic of all that gives security and a sense of self—first womb, then mother, family, race (or tribe), society, and finally the collective wisdom of the time—yet all these can create a sense of dependency and attachment so that the individual is unable to function as an independent, emotional unit. To pass this test, the individual must be able to disconnect these "umbilical cords" while still acting with an awareness that he is organically bound with the rest of humanity and Creation. If he is successful in severing his dependency ties but has in the process withdrawn his empathy from the whole, vestiges of doubt and insecurity will remain to goad him back into human relationships. To be independent while staying connected is an ideal that can only be realized at a higher level of being. It is only accomplished when loyalty to the Christ ideal takes precedence over loyalty to family and relationships, while at the same time the individual remains open and receptive to the needs of others.

If the individual is not to confuse the orders which emanate from Christ with those which emanate from the unintegrated contents of his own psyche, the test of independence is necessary. Also, an apostle must get used to the fact that he may be hated for his faith and testimony. We know that the test for discipleship was strict, as on the occasion when Jesus said: "If any man come to me, and hate not his father, and mother, and wife, and children, and brethren, and sisters, yea, and his own life also, he cannot be my disciple."[5] Thus, the test of apostleship must be even stricter.

The second test is given by Capricorn and its "ruler," Saturn. This is the test of patience, which is conducted through the manipulation of the ambition. In being an emissary of the "kingdom of Christ," the would-be apostle must expend a great deal of energy, yet he must do so without any sense of personal ambition. In a sense, he must have one ambition: to be ambitionless. Nevertheless, in his ambitionlessness, the apostle must labor unceasingly and must outdo those who are motivated by personal ambition. This is the test of Capricorn and Saturn, which many fail. If the would-be apostle does not rid himself of his ambition, he becomes a cult-hero, and in the process, sets a stumbling block in the way of those who would confuse devotion to the message with devotion to the messenger.

The Apostle Paul was subjected to the same test but passed with distinction, and in the process, reprimanded those who would have made him the object of worship:

> *For ye are yet carnal: for whereas there is among you envying, and strife, and divisions, are ye not carnal, and walk as men? Who then is Paul, and who is Apollos, but ministers by whom ye believed, even as the Lord gave to every man? I have planted, Apollos watered; but God gave the increase. So then neither is he that planteth any thing, neither he that watereth; but God that giveth the increase.*[6]

From this we can see that an apostle points the way and does not encourage those to whom he is sent to seek answers through him.

Criticism and Threat

The criticism directed at Ephesus is that it has left the first love and it is warned that it should repent and do the first work or else its candlestick will be removed from its place.

Leaving the first love implies fickleness, but in the sense that it is used here, it can also mean a dilution of the affection. In the case of the principles that Cancer and Capricorn embody, to leave the first love is to poorly reflect the principle of purposive activity. There is activity, but it has become routinized. What must be noted is that leaving the first love can be atoned for by doing the first work. Loving and working—being and doing—are inseparable. When activity is no longer undertaken because it is the emanation of a purified nature, but undertaken rather for gain, the Cancer–Capricorn principle is departing from its pure expression in its application.

The call to repent and to do the first work is really the call for the expression of the principle of work to be returned to its pure state: work without the enticement of reward.

Christ's threat that He would come to Ephesus quickly and remove the candlestick from its place means that the consequence of a misuse of Cancer–Capricorn energy will quickly be felt in the consciousness. This result, which is symbolized as a removal of the candlestick from its position, is the lack of consecration of one's efforts. There may be gains from striving, but these will not bring satisfaction and peace of mind since striving was undertaken for the wrong reason and with the wrong attitude. In the sense of the *chakra*

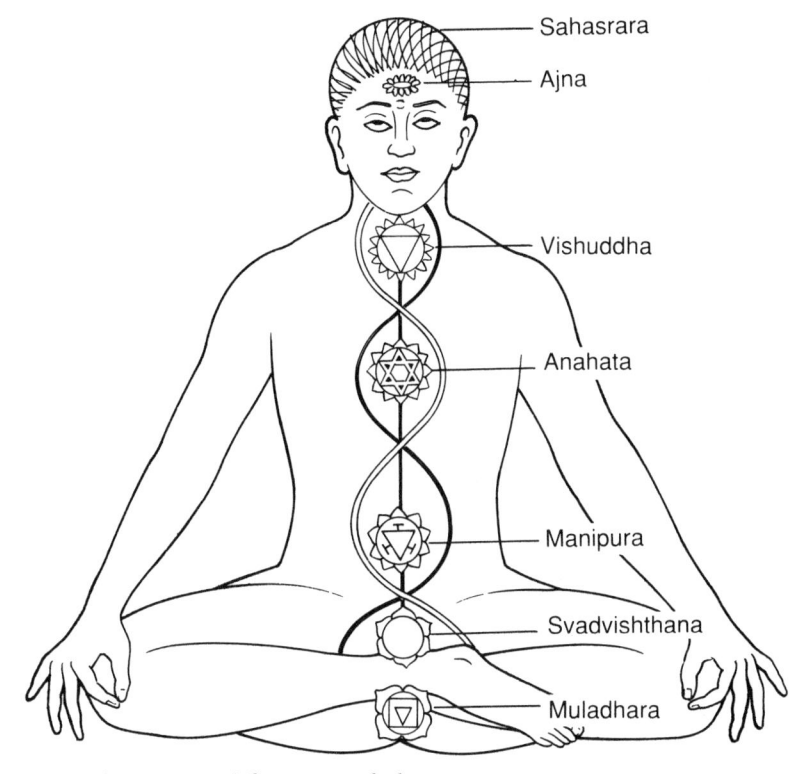

Figure 11.1 *The Seven Chakras*

that Ephesus (and hence the Cancer–Capricorn polarity) represents, a removal of the candlestick would imply that this *chakra* not be synthesizing its energy with the others, and as a consequence, will not add to the growth of consciousness.

Encouragement and Promise

By way of encouragement, Ephesus is told, "This thou hast, that thou hatest the deeds of the Nicolaitans, which I also hate." Many inconclusive attempts have been made to explain the deeds of the Nicolaitans. However, to try to find out who the Nicolaitans were or what their deeds consisted of is, perhaps, a case of misplaced emphasis. If, instead, we ask what it means for Christ to hate, we would be able to get a clearer insight into what the Nicolaitans and their deeds symbolized.

For Christ to hate is not the same thing as for a human being to hate. This is because Christ, as a universal principle, has no mind with which to hate. What it must mean—if the meaning is to harmonize with everything else that is known about Christ—is that the deeds of the Nicolaitans are the very antithesis of what it means to be Christ. When Christ also credits the church at Ephesus with hating the Nicolaitans, He is demonstrating that a certain affinity exists between his being and some particular characteristic embodied by Cancer–Capricorn as a principle. The only "deeds" that would meet these qualifications, particularly in light of the principle that Cancer–Capricorn represents, is *indifference*. Thus, Ephesus can never be accused of being on the side of indifference, and this characteristic, it shares with Christ.

In the promise to "him that overcometh," that he would "eat of the tree of life which is in the midst of the paradise of God," we are again dealing with a principle concerning the successful resolution to the paradox the Cancer-Capricorn polarity represents in the consciousness.

"Overcoming" in this context means "doing the first work," or laboring from a sense of inner purpose rather than for reward. The fact that each task accomplished by each church brings its own reward implies that the rewards themselves are tied up in, and form an integral part of the resolution to the conflict. This interrelationship of challenges and rewards is like someone saying to us: "If you can open this box, the contents will be yours." The specific promise in this case is that if we can become an emissary of purpose, able to act consciously—and that means to act neither from need nor from the expectation of reward—we will be able to "eat of the tree of life." The reward balances out our sacrifice: For if we always act consciously and independently of a reward system, then we will be contributing to something from which we will ultimately gain an endless supply of nurturance.

One cannot act out of a principle consciously, without eventually becoming that principle in embodiment. And in the present case of Cancer–Capricorn, we are dealing with the expression of Being and Purpose. Thus, the end result will be that the human vehicle that expresses Being and Purpose will become permanently attuned to the reservoir of Being which comes from God, and is God.

Chapter 12

The Smyrna Letter:
Instructions on Integrating Virgo–Pisces Energy

The Letter

King James Version
And unto the angel of the church in Smyrna write; These things saith the first and the last, which was dead, and is alive;

I know thy works, and tribulation, and poverty, (but thou art rich) and I know the blasphemy of them which say they are Jews, and are not, but are the synagogue of Satan.

Fear none of those things which thou shalt suffer: behold, the devil shall cast some of you into prison, that ye may be tried; and ye shall have tribulation ten days; be thou faithful unto death, and I will give thee a crown of life.

Revised Standard Version
And to the angel of the church in Smyrna write: "The words of the first and the last, who died and came to life.

"I know your tribulation and your poverty (but you are rich) and the slander of those who say that they are Jews and are not, but are a synagogue of Satan. Do not fear what you are about to suffer. Behold, the devil is about to throw some of you into prison, that you may be tested, and for ten days you will have tribulation. Be faithful unto death, and I will give you the crown of life. He who has an ear, let him hear what the Spirit says to the churches. He who conquers shall not be hurt by the second death." 2:8–12

Interpretation

Introduction

To the church at Smyrna, Christ introduces Himself as "the first and the last," and He "which was dead and is alive." Here, as in the previous letter, the authority is established from the perspective of the pure idea, or the "essence" that the church at Smyrna is to strive toward reflecting.

The title of "the first and the last" is commonly attributed to the being of Jesus Christ. It is sometimes rendered as the "Alpha and the Omega." This designation embodies a most profound mystery as nothing is said about the middle. Since the Divine Reality exists outside of time, "the first" must mean the source of all manifestations, and "the last," their culmination. The implication is that all that is in between is impermanent or ephemeral. This explanation may at first sound confusing, but what it means in simple terms is that the process of the growth of consciousness within an individual has its beginning in a need deeper than a personal one and would have its culmination in a state far beyond human conceptualization. In terms of the human life drama, the implication is that it is Christ who starts the work within the human consciousness to bring it to a fuller comprehension of the reality of God, and that when the maximum comprehension is achieved, it will be revealed that the result of that realization is the very Christ Himself.

This type of introduction to Smyrna fits the characteristics of the energies of the Virgo–Pisces polarity. The Virgo pole represents the beginning of the process of gestation that will eventually lead to a fully formed Christ Consciousness in the individual. Virgo deals with the verification impulse, with analysis, and with the termination of complacency about life. Virgo represents the phase in consciousness where one begins to consciously accumulate experiences. Virgo energy asserts itself in one's consciousness when one stops taking things for granted. However, by expressing itself in the form of the accumulation of experiences, the energy of Virgo exposes one to the danger of being lost in the experiencing itself.

The opposite pole, Pisces, deals with conclusions and endings in all their symbolic forms, including physical death itself. The problem generated by these two energies—which are antithetical—is in the form of finding a set of criteria for determining where one should finally place one's attention. The Virgo energy makes one too hesitant to conclude a matter, while the Pisces energy makes one all too readily agreeable. Therefore, by introducing Himself as "the first and the last," Christ is in effect saying that just as He unifies two poles within Himself, so too will the two poles of the self-assessment principle—i.e., verification and confirmation, experiencing and believing—be unified within oneself if Christ Consciousness is the target of living. This means that no matter how intricate the dilemma, as long as the motive that gave rise to it is pure, so too will be the conclusion.

The words, "which was dead and is alive" refer more to Pisces than to Virgo. Although this attribute may be interpreted as referring to the death and resurrection of Jesus Christ, it is really used to symbolize the continuing processes of death and rebirth that characterize the growth of consciousness. Death in this sense means a process rather than a state. As such, it refers to an attitude to life in which the individual continually dies to a separate existence to be born as part of a larger, Collective Body.

This process is accomplished by the individual fostering a consciousness that is free from clinging, always parting so that room for the new is created. The death that Christ refers to is a process that always prepares the way for something new. During his ministry, Jesus talked a great deal about death as a particular attitude to life. On this score, he said, "He that findeth his life shall lose it: and he that loseth his life for my sake shall find it."[1] In a slightly different context, He emphasized death as a precondition for growth of consciousness: "Truly, truly, I say to you, unless a grain of wheat falls into the earth and dies, it remains alone; but if it dies, it bears much fruit."[2]

Address

In Christ's address to it, Smyrna is recognized for the tribulation and poverty that it is going through. However, it is told that it is really rich. Christ also points out that He knows the blasphemy of those who say that they are Jews but who are really of the synagogue of Satan.

In many ways, tribulation and deprivation can be said to be the lot of the Virgo–Pisces polarity. As the archetypal energy of the verification and confirmation impulse, the Virgo–Pisces axis impels an individual to leave the security of well-established, albeit, stereotyped modes of being to ascertain reality for himself. Because of this impulse to venture forth into the unknown, tribulations come upon an individual through encounters with constructions of his own unconscious.

In a sense, individual experiences, which are encountered on the path of knowledge of the Self, are really experiences with the projected contents of one's own psyche. This reality is cryptically expressed in the saying, *The path lies within*. The meaning of this saying is that whatever we encounter is an emanation from our inner being, and that, to arrive at a knowledge of the Self, one must effectively deal with the mental and emotional states that give rise to external encounters. Consequently, we ought to regard the physical world as a mirror from which we can obtain information concerning hidden blemishes of the psyche.

In terms of the poverty that is also the lot of Smyrna, this astrologically has to do with the erosion of ego that may characterize one's spiritual work on oneself. Poverty can be better associated with Pisces than with Virgo since Pisces represents, more closely than all the other zodiacal signs, that psychological state in which an individual's sense of separateness becomes eroded. This erosion of ego allows the individual to identify with what is common to all rather than with what is peculiar. Because of this disposition, we can say that the erosion of ego is an act of sacrifice, and as such, acquaints one with poverty. However, from the point of view of Christ Consciousness, to be poor in this way is to be rich since sacrifice and "not being anyone special" are the very stuff of one's consciousness of Christ.

The idea of poverty can also apply in the literal sense, for indeed, the energies of Pisces and Virgo in their outer world expressions deal with the care of the sick and with institutionalization in its various forms. Again, this poverty could be attributed to the phenomenon of psychological projection. The energy of Virgo gives special insights into dealing with the sick because it gives special ability to deal with intricacies of "machines" and the human body is one such. On the other hand, the energy of Pisces gives one the patience to deal with groups and group needs such as those represented by institutions.

"The blasphemy of them which say they are Jews" has to do with the delusion that some individuals perpetrate upon themselves by thinking that they are on "the path of discipleship," or "in the church," while their activities totally contradict such a claim. Blasphemy in the spiritual sense does not mean to literally say things against God, but rather to misrepresent a Divine Reality, to counterfeit it. When we view blasphemy in this manner, the idea of those who misrepresent themselves being of the synagogue of Satan follows naturally. Being of Satan's synagogue means that one is in league with confusion and disorganization. Such a state is pertinent to the Virgo–Pisces polarity, for, as touched upon earlier, there could be a tendency for the one giving expression to the energy to get lost in the experiencing from the Virgo pole, and to prematurely retreat from life from the Pisces pole. In the latter case, the individual may lose his sense of separateness, not from labors of love, but from alcohol, drugs, and an abandonment of personal responsibility such that he may become a burden to others.

Criticism and Threat

There are no criticisms and threats in the Smyrna letter. Rather, there are words of encouragement concerning the tribulation that will descend upon it. The church is told that it must not fear those things that it shall suffer, that the devil will cast some of them into prison to be tried and that the tribulation will last for a period of ten days.

The lack of criticism does not mean that the Smyrnian church is beyond reproach. Surely, it is better to be rebuked than to be told that suffering will descend upon one. Here, in contrast to the letters to most of the other churches, there is no call to repentance such that Smyrna can avoid this fate. It seems as if it is too late for a change of destiny.

It is true that suffering is the lot of the Virgo–Pisces energy of which Smyrna is an objectification. This suffering comes from psychological projection and identification. With projection, we learn to objectify and purify the contents of our own psyche. In some cases, there is physical, personal suffering, while in other cases, if we are able to empathize strongly enough with others, the suffering occurs through a sharing of burdens.

There are also two further avenues of suffering related to the negative sides of projection and identification. First, when we evade personal responsibility for change by unfairly or inappropriately ascribing what belong to ourselves to others, the time comes when we must withdraw all these projections and personally deal with the psychological reasons for having made them in the first place. This can be a time of great suffering, but nevertheless great awakening.

Second, when we fail to properly respond to opportunities to broaden our sense of Self—as in sharing resources, empathy, and so forth—other unconscious factors set in so that encrustations around our concept of Self are dissolved. This must take place so that the efficacy of the transformational process at the cosmic level is preserved. Although the process of spiritual growth and transformation might be regarded as a personal undertaking with the aim of self-improvement in mind, it is really a response to a cosmic need more than a personal one. At one level, it might appear that we each make voluntary choices concerning our personal, spiritual growth; yet at another, we are only responding to the agenda that God (or Life, if you will) has for us.

The idea of objectifying the tribulation of Smyrna by attributing it to the devil is a way of saying that as we recognize that tribulation and suffering are necessary for our inner growth, we ought not to identify with this suffering or to seek it for its own sake. If we were to do so, a perverse sense of superiority might transpire.

In a psychological sense, the devil that will cause one to be thrown into prison consists of everything within oneself that contributes to narrowness and insufficiency of Being. To be thrown into prison really means to have one's focus narrowed. The relevance of this kind of "prison" for Virgo–Pisces is that this pair of signs represents spiritual seeking in the overt sense, and for the search to be successful, the focus must be narrowed to the realm within oneself. Even if the reference to prison in the Smyrna letter is interpreted as referring to actual, physical confinement, the restriction imposed by such a tribulation forces the spiritual seeker to focus the search within.

To have tribulation for ten days has significance only in the context of the rest of Revelation. This ten-day period refers to a ten-degree segment of the zodiac known as a decanate. There are thirty-six such decanates on the zodiacal wheel, three per sign. The equivalence of ten days and ten degrees stems from the correlation of the 360-degree zodiac and the 360-day year that Revelation uses. The reason for regarding this ten-degree segment as an indivisible unit perhaps stems from the idea that a ten-degree area of the zodiac possesses a characteristic energy that one must focus upon and then integrate.

Encouragement and Promise

The encouragement extended to Smyrna is that it would receive a crown of life if it continues faithful unto death. The church is also promised that he who overcomes will not be hurt by the second death.

The call to be faithful unto death does not seem like an exacting demand when viewed in the context of the Virgo–Pisces principle. This principle, since it spans two poles of the verification impulse—namely, experiencing and acknowledging—can take an individual to extremes of doubt and criticism on one hand, and extremes of gullibility on the other. It takes faith to keep the individual true to his original purpose in these circumstances. The faith that is called for is that which will enable us to use Virgo energy to understand our overall life-purpose even as we are caught up in examining the components of life. With regard to the use of Pisces energy, the faith that is required is that which allows us to visualize the tangible, practical reality of the truths that we adhere to.

In a general sense, it can be truly said that death freezes the inner posture of life as in a still photograph. It is therefore important that death should not find one in a compromising posture of faithlessness. It is not Christ's intention to make heroes of the Smyrnians, but rather to stress that it is the moment of death that counts in deciding the outcome of one's entire life's sojourn.

Basically, the two promises extended to Smyrna have the same implication. To be given a crown of life means that one would have dominion over death. Consciousness of identity is preserved such that one would have conquered death. The other promise, that he that overcomes will not be hurt by the second death, also refers to this continuity of existence. The second death refers to the only true death of which we might be aware, even as we may fear the first. The first death is ego death. This is what the Virgo–Pisces principle brings us to terms with. When we die to the separate, self-seeking self, we are reborn in a Collective Self that is more enduring. However, resisting the influences that are working within the Universe to bring about a harmony of wills, we become susceptible to the second death. This is spiritual death.

Chapter 13

The Pergamum Letter:
Instructions on Integrating Gemini–Sagittarius Energy

The Letter

King James Version

And to the angel of the church in Pergamos write; These things saith he which hath the sharp sword with two edges;

I know thy works, and where thou dwellest, even where Satan's seat is: and thou holdest fast my name, and hast not denied my faith, even in those days wherein Antipas was my faithful martyr, who was slain among you, where Satan dwelleth.

But I have a few things against thee, because thou hast there them that hold the doctrine of Balaam, who taught Balak to cast a stumbling block before the children of Israel, to eat things sacrificed unto idols, and to commit fornication.

So hast thou also them that hold the doctrine of the Nicolaitans, which thing I hate.

Repent; or else I will come unto thee quickly, and will fight against them with the sword of my mouth.

He that hath an ear, let him hear what the Spirit saith unto the churches; To him that overcometh will I grant to eat of the hidden manna, and will give him a white stone, and in the stone a new name written, which no man knoweth saving he that receiveth it.

Revised Standard Version

And to the angel of the church in Pergamum write: "The words of him who has the sharp two-edged sword.

"I know where you dwell, where Satan's throne is; you hold fast my name and you did not deny my faith even in the

days of Antipas my witness, my faithful one, who was killed among you, where Satan dwells. But I have a few things against you: you have some there who hold the teaching of Balaam, who taught Balak to put a stumbling block before the sons of Israel, that they might eat food sacrificed to idols and practice immorality. So you also have some who hold the teaching of the Nicolaitans. Repent then. If not, I will come to you soon and war against them with the sword of my mouth. He who has an ear, let him hear what the Spirit says to the churches. To him who conquers I will give some of the hidden manna, and I will give him a white stone, with a new name written on the stone which no one knows except him who receives it." 2:12–17

Interpretation

Introduction

Here, Christ introduces Himself as He who has the sharp sword with the two edges. There can be no doubt that this introduction implies power. But, it is not the power of a material force; rather, it is the power of the mind. The sword with two edges is a symbol of skill and mastery at carving one's way through mysteries and illusions. It is therefore indicative of powers of mental penetration and discernment.

The church at Pergamum, representing the Gemini–Sagittarius polarity, is reminded that there is a point of mastery of this dual-purpose tool. The two edges of the sword represent the two functions of the mind, one being theoretical and the other application oriented. It is significant that John saw the two-edged sword as coming out of Christ's mouth (Rev. 1:16). The meaning of the sword issuing from the mouth is that, first, the mouth is symbolic of consciousness, and second, this consciousness is capable of dispelling illusions and falsehoods. The idea of the mouth being symbolic of consciousness is not new. For example, Jesus had said that is not what goes into the mouth of a man that defiles him, but what goes out,[1] implying that the mouth is the point of objectification of consciousness. Jesus was even more explicit on another occasion when he said that it is out of the abundance of the heart that the mouth speaks.[2]

Address

Pergamum is told: "I know thy works, and where thou dwellest, even where Satan's seat is: and thou holdest fast my name, and has not denied my faith." If we apply a connotation of evil to the statement that the church at Pergamum dwelt where Satan's seat is, we will come up with a very confused address—the very next comments on the work of the church are extolling its virtues; it holds fast the name of Christ, and has not denied the faith of Christ. It is only when we acknowledge the astrological significance of Pergamum that we get a clear idea as to what it means to hold fast the name and faith of Christ.

To dwell where Satan's seat is means to operate in the domain of ideas—in the region of the mind. Satan's seat, or the means of Satan's accommodation, is the human mind. Outside of the mind, Satan cannot and does not have a reality or existence.

In the realm of the mind, an individual encounters innumerable ideas and it is up to him to choose which of these many possibilities he will give expression to in his being. There is therefore a certain hazard in dwelling where Satan's seat is, but even while this exposes one to possibilities that are contradictory to what Christ represents, it also opens up to him the possibility of becoming clearer on how he can more fully reflect Christ.

The Gemini–Sagittarius polarity, more than any other, represents freedom of thought and choice. With this freedom comes the power that enables the individual to define reality for himself and be what he wants to be. This expression of being is the basis of individual freedom, and it is in this sense that Gemini–Sagittarius energy is the means of the accommodation of Satan.

To hold fast the name of Christ is to hold onto the consciousness of Christ in one's thinking. The Christ Consciousness, or the Christ energy in us is that part of our nature that uplifts our striving and redirects our energy from self-seeking and stagnation to activities beneficial to others. This expression of Christ Consciousness is nevertheless only the beginning, for we also have to hold the faith of Christ, meaning, to be in resonance with what Christ is and represents. This is known as letting Christ dwell in the heart. In the epistle of Paul to the Ephesians, he expressed his hope that God would strengthen them by his spirit in the inner man so that, "Christ may dwell in your hearts by faith."[3] When Christ lives in the heart, we will be able to live by the principles Christ represents as if these are a natural emanation of our nature.

Criticism and Threat

Pergamum is criticized for harboring those who hold the doctrine of Balaam and those who hold the doctrine of the Nicolaitans. They are told that these things are hated by Christ. In order to ascertain what significance holding the doctrine of Balaam has for the expression of the Gemini–Sagittarius principle, it is necessary to review the events that led to Balaam becoming a symbol of notoriety.

According to the account given in the Numbers,[4] Balaam was a man of mystical consciousness who was called by Balak, King of Moab, to make a curse on the Children of Israel as they camped in the land of Moab on their way to the Promised Land. Balak was afraid they would devastate the land by their consumption and wished to drive them out. However, he was afraid to go into battle against them because the Israelites had just beaten the Amorites. He wanted Balaam to use his occult powers against Israel so that he could derive an advantage against them. When Balak's messengers reached Balaam and petitioned him, he was shortly thereafter warned by God that he should not go to Balak and that he should not curse the Children of Israel because they were blessed.

The story takes a confusing turn here, however, for according to the account in Numbers, Balaam refused to comply with Balak's request on this occasion. When Balak sent his princes to beseech him a second time, Balaam waited for the authorization of God before consenting to go. He was told by God, "If the men come to call thee, rise up, and go with them; but yet the word which I shall say unto thee, that shalt thou do."[5] Consequently, Balaam saddled his ass and went with the princes of Moab.

For some inexplicable reason, we are told in this account that, "And God's anger was kindled because he went."[6] An angel was sent to obstruct the path of Balaam's ass. The angel was visible to the ass but not at first to Balaam whose persistence at spurring on the ass caused it to talk to him and rebuke him.

To summarize the rest of this intriguing episode: Balaam was told by the angel to go with the men but only to say what the angel told him to. Balaam did not curse the Children of Israel, but blessed them on three occasions. Each occasion was accompanied by a burnt offering prepared by Balak according to Balaam's instructions. On each occasion that he blessed Israel, Balaam also made certain prophecies about the future victories that Israel would have over the land of the Moabites. These prophesies infuriated Balak so much that he chased Balaam away.

The next turn in the story is that

> *Israel abode in Shittim and the people began to commit whoredom with the daughters of Moab. And they called the*

> *people unto the sacrifice of their gods: and the people did eat, and bowed down to their gods. And Israel joined himself unto Baal-peor: and the anger of the Lord was kindled against Israel.*[7]

Here, we must leave the story and try to come to grips with the treatment that Balaam has received at the pens of Old Testament prophets and New Testament apostles.

In the books of Joshua, Nehemiah, Micah in the Old Testament, and of Peter and Jude in the New, Balaam is described as a transgressor.[8] These accounts have placed at his feet the blame for the idolatry and fornication that the Children of Israel committed with the daughters of Moab. However, if we accept the story recorded in the book of Numbers, then any transgression imputed to Balaam must have occurred at another level than the outward, verbal one.

If we must fault Balaam on the basis of this story that is preserved for all to read, then we must look below the surface for his shortcoming. It must be remembered that Balaam was a seer—a man who had access to occult powers. He described himself as

> *which heard the words of God, and knew the knowledge of the Most High, which saw the vision of the Almighty, falling into a trance, but having his eyes open: I shall see him, but not now; I shall behold him but not nigh.*[9]

This means that he had experienced the "Beatific Vision" in the terminology of Christian mysticism, and that he is able to go into "Samadhi," according to the Eastern mystics. Because of these powers, there would be no difference for Balaam between appearance and Reality.[10]

When he gave in to Balak's wishes by going through the motions at various altars, albeit humoring him, he showed not only a lack of forthrightness, but also a great deal of ambivalence. The lesson here is that, when powers such as those possessed by Balaam are aroused, the possessor of them cannot be ambivalent in his actions; otherwise he can unwittingly unleash occult forces in an unpredictable manner. Also jesting must be held in check. In Balaam's case, by actually humoring Balak, he unwittingly convinced Balak not to take military action against the Israelites. Had he not done so, Balak might have gone into combat and been defeated. But, hearing Balaam's blessings and prophecies concerning the triumph of Israel, military action was stayed and, having free access to the pleasantries of the land of Moab, the Israelites demoralized themselves.

In the criticism to Pergamum, it is the misinterpretation of the

Gemini–Sagittarius principle of knowledge and wisdom (or knowing and understanding) that is being attacked. To say that Pergamum had those that held the doctrine of Balaam does not mean that there was an organized doctrine. What it means is that the Gemini–Sagittarius principle can be inappropriately expressed in our consciousness. The relevance of bringing up Balaam's name here is that the principle of knowledge and wisdom that the astrological polarity of Gemini–Sagittarius represents could be misused. An individual could become a super-rationalist, could become ambivalent, could become lost in the games and roles—the motions—he is going through. Since the energy of Gemini expresses itself in the search for knowledge and intrigue, and the energy of Sagittarius expresses itself as farsightedness—i.e., the prophet and visionary—the doctrine of Balaam is very significant for this astrological polarity.

The crimes for which the Balaamites are here faulted are eating things sacrificed to idols and committing fornication. In the context of Revelation, these must be regarded as symbolic acts. The meaning of eating things sacrificed to idols pertains to the impersonal principle of Gemini–Sagittarius insofar as we live out of the lower aspects of our human nature. For example, all the energy that a human being takes in, in the form of food and drink, is raised up ultimately into higher functions such as thoughts and feelings. If these thoughts and feelings are used to get a better fix on the Divine Ideal, then the food that was taken in initially is raised up to God. If, however, these thoughts and feelings are used to further service the appetites, they are sacrificed to idols. On this score, the Apostle Paul said that the Children of Israel committed idolatry because they sat down to eat and then got up to play: "Neither be ye idolators, as were some of them; as it is written, The people sat down to eat and drink and rose up to play."[11]

The fornication that Revelation—and the Bible for that matter—is concerned about is not the physical act of sex out of marriage. Sex in and out of marriage is the same physical act; consequently, Revelation, or the Bible in general, is not concerned with an act that cannot be experientially distinguished from another.[12] Rather, it is the attitude that leads one to form liaisons on the basis of expediency and not the act itself that is at issue.

Symbolically speaking, sexual union signifies the uniting of two beings in mind, emotion, and will. It is the last contact in a hierarchy and bears witness to the completion of a union that has its origin at a much higher level. Traditionally, the act of marriage was a means of expressing these other states of union. Thus, the sex act was somewhat solemnized by the marital commitment. When Revelation uses the word fornication, it is doing so with the general idea of addressing all human tendencies to "prematurely conclude a matter."

In terms of the signs of Gemini and Sagittarius, the sin of eating things sacrificed to idols fits the misrepresentation of Gemini energy better than that of Sagittarius. One of the ways in which the Gemini facility with ideas can be misused is for it to express itself as an unconcern for moral issues. On the other hand, committing fornication, in its symbolic sense, befits the shortcomings of Sagittarius. The energy of the Sagittarius pole deals with induction—going from particulars to general principles. Sagittarius energy can easily lead to rashness in organizing fragments of truth for Truth, or, to say it another way, the energy of Sagittarius can be misused by an individual's being too quick to conclude a matter.

Adherence to the doctrine of the Nicolaitans is also one of the shortcomings of Pergamum. Apart from the Ephesus letter, there is no reference to the Nicolaitans elsewhere in the Bible. The church at Ephesus was commended for hating the deeds of the Nicolaitans, and here, Pergamum is accused of having the doctrine. If hating the deeds of the Nicolaitans means not being indifferent, as was explained in the interpretation of the Ephesus letter, then holding the doctrine should mean holding on to whatever it is that gives rise to the deeds. This doctrine is a preoccupation with the world of ideas to the neglect of the concrete world of action. Thus, it can be seen why holding this "doctrine" would lead to the deeds, which are really various degrees of indifference.

The threat expressed to Pergamum is that unless it repents, Christ will come to it quickly and fight it with the sword of His mouth. This call to repentance, combined with a threat, is a reminder to individuals that all their theoretical and mental constructs will collapse if they stray from the essential feature of Christ Consciousness. To repent, one must change from flippancy, megalomania, indifference, and idolatry to discernment, balance, and compassion.

Encouragement and Promise

To the church at Pergamum, and consequently to the consciousness working at integrating the Gemini–Sagittarius principle, those that overcome will be granted to eat of the hidden manna and will be given a white stone with a name written *in* it that no one else will know except the one to whom it is given.

The task of overcoming for the consciousness working with the Gemini–Sagittarius principle has to do with intellectual mastery and the harmonization of the rational, task-oriented aspects of the mind with the inductive, speculative aspects. The reciprocity that can be established between these two mental aspects allows a person to directly interpret Divine Will and to formulate it into a mandate for action. The Gemini pole is also familiar with the pursuit of ideas and with the determination of equivalents. However, with the mind functioning in the Gemini mode, an individual might not be patient enough to explain the significance of ideas perceived to others or to formulate their implications at a more down-to-earth level. Consequently, mental functioning in the Gemini mode takes on some of the characteristics of play.

In direct contrast to the Gemini mode of functioning that wants to take earth to heaven as it seeks to find correspondences everywhere, the Sagittarius functioning of mind wants to bring heaven to earth. Together, these two sign energies unite heaven and earth. The blending of their opposite energies means that human existence can be infused with Divine ideas and the methods of using them at one and the same time.

To eat of the hidden manna is therefore to have access to planes of Reality other than the physical one, and planes not conditioned by experiences on the physical one. To eat of the hidden manna contrasts with eating food sacrificed to idols—a fault charged to Pergamum. The resolution of the dilemma presented by the energy of this polarity would no longer be seen in terms of compromise and expediency, but rather in terms of commitment and clarity.

The white stone is symbolic of how the Gemini–Sagittarius principle will resolve itself if properly applied. In a sense, it is a symbol for the purified new world that the energies of these signs are assisting to create. Since these energies deal with the mind and with ideas or, in a sense, with the discovery of Truth, the white stone is symbolic of a permanent piece of this Truth given as a keepsake. An individual will have his own, tangible, personal Truth. No longer will he have to speculate when Truth has made its permanent abode on earth.

The name that will be written *in* this white stone will be known only by the person who receives it. What then is this name? What does it mean to have a name that is known only to the one having it when, in ordinary, earthly existence, a name is used as a label to identify and wield objects and concepts about? In the highest sense of the word, a name and what the name implies are synonymous. Duality does not exist in "Heaven," and to be given a permanent keepsake from "Heaven" means that the name that is written in or on that keepsake is the same as having one's identity contained in it. This is the meaning of the name that no one else will know about because the name and the identity are one.

It is significant that the name is written *in* and not *on* the stone, although the RSV translated it as on rather than in. This means that the name is at the core of the stone, forming the basis of it. This is not unlike the construction of a pearl where a grain of sand may form its innermost core. In the same sense, it is to this name that the white stone—this permanent keepsake of Truth—owes its existence.

When one has received his name in the cosmic sense, he has received his identity—which is to say that he has come to know, exactly, precisely, and unequivocally, his place in the universal scheme. This place no one else will be able to fill, and it will be as if it was created specifically with the individual in mind. Thus, when one receives his identity, he has received his name, and no one else will be able to decipher this name. This process may be called *individuation* and forms the basis of the state of existence called *illumination*. The white stone signifies *illumination* or a "piece" of the *Universal Mind*, just as a literal stone is a solid representative piece of the earth.

Chapter 14

The Thyatira Letter:
Instructions on Integrating Aries–Libra Energy

The Letter

King James Version
And unto the angel of the church in Thyatira write; These things saith the Son of God, who hath his eyes like unto a flame of fire, and his feet are like fine brass;

I know thy works, and charity, and service, and faith and thy patience, and thy works; and the last to be more than the first.

Notwithstanding I have a few things against thee, because thou sufferest that woman Jezebel, which calleth herself a prophetess, to teach and to seduce my servants to commit fornication, and to eat things sacrificed unto idols.

And I gave her space to repent of her fornication; and she repented not.

Behold, I will cast her into a bed, and them that commit adultery with her into great tribulation, except they repent of their deeds.

And I will kill her children with death; and all the churches shall know that I am he which searcheth the reins and hearts: and I will give unto every one of you according to your works.

But unto you I say, and unto the rest in Thyatira, as many as have not this doctrine, and which have not known the depths of Satan, as they speak; I will put unto you none other burden.

But that which ye have already hold fast till I come.

And he that overcometh, and keepeth my works unto the end, to him will I give power over the nations:

And he shall rule them with a rod of iron; as the vessels of a potter shall they be broken to shivers: even as I received of my Father.

And I will give him the morning star.

He that hath an ear, let him hear what the Spirit saith unto the churches.

Revised Standard Version

And to the angel of the church in Thyatira write: "The words of the Son of God, who has eyes like a flame of fire, and whose feet are like burnished bronze.

"I know your works, your love and faith and service and patient endurance, and that your latter works exceed the first. But I have this against you, that you tolerate the woman Jezebel, who calls herself a prophetess and is teaching and beguiling my servants to practice immorality and to eat food sacrificed to idols. I gave her time to repent, but she refuses to repent of her immorality. Behold, I will throw her on a sickbed, and those who commit adultery with her I will throw into great tribulation, unless they repent of her doings; and I will strike her children dead. And all the churches shall know that I am he who searches mind and heart, and I will give to each of you as your works deserve. But to the rest of you in Thyatira, who do not hold this teaching, who have not learned what some call the deep things of Satan, to you I say, I do not lay upon you any other burden; only hold fast what you have, until I come. He who conquers and who keeps my works until the end, I will give him power over the nations, and he shall rule them with a rod of iron, as when earthen pots are broken in pieces, even as I myself have received power from my father; and I will give him the morning star. He who has an ear, let him hear what the Spirit says to the churches!" 2:18–29

Interpretation

Introduction

In introducing Himself to Thyatira, Christ displays the most authoritative descriptions of Himself in the seven letters: "These things saith the Son of God who hath his eyes like unto a flame of fire, and his feet are like fine brass."

First, by introducing Himself as the Son of God, Christ is reminding the church at Thyatira—and consequently the consciousness struggling with the Aries–Libra principle—that there is another aspect to our human heritage that is all too easily forgotten in daily life. This aspect of our heritage is the spiritual side, and as the physical side is given expression, the spiritual side usually gets underrepresented. The introduction is a reminder that the entire earthly life ought to be viewed from the perspective of the Son of God, and not just from the human side. The Son of God does not refer only to the historical Jesus, but the Son of God as a *principle* of which Jesus was an expositor.

The special significance this introduction has for the Aries–Libra polarity is that one side of this polarity, the Aries side, relates to the consciousness of self as an individual entity—as an ego. Astrologically speaking, the vibration of Aries is summed in the theme, *I Am*. In reminding Thyatira that He is the Son of God, Christ is saying that the affirmation of being, represented in the human consciousness as *I Am*, is never complete unless in saying this, we are affirming the existence of the Eternal Unchanging within. It is only when we say *I Am* with the conviction of the Son of God that the conflicts represented by Aries–Libra can be resolved. It would have been an equivalent rendition if this was introduced as "These things saith the *I Am*", for the authority would have been the same.

The Son of God is the final authority on all matters concerning the transformation of the being of man. It is this truth that is being conveyed in the Gospel of John: "The Father judges no one but has given all judgment to the Son."[1] This means that every life, and every activity even, will be assessed from the perspective of how much that life or that activity has contributed to a person's being able to say *I Am* with authenticity. Alternatively, each life will be assessed on the basis of how much closer it has brought the consciousness to that of the Son of God.

In affirming one's existence from the perspective of the Son of God, one is also affirming the existence of others. This does not come naturally for the Aries side of this polarity for the reason that the impulse to act, which originates from Aries energy, may only be an emanation of the ego. Even when actions are undertaken with the best of intentions, they may still be ego-directed, and consequently there is no guarantee that the results that are anticipated from one's acts will manifest. To compensate for the unpredictability of the results of one's actions, the individual will have to consider whether or not an act will take one closer to the consciousness of the Son of God. Only then will any untoward consequences stemming from the Aries impulse to act be minimized.

The part of the introduction referring to the eyes being like a flame of fire relates to the Libra side of this polarity. Libra, far more than Aries, deals with relationships and attraction generally.

As for the meaning of the symbolism of eyes like a flame of fire, we have to consider the importance of eyes in forming attractions. They normally unify the inside with the outside by opening up the individual to impressions from the external world. They are thus the point of contact where the contents of individual consciousness meet and interact with what is in the external world. So it is that the eyes make lust, and consequently, "sin" possible. For in the sense that an individual is able to see opportunities to realize inner desires, attractions are set up. Properly speaking, what is called sin is really a condition of the mind, and any manifestation of sin in the material world preexisted in the mind.

Eyes that are like a flame of fire, rather than attracting, erode the boundary between the outer and the inner so that the individual does not see anything outside that cannot be realized inside. Everything that comes within the range of vision is set ablaze. Consequently, instead of being a means of drawing one into entanglements, eyes that are like a flame of fire are a means of consecrating everything to the Source of life, or existence in its unmanifest form. This way, the Libra impulse to establish relationships can be converted into an opportunity to purify and increase the consciousness.

The feet of fine brass that Christ ascribes to Himself suggest a strong base or foundation. The feet are that part of the anatomy on which everything else rests, and being closest to the ground and furthest from the head, they are sometimes the most neglected parts. Consequently, feet in this context are symbolic of a person's accumulated weaknesses, most of which may be hidden from the individual himself. The properties or characteristics that brass represents are durability, hardness, resistance to corrosion, and strength. The brass referred to in Revelation must belong to one of the early copper alloys, and it is quite likely that it is a mixture of copper and tin that constitutes this brass as most of the other types of brasses now available are recent metallurgical innovations.

Feet of fine brass has a psychological meaning as well, and this meaning is obtainable from the symbolic language of alchemy. For example, medieval alchemists twinned all of the then known planets and the sun and moon with a particular metal to arrive at a symbolic language by which they could represent certain inner processes in terms that facilitated communication among themselves. This allowed them to keep their knowledge secret from the general public. By this allocation, *gold* was ascribed to the sun, *silver* to the moon, *mercury* or *quicksilver* to the planet Mercury, *copper* to Venus, *iron* to Mars, *tin* to Jupiter, and *lead* to Saturn.[2]

Since the brass that was made in the time of Revelation was obtained by a blend of copper and tin, it would be associated with the astrological influences of Venus and Jupiter. In the psychological sense, Venus symbolizes the impulse to set up attractions based on our desires and values. Venus also represents our propensity to attribute value to things. It also signifies attraction in the objective sense. Jupiter, on the other hand, symbolizes fulfillment and all the factors that contribute to it. In the external sense, Jupiter's influence includes reward systems and processes of compensation.

The combination of these two polar energies of desiring and fulfillment—or attraction and compensation in the external sense—gives rise to a sense of self-contained or self-generated contentment. What the combination of copper and tin, or Venus and Jupiter, implies in the psychological sense is that an individual does not infuse anything outside of himself with power over his sense of contentedness. Thus, with feet of fine brass, contentment becomes a base for striving rather than the conclusion of striving. This is in stark contrast to ordinary life functioning where most of our striving is undertaken with the goal of contentment in mind. The term, "feet of fine brass" therefore implies that Christ's lowest is greater than the ordinary person's highest.

Address

In this address, Thyatira is commended for its charity, service, faith, its works, and its sense of justice—represented here by the last being more than the first. The praises are similar to those given out to Ephesus, because in astrological terms, these two churches represent the two pairs of Cardinal signs. In this particular instance, Christ is addressing the ideals of the signs of Aries and Libra, but in such a way as to imply that these ideals are already being realized. This is rather ironic, since charity and community service are the opposites of the normal expressions of the Aries impulse, and faith and jurisprudence the opposite of the normal outcome of Libra actions. This method of addressing the church at Thyatira is used as a sort of encouragement.

For the Aries pole, the church is challenged to express self-consciousness in the form of the qualities of charity and service. For the Libra pole, which is susceptible to wavering and procrastination, it is challenged to act with certitude and prudence.

Criticism and Threat

Thyatira is accused of harboring a prophetess called Jezebel who teaches and seduces the servants of Christ to commit fornication and to eat things sacrificed to idols.

As with all the churches, the rebukes reflect the undesirable expression of the energy of the astrological polarities that they represent, just as the praises reflect the positive expressions. Here, Jezebel is used to symbolize a principle, just as Balaam was used for the same purpose in the Pergamum letter. The offenses are also similar to those of the Gemini–Sagittarius polarity represented by the Pergamum church—that was also rebuked for fornication and eating things sacrificed to idols. These faults seem to be the built-in biases to error of the Fire and Air polarities which Aries and Libra, Sagittarius and Gemini are respectively.

The idea of a self-appointed prophetess conjures up images of misinterpretation of Divine Ideas for some specific, personal purpose. The prophetess, as opposed to a prophet, entices and preys on the natural weaknesses of the psyche instead of appealing to the strengths of it. She commits "fornication" with her followers by her skill at estranging their affection from what is pure to that which is exciting and mysterious. Jezebel seems to embody everything that is negative about the planetary ruler of Libra, Venus. Astrologically speaking, Venus deals with relationships, and the negative pole of relationships is the desire to be loved, appreciated, catered to. The more fulfillment is sought through being the object of affection, the more the individual will open him/herself up to false joys, false hopes, and eventual disappointments.

The meaning of eating things sacrificed to idols has more to do with the Mars energy associated with Aries. In the symbolic language of astrology, Mars rules Aries, and Mars, in its negative expression, may be crude and undiscriminating. As with the Gemini–Sagittarius polarity, eating things sacrificed to idols means that one takes in energy in its various forms only to squander it on "lower" functions. One is thereby in league with idol worship, since the objective of striving is still confined to the material reality.

The threats directed at Thyatira have to do with the woman Jezebel who, Christ says, will be cast into a bed and into great tribulation as will those who commit adultery with her. Also, her children will be killed with death so that all the churches will know that

Christ searches the reins and the hearts. The threats end with the statement, "I will give unto every one of you according to your works."

The tribulations that will descend upon Jezebel and those that commit adultery with her are the natural consequences of the misinterpretation of Truth and the misspecification of the ideals of life. Jezebel is a symbol for temporal joys and incomplete Truths. Thus, when Christ says that He will kill her children with death, the meaning of this in terms of the principles addressed is that the offspring of such temporal joys and such half-Truths will not be able to stand up to the test of time. These offspring are false hopes, a mistaken sense of mission, and a muddled and confused personal consciousness. In order for Thyatira to escape the tribulation that would descend upon it, it will have to query the source of the instructions it is responding to, and it must query its own motives. Again, we must bear in mind that Thyatira is a symbol for the principles embodied by the Aries–Libra polarity.

Christ also reminds Thyatira that He is the one who searches the reins and the hearts. This means that the Christ presence, which lives below the level of awareness, is very much aware of the true motives and impulses that cause the individual to act. First, the act of searching implies the act of careful study for something in particular. Second, searching the reins means the act of observing the center in the individual that governs the actions, meaning the will. Just as the reins are used to regulate the speed and direction of a riding horse, so too does the will govern all the actions of an individual.

By also saying that he searches the hearts, Christ is expressing that the impersonal Christ presence looks beyond our subjective or self-centered view of the world. The heart has always been used to symbolize our subjective view of the world and the "seat" of the emotions. To search both the reins and the hearts is to scrutinize and assess the individual at a level that lies beyond the actions and the motivations that prompted them. This type of assessment is to determine whether or not the individual has the *Will* to will. If we regard the will as the power of holding the attention on a particular matter, the *Will* to will would mean the power over the attention such that it can be taken from one matter and placed on another that is perceived to have a higher priority as far as an individual's well-being is concerned. This is, of course, a tremendous power, for it will result in the individual undertaking only those activities that are in accord with the reason. True reason and rationality are gifts of the Spirit and are inseparable from Will, without which rationality degenerates into an unlimited capacity to make excuses and reason becomes delusionary. Basically, this is what Christ is looking for in the individual, the power that will release the potential resident within the individual to take him to the Consciousness and Reality of Christ.

The idea that everyone will receive according to his works permeates both the Old and New Testaments, but more so in the New. Despite very clear depiction of how Divine justice operates, there are still many of us who see only an either-or outcome—*heaven* or *hell*—to infinitely variable conditions of our human existence. When the possibilities before each of us are seen only in terms of *heaven* and *hell*, this limited perspective combines with our human propensity to judge one another—and to judge only in favor of the first person singular—to deny ourselves valuable opportunities for the transformation of our beings. Perhaps, rather than measuring ourselves in terms of our own possibilities and potentials, we are content to try only to be not-as-bad-as those persons whom we think will go to *hell*. We choose *heaven* for ourselves by default in the process.

However, the situation is otherwise, for in as much as there are individuals, there are different qualities of works, and there are different "rewards" for these works. The idea may be expressed in terms of the concept of *karma* that was looked at in Chapters Seven and Nine. It was stated there that this concept means the inseparability of cause and effect. Another way of putting it is to say that an individual reaps the fitting rewards of his own works: "He that kills with the sword shall be killed by the sword," says John in Revelation 13:10.

The judgment is therefore tied up in the works, and in actuality, whether we act or do not act, we are judging ourselves. Works and judgment go hand in hand, and together, they express the process of self-creation. It may not be too far from the truth to visualize this process as that of a sculptor who is carving from a block of stone an image that he wants to be, and may eventually become. This sculptor will be rewarded according to his works, and the judgment that prescribes his destiny will be beyond reproach. Likewise, we are reminded by the words of Christ that the impulse that lies within each of us, prompting us to act, is in every respect acting as a sculptor to carve out our destiny.

Encouragement and Promise

Those in Thyatira who did not subscribe to the doctrine of Jezebel, and who did not know the depths of Satan as they speak, were encouraged to hold fast to that which they had until Christ comes.

Not knowing the depths of Satan could be related to the idea of Satan's seat as expounded in the interpretation of the Pergamum letter. If Satan's seat is in the mind and the realm of ideas, the depths of Satan must refer to the aspects of a person's mental and intellectual functioning that is most opinionated and idiosyncratic.

The instructions that they should hold fast that which they have until Christ comes means just that. The coming of Christ occurs by process, by the individual engineering the proper circumstances in the consciousness that will bring this "event" about. This "Coming of Christ" is dealt with more fully in the discussion of the Philadelphia letter. Anyway, this much can be said at this point, that it is the very act of holding fast in the Spirit of Christ that makes it possible for one to be reunited with Christ.

In terms of promises, Thyatira, and therefore the Aries–Libra principle, is told that he who overcomes and keeps Christ's works to the end will be given power over the nations so that he can rule them with a rod of iron. He is also promised the morning star.

The idea of being given power over the nations really means that those who master the Aries–Libra principle will become part of the process that will effectively reduce the man-made barriers that have kept people apart and at war amongst themselves. These barriers are of every sort—political, religious, ideological, racial, cultural, and more. First, these barriers have to be overcome in the personal consciousness, then in the collective consciousness. The personal battle can be won by the individual breaking free from the shackles of self-seeking self-consciousness. This power is already demonstrable as can be observed when two or more persons who possess any substantial degree of Christ Consciousness get together. No matter how diverse the customs or culture, they immediately find that they share a unity of spirit. This communion is not only reserved for persons of the Christian Faith, for the reality of Christ Consciousness does not respect institutionalized boundaries.

The rod of iron referred to has implications more for the Aries pole through the association of Aries with Mars. The planet Mars is known as the "red" planet, and in alchemy, it is related to the metal iron. Mars represents the objectification of personal, individual consciousness. Thus, it has everything to do with the release of energy, with assertiveness, and with carving out one's individual place in the material world. This energy is not, however, free from the frustrations and barriers that beset all expressions of individual power. With the rod of iron that is promised to those who triumph in the expression of this Aries–Libra principle, all that stands in the way of personal fulfillment will crumble, since all actions taken will no longer be taken for personal gratification, but for the good of the collectivity.

The morning star, which will also be given to those who overcome, refers to Venus, the planet that "rules" the Libra side of this polarity. Venus is a morning "star" during the time when the sun is in the sign of Libra—September 23rd to October 24th, approximately. This means that Venus is ahead of the sun in its position on the ecliptic—i.e., the zodiac. Venus at this time of year becomes a herald of the day. In this sense, it is symbolic of something more substantial to come. In the spiritual sense, the morning star is a symbol of what may be called *Cosmic Consciousness*, as much as it is possible to embody and express this in earthly life.

Chapter 15

The Sardis Letter:
Instructions on Integrating Leo–Aquarius Energy

The Letter

King James Version

And unto the angel of the church in Sardis write; These things saith he that hath the seven Spirits of God, and the seven stars; I know thy works, that thou has a name that thou livest, and art dead.

Be watchful, and strengthen the things which remain, that are ready to die; for I have not found thy works perfect before God.

Remember therefore how thou hast received and heard, and hold fast, and repent. If therefore thou shalt not watch, I will come on thee as a thief, and thou shalt not know what hour I will come upon thee.

Thou hast a few names even in Sardis which have not defiled their garments; and they shall walk with me in white; for they are worthy.

He that overcometh, the same shall be clothed in white raiment; and I will not blot out his name out of the book of life, but I will confess his name before my Father, and before his angels.

He that hath an ear, let him hear what the Spirit saith unto the churches.

Revised Standard Version

And to the angel of the church in Sardis write; "The words of him who has the seven spirits of God and the seven stars.

"I know your works; you have the name of being alive, and you are dead. Awake, and strengthen what remains and is

on the point of death, for I have not found your works perfect in the sight of my God. Remember then what you received and heard; keep that, and repent. If you will not awake, I will come like a thief, and you will not know what hour I will come upon you. Yet you have still a few names in Sardis, people who have not soiled their garments; and they shall walk with me in white, for they are worthy. He who conquers shall be clad thus in white garments; and I will not blot his name out of the book of life; I will confess his name before my Father and before his angels. He who has an ear, let him hear what the Spirit says to the churches" 3:1-5

Interpretation

Introduction

Christ introduces Himself to Sardis as "He that has the seven spirits of God and the seven stars." The seven spirits of God seem to be another hierarchy of powers, superceding the seven stars, which we are told (Rev. 1:20) are the seven angels, and the seven candlesticks, which are the seven churches. This means that the instructions, which are to follow, are to be taken as coming from one whose power goes beyond the seven stars and the seven spirits.

Christ is here portraying Himself as the one who represents the point of synthesis of all these powers. This is a message concerning the integration of the human psyche at the highest level possible.[1] It is no coincidence then that Sardis represents the energies of Leo and Aquarius, which promote the process of psychological integration through the faculties of Will and intuition. This polarity of signs represents the powers of creativity latent in man. The sign of Leo, which is "ruled" by the Sun, represents human creative potential, while its opposite, Aquarius, represents the urge to release this creativity and give it validation in time–space. Both of these signs deal with freedom in one sense or another. With Leo, it is freedom in time–space, freedom to associate; while with Aquarius, it is freedom of expression in the realm of ideas. This freedom with ideas gives inventiveness and creative genius to those who can embody it as part of their being.

By introducing Himself as the possessor of the seven stars and the seven spirits of God, Christ is setting Himself up as a developmental target to be aimed for. He is making the point that one must not even look to any of the seven individual spirits of God for direction. Each of these is a partial revelation of something greater, and in giving expression to one without consideration of the others, we can end up in lopsided development. We must strive to possess and give expression to all the spirits before we can be sure of their harmonious functioning. It may not be out of line to make a comparison between the seven spirits of God and the seven colors of the rainbow that originate from white light. In like manner, the spirits of God are the "agents" of God, and to be able to have an interaction with more than the agents, one must learn to integrate these spirits within oneself. This is the significance of the introduction—that the one who is sending the instructions has already integrated these powers within himself.

As for what these powers represent, the following explanation suggests itself. We can divide the spirits or powers into two groups, one group of three and another of four. The first group of three is the higher of the two groups. Paul enumerated these in his epistle to Timothy as "power, love, and a sound mind."[2] They are also described in many other contexts and traditions as *Will, Love,* and *Wisdom*. The three are embodied in the trinitarian concept of the *Father*, the *Son* and the *Holy Ghost*. For the work of integration in us to be successful, we must first give these three harmonious expression then integrate them with the "lower" four.

The four spirits of the "lower" order comprise what we may regard as Nature, or Providence. These spirits are known as the four Elements, discussed in Chapters Three and Seven. These Elements are Fire, Earth, Air, and Water. Actually, these are only metaphors for different processes at work shaping the phenomenal Universe. Thus, Fire is the principle of Striving; Earth, the principle of Consolidation or Crystallization; Air, the principle of Association; and Water, the principle of Cohesion. These processes can express themselves in various modes. However, with respect to human psychology, Fire expresses itself as Desire, Earth as Sensation, Air as Curiosity, and Water as Attachment. Each of these Elements must be properly expressed and mastered before integration with the higher three can be achieved.

Address

During the address, Sardis is told that it has a name that it lives, but that it is dead. It should be noted that there are no praises extended to the church at Sardis, or to the polarity of Leo–Aquarius that it represents. To tell Sardis that it has a name that it lives but that it is dead, is to call Sardis a "living-dead." This is not a contradiction in terms, but a figure of speech that treats death in the same sense in which Jesus told one of his would-be disciples to let the dead bury their dead.[3] The idea is that one might exhibit all the signs of biological life yet be dead to the world of the Spirit and the things that really matter.

The polarity of Leo–Aquarius should be the polarity that comes closest to expressing, in an earthly context, what it means to be alive. The true expression of life is creativity. When we cease to be creative, we become a living-dead. However, the creativity that attests to life in the spiritual sense is not the same creativity people ordinarily refer to when they mention the word. In the sense that it is used here, creativity involves the act of bringing newness into manifestation. This, in turn, involves channelling Spirit into matter, into time–space coordinates.

The theme of Leo, as was said previously, is *I Will*, implying power to be, to create. However, if when "I Will" resonates in an individual's mind without that individual allowing himself to become a channel to the Spirit, then this "I Will" becomes just a hollow echo, an empty promise. This is because a true act of will only occurs if in affirming this, we are giving expression to our essence.

As for the Aquarius pole, creativity is implied in the theme of the sign, *I Know*. The theme of Aquarius is an expression of the quiet self-determination that comes to the consciousness when the intuitive faculties are in operation. This knowing is knowing by being one with that which is known, and it must be expressed outwardly. Failing this, the energy of the sign will become blocked. This will be another form of death.

The criticism that is leveled at Sardis is that it should be watchful because its works have not been found to be perfect before God. Sardis is also warned to strengthen the things that remain and are at the point of death.

These criticisms and rebukes must be understood in the context of the earlier statement that Sardis had a name that it was living but that it was really dead. Death is a process of crystallization and hardening, and Sardis is warned that before life is totally overcome by death, it must do something to rekindle whatever sparks of life may remain. This is in line with the saying of Jesus that "... whosoever hath, to him shall be given, and he shall have more abundantly: but whosoever hath not, from him shall be taken away even that he hath."[4] This must be so because there is really no such thing as a *steady state* in life when it is viewed from the spiritual perspective. There is either growth or decay.

The call to be watchful draws attention to the means by which the things that remain and are destined for death may be salvaged. This call is a call to awareness, a call to consciousness. It is the means by which the process of death in the human being can be reversed. This idea of reversing the process of death applies to the physical level as well. It is a recognized medical fact that organs and faculties that are not exercised lose their efficacy for want of attention. This process is called atrophy. However, the watchfulness that Sardis is asked to practice can also be called attentiveness or Self-remembering. It justifiably may be said that the origin of sin is Self-forgetfulness and the ignorance that results.

For no other polarity is a call to Self-remembering more apt. Aquarius and Leo, representing the archetypal energies of Intuition and Will, are usually the first victims of Self-forgetfulness. Actually, loss of Will and Intuition even precede Self-forgetfulness and can be said to cause the same. By exercising these faculties through creativity, we can stop the crystallization and turn the whole process toward growth.

Further Criticism and Threat

Sardis is also told to hold fast and to repent, and is warned that if it does not watch, Christ will "... come on thee as a thief, and thou shall not know what hour I will come upon thee." This call to hold fast is a call to stop the deterioration so that the process can move from decay to growth. Holding fast is not meant to be a final solution to Sardis' catalepsy, just a means of bringing about the necessary reversal.

The threat that Christ will come to it, as a thief at an unannounced hour, is made to Sardis if it is not watchful. We can look at this statement that Christ will come upon Sardis as a thief from a psychological perspective. The coming of Christ as a thief has to do with the lack of contact that may exist *at all times* between an individual's personal way of life and that of the Christ energy, or Christ Consciousness. Just as a thief can come and go unnoticed in the house of a person who is not watchful, Christ's presence goes unrecognized in the lifestyle of the unaware. This means that the unaware person does not make conscious contact with Christ since all opportunities for him to do so are missed.[5]

The fact that a person does not make contact with Christ does not mean that he does not somehow figure in the cosmic process of God reconciling the world unto Himself.[6] The problem is that the energy builds in the unconscious, and, when it finally breaks forth into consciousness, can be very destructive to one's continued

170   MEDITATIONS ON THE APOCALYPSE

personal existence. Conscious participation in the psychological process of mankind being reconciled to God through Christ ensures that consciousness of individuality will persist to the end. Unconsciousness or unawareness is a result of denial and repression, and this means that Christ will come as a thief in the night. Christ is a process at work in the Universe, and it does not need our personal authorization to do its all important and impersonal work.

At a more personal level, the coming of Christ as a thief deals with the personal ego. When this event occurs, the barrier disappears between the individual will and Divine Will. When an ego is overwhelmed by external influences, the result can be very damaging to the continuance of personality. A person is then said to be mad. There are many ways through which mankind can lose the ego. Of these many ways, the only safe one is to actively seek to express, through one's mode of being, the principles that characterize Christ. These are love for one's fellow man and awareness of God's love in one's life. This amounts to spiritual clarity. Love and spiritual clarity must be entertained to the point where the boundary between one's personal concerns and those for one's fellow man and for humanity at large become obscured. This way, Christ can come to find the individual awake and watching.

Encouragement and Promise

Sardis is told that for the few who have not defiled their garments, they would walk with Christ in white because of their worthiness. The promise is also given to those who overcome, that they will be clothed in white raiment and that their names will not be blotted out of the book of life, but that Christ will confess their names before the Father and his holy angels.

These promises are quite complex and are tied to the process of psychological integration in the individual. Those who have not defiled their garments refer to those who are working at integration at a higher level, who have been successful in placing their ideals into expression as a natural emanation of their being. One's garment, in the literal sense, is one's covering and that which serves as a protection against the elements. In psychological terms, however, the "garments" that protect an individual and give whatever nobility there may be to the thoughts and actions of that person are the ideals within that person.

The word "ideal" is chosen because this is the first stage of recognition in the mind of higher levels of the being. An ideal is the reality an individual will create for himself if everything he perceives as a barrier to his self-expression and fulfillment is dissolved. If, in the face of difficulties, we still hold on to our ideals and do not downgrade or dilute them, we are keeping our garment clean. This is how integration is eventually achieved, by making the ideal and the "perceived Real" one. At this point, the ideal will merge with the mental and the instinctual parts of the nature.

The idea of a mode of being or state of consciousness acting as a protection is not new. The Apostle Peter said in this context that "charity shall cover the multitude of sins,"[7] implying that *charity*,[8]— the highest mode of expression of individual human consciousness on earth—shall provide a garment against all possible risks of the individual losing touch with the Divine as he is caught up in the complexities of life. It should be remembered that this thing, *charity*, is also that which the Apostle Paul upheld as that one mode of being that supercedes every other. The protection that comes from being clothed in white raiment, or to say the same thing, from being unified with one's ideals gives a clear conscience and the "peace of God which passeth all understanding."

The statement that Christ will not blot out one's name from the book of life but will confess it before the Father, raises questions about what the book of life is and what it means to have one's name blotted out from it. This promise implies that everyone's name is found in the "book of life" to begin with, and that at some point, the decision has to be made to either blot out the name or validate the entry. The key to the meaning of this promise must be sought in the deeper meanings of words and expressions such as "name," "book of life," and "confess one's name before the Father."

First, one's name is a symbol for one's individual consciousness. The church at Pergamum was promised a name that no one else will know except it alone. This is the same idea. The "book of life" will consist of "names" of individuals, meaning that it is a state of Collective Awareness, or Collective Consciousness, or Cosmic Consciousness.

The fact that one's name is automatically present in the "book of life," that one does not have to earn an entry into it, means that every individual has within him the power to grow in this Divine Consciousness, but that this power is in latent form only. It is only when the individual begins to actively confess the "name" of Christ that Christ in turn confesses his "name" before the Father.

For an individual to confess Christ is for that person to give expression and exposure to the Christ principle. This is the only true confession. If an individual takes this literally and verbally confesses his allegiance to Christ before his friends and acquaintances, the confession will only become a true confession if, by this public act, he has set up "enforcement factors"[9] in his environment that will facilitate this expression of the Reality of Christ.

To confess Christ is to live, as a matter of faith, to the Divinity resident in oneself. Initially, this must be done by faith because the individual will be living at a level of being that he is unaccustomed to, and consequently, this will involve living under extreme sacrifice. But if he learns eventually to live to the best that he can perceive in himself, later on he will get the power of Christ to make irreversible the consciousness of Christ in him. At this point, when one becomes irreversibly established in Christ Consciousness, Christ "confesses" his "name" before the Father.

Jesus had also told his disciples that "Whosoever therefore shall confess me before men, him will I confess also before my Father which is in heaven."[10] In everyday language, one can paraphrase this process as, "Anyone who lives to the best that he can perceive in himself, i.e., to Christ, will find that the best in him grows until he is fully consumed and illumined by this inner reality—Christ confesses him before the Father." When this happens, the individual's God–Consciousness will become a psychological reality.

The archetypal Leo–Aquarius energy expresses this mystery quite aptly. Leo represents the expression of the Self, as was mentioned previously, and therefore represents creativity or the act of bringing newness into manifestation. The Aquarian pole represents the widening of this aperture in the personal consciousness to increase its receptivity to the Divine. Leo energy is therefore man confessing Christ—or man living to the best that is in himself, while Aquarius energy is Christ confessing man before the Father—the process by which the best in man grows.

Chapter 16

The Laodicea Letter:
Instructions on Integrating Taurus–Scorpio Energy

The Letter

King James Version

And unto the angel of the church of the Laodiceans write; These things saith the Amen, the faithful and true witness, the beginning of the creation of God;

I know thy works, that thou art neither cold nor hot: I would thou wert cold or hot.

So then because thou art lukewarm, and neither cold nor hot, I will spew thee out of my mouth,

Because thou sayest, I am rich, and increased with goods, and have need of nothing; and knowest not that thou art wretched, and miserable, and poor, and blind, and naked:

I counsel thee to buy of me gold tried in the fire, that thou mayest be rich; and white raiment, that thou mayest be clothed, and the shame of thy nakedness do not appear; and anoint thine eyes with eyesalve, that thou mayest see.

As many as I love, I rebuke and chasten: be zealous therefore, and repent.

Behold, I stand at the door, and knock: if any man hear my voice, and open the door, I will come in to him, and will sup with him, and he with me.

To him that overcometh will I grant to sit with me in my throne, even as I also overcame, and am set down with my Father in his throne.

He that hath an ear, let him hear what the Spirit saith unto the churches.

Revised Standard Version

And to the angel of the church in Laodicea write: "The words of the Amen, the faithful and true witness, the beginning of God's creation.

"I know your works: you are neither cold nor hot. Would that you were cold or hot! So, because you are lukewarm, and neither cold nor hot, I will spew you out of my mouth. For you say, I am rich, I have prospered, and I need nothing; not knowing that you are wretched, pitiable, poor, blind, and naked. Therefore I counsel you to buy from me gold refined by fire, that you may be rich, and white garments to clothe you and to keep the shame of your nakedness from being seen, and salve to anoint your eyes, that you may see. Those whom I love, I reprove and chasten; so be zealous and repent. Behold, I stand at the door and knock; if any one hears my voice and opens the door, I will come in to him and eat with him, and he with me. He who conquers, I will grant him to sit with me on my throne, as I myself conquered and sat down with my Father on his throne. He who has an ear, let him hear what the Spirit says to the churches." 3:14–22

Interpretation

Introduction

In this letter, Christ introduces Himself as "the Amen, the faithful and true witness, the beginning of the creation of God." This is perhaps the most difficult of the seven introductions to interpret. The indication is that Christ is regarding the titles of the Amen, the "faithful and true witness," and "the beginning of the creation of God" as equivalent renditions of the same function. In this sense, the Amen must be interpreted to be a precondition of creation or an agency without whose agreement creation would not have been possible.

We must at this stage return to the Gospel of John for a parallel. John, in the Gospel, says that in the beginning was the Word, and that the Word was God, and that all things were made by the Word. The difference between these two concepts of the Word and the

Witness is that the Word is the creative impulse, while the Witness is the medium within which this creation is made possible. The Amen, the Faithful and True Witness, the Beginning of God's Creation, are all synonyms for the *Spirit of Concurrence* prevailing in "heaven" that made creation possible.

The fact that Christ introduces Himself with these titles means that the energy of the polarity of Taurus–Scorpio must attune itself to source of origin. It must repolarize itself to neutral coordinates. Taurus and Scorpio deal with resources for personal and partnership usages respectively. Taurus deals with money as an energy form and as an outer symbol of the fruits of productivity. The problem, however, is that the energy of Taurus, namely the ability to accumulate what is of value, may lead one to regard money and wealth as ends in themselves.

When a proper understanding of money and wealth is achieved, it will be seen that they are psychological states of matter. Thus, to return to source for the Taurus energy will be a recognition of the purpose of money as a way of directing energy. When this higher understanding of money is achieved, it will be rather difficult not to see that life's striving does not end with the accumulation of wealth.

The Scorpio pole deals with sex energy and the ability for sustained human relationships. The partnership consciousness of Scorpio gives rise to the sexual tension in the being otherwise known as "libido." This sexual tension, or libido, is not to be regarded as something negative. It is a neutral state that may vent itself in the form of sexual energy—which may or may not be released in the sex act—or in the form of creativity. The level of a person's consciousness determines the manner in which this tension will seek release. Release of sex energy through sexual encounters serves the purpose of Nature, while release through higher creative channels helps to directly expand consciousness.

The use of sex energy at the physical level is a fail-safe device of Nature to ensure that God's creation will continue even if we do not give our conscious cooperation to the process. This is why sex energy is tied to reproduction; every new human being brings into the physical world a fresh possibility of God realizing Himself—or Itself—on the material plane.

Recognition at the personal level that sexual tension can serve dual purposes assists in the return of Scorpio energy to a neutral function. This is the first step in mastering sex energy. The individual will not have to seek ways to release this energy as it is built up, but will be able to use it to hold his attention on matters that he finds of interest. And, it is this holding of the interest that enables one to break out of repetitive cycles of thinking and behaving. Further, this sustained interest leads to a person being able to gain insights into the mysteries of existence and to directly transform his being.

The alternative to this direct growth is the indirect and impersonal option of growth through many, many lifetimes.[1] The ability to directly transform consciousness is directly proportionate to the ability to hold the interest on a particular matter.

The Beginning-of-the-Creation-of-God, the Amen, the Faithful and True Witness, is therefore the *Logos*, cosmically speaking, and its human equivalent is the libido. This libido will also be a Faithful and True Witness if it is held as it is built up and not dissipated in the manner of an automatic flush toilet. If it is so dissipated, it is not the Faithful and True Witness. Thus, when Christ introduces Himself as the Faithful and True Witness, He is giving directions for the manner in which the Taurus–Scorpio polarity must resolve itself. This tension must be held, as this is the only way that a resolution can be achieved.

Address

Laodicea joins Sardis in not receiving any praises at all. Instead, Laodicea is told:

> *I know thy works, that thou are neither cold nor hot; I would that thou wert cold or hot. So then because thou art lukewarm, and neither cold nor hot, I will spew thee out of my mouth. Because thou sayest, I am rich and increased with goods and have need of nothing; and knowest not that thou art wretched, and miserable, and poor, and blind and naked.*[2]

The reason that Laodicea is treated with such severity is that the Taurus–Scorpio principle of fertility and sexual energy is neutral in its effects. This also accounts for Laodicea being called lukewarm. This lukewarmness, perhaps, means that the energy is allowed to sit and cause discontent and confusion in the psyche. If this is the case, then the statement "I will spew thee out of my mouth" is more easily understood. At this stage, it is important for us to remember that the Christ who is speaking is the impersonal energy of Christ Consciousness that is available to every individual human being. Therefore, when this impersonal Consciousness says, "I will spew thee out of my mouth," what it really means is that the psyche that is confused, and in a quandary because of the tension of the creative energy, is not what Christ Consciousness is made of. It takes concentration and creativity to nourish the growth of the Christ in one. Just as a particular food may be spat out if its taste is not satisfactory, or if it is suspected of being the source of future digestive problems, so it is that a festering of sexual energy in the psyche must be met with expulsion—meaning that the energy may lead to neurotic tendencies and behavior.

By accusing Laodicea of smugness, Christ is chastising the Taurus pole more than the Scorpio pole. "Thou sayest that I am rich," begins the criticism. As mentioned earlier, the theme that sums up the Taurus energy in the consciousness is *I Have*. Taurus may not represent only money, but also what one values. In other words, it is up to the individual consciousness to determine how valuables are determined. In Laodicea's case, the consciousness has opted for material goods. By being smug, and thinking that it is rich because it is increasing in goods, the consciousness is giving external things power over itself. This is why Christ must remind it that it is wretched, poor, blind, and naked. This is just another way of saying that material possessions do not bring peace of mind (alleviate wretchedness), nor cessation of anxiety (alleviation of poverty), nor understanding (the opposite of being blind), nor a sense of confidence (being clothed).

Criticism and Threat

When Laodicea is told, "I counsel thee to buy of me gold tried in the fire, that thou mayest be rich; and white raiment that thou mayest be clothed, and that the shame of thy nakedness do not appear; and anoint thine eyes with eyesalve, that thou mayest see," it is really being told that it does not have a sense of values.

Laodicea does not know a good bargain when confronted with it, and this is the message that is being put across. The gold that Christ wants Laodicea to buy from Him is gold that has been refined, that has had all its impurities burned away. The process of obtaining refined gold is symbolic of the process of how consciousness expands, and the refined gold itself is symbolic of the highest levels of consciousness available to human beings. It is, therefore, symbolic of the illumined mind. The gold that Christ is counselling Laodicea, and thus the Taurus–Scorpio polarity, to buy from Him is this higher state of consciousness. *This has to be bought* in the sense that one must give up something to get it. But since this process of exchange is all an internal one—buyer and seller are both internalized—it is equivalent to the act of refining one's own energy. The libido, or the sexual energy that Scorpio and Taurus symbolize, must be raised up in a higher level of expression.

In a sense, Taurus symbolizes the lower gate, and Scorpio the higher, in terms of the routes one can take with this energy. Scorpio as a psychological principle is associated with regeneration, death and rebirth, and metamorphosis. The underlying theme of the sign is *I Desire*, meaning that the energy of the sign embodies an intensity of stored up interest. Scorpio in psychological functioning is the ability to penetrate through the veils of existence to touch the very bedrock of creativity itself. If an individual has no libido, no tension in the being, then he does not have the fuel required to hold his own interest and to dissolve mysteries. Consequently, he will not be able to consciously participate in his own spiritual growth. This is similar to the mundane sphere, where, if an individual does not have purchasing power, or something with which to make exchange, he is not able to buy anything.

Laodicea is also rebuked for not purchasing white raiment to clothe its nakedness, and eyesalve to anoint its eyes that it might see. Being naked is symbolic of not having protection against the external elements, and not being able to see symbolizes a lack of understanding. White raiment suggests the protection that purity of thoughts and feelings give to the psyche. This symbol was also used in the case of Sardis.

It must be remembered that Sardis and Laodicea have a great deal in common in terms of how the astrological energies they represent function in human consciousness. These churches represent the Fixed signs of the zodiac. In the case of Sardis, it was told that those who are worthy and have not defiled their garments would walk with Christ in white. The purity suggested by white raiment can be said to bubble up as an everlasting spring.[3] Also with it comes continuous self-forgiveness, continuous innocence, and peace. The Taurus–Scorpio polarity as a principle holds, in the psychical body, the secret of everlasting life that will not be revealed until one is able to accumulate the purchasing power necessary to buy gold, white raiment, and eyesalve.

The eyesalve referred to has to do with, in a physical sense, a sort of eye ointment made from Phyrgian stone, according to Sir William Ramsay.[4] Here, however, it is a symbol for the more general remedy, of working therapeutically on the eye of understanding so that one can directly comprehend Reality instead of being satisfied with encountering it only through all its symbolic forms.

The call to Laodicea to repent is preceded by a call to be zealous and a warning that Christ rebukes and chastens those whom He loves: "As many as I love, I rebuke and chasten," says the letter. This statement makes sense only when interpreted symbolically. If a literal interpretation is attempted, it would suggest that Christ acts as a human being would, selecting those whom He wants to love, then going about the task of rebuking and chastening them. This is an unacceptable interpretation since it implies that Christ discriminates and plays favorites among individuals.

A more meaningful interpretation would be that Christ, the impersonal energy in us, is released only when we divest ourselves of materialistic and sensual pursuits. This divestment, or disinvestment, is generally accompanied by pain and suffering, and it is in this sense that it may be said to the chastening of the Lord. In the life of any individual who is ready to be initiated into the deeper mysteries of existence, he will find that almost everything in the external world that he invests his interest and energy in turns against him, forcing him to withdraw the investment so that he can, in turn, put in toward further self-examination and Self-discovery.

The call to zeal is addressed more to the energy of Taurus that can lead one to a rather mundane functioning. With this energy, the tangible, material world is given preeminence, and in this sense, it requires some zeal to let go and seek higher things. The call to repentance is a call to acquire a true sense of value, a sense of that which really lasts, which cannot tarnish or depreciate.

Encouragement and Promise

There is no final encouragement to Laodicea, at least not in the sense that it has occurred in the other letters. However, Laodicea receives a double promise. It is told by Christ that He stands at the door knocking, and that if any man hears His voice and opens the door, that He will come in to him and sup with him. It is also promised that he who overcomes will be granted to sit with Him in His throne just as He overcame and is set down with His Father in His throne.

The first of these promises is an enticement to the Taurus side of this polarity, while the second is tailor-made for the Scorpio pole. By saying that He stands at the door knocking, Christ is saying that He has already taken the first step and that any communion between Him and an individual depends on the individual responding to His knock. In other words, the ball is in the individual's court, in a manner of speaking, and any possibility of interaction with Christ depends on a conscious act on one's part.

Christ's knocking signifies that He makes His presence known to every individual, and that it is up to each person to sense that presence. Both the knock and the voice relate to the conscience of an individual, which is always the first to declare the coming of Christ to the consciousness. Conscience has sometimes been called "the still, small voice," but it is really that nagging sense of uncertainty that we may feel to indicate to us that everything is not right with our world after all.

Generally speaking, an individual lives in a rather tight time–space compartment that keeps out everything that does not directly figure in making that time–space box comfortable. This mode of being creates a closed system within which desires are generated and within which one's energy is expended finding ways of fulfilling them. As soon as these desires are satisfied, more are generated. By standing at the door knocking, Christ is offering the individual an opportunity to have an exchange with the Reality outside of his time–space reality box.

The idea of "standing at the door" can also apply to the figurative door of the heart. This door is the desire nature of an individual—the configuration of one's view of the world structured psychologically around what one expects to take from life—and it is usually the only way that anything new can enter and form part of the ordinary person's reality. This is because Taurus represents attraction through desiring, and the planet that "rules" Taurus—Venus—is the very epitome of attraction. By saying that He is standing at the door knocking, the Christ energy is recognizing that if it is ever to make an inroad into the ordinary person's consciousness and form part of one's world, it must go through the desire nature.

Christ Consciousness may begin in the individual's consciousness as a "higher" desire such as the desire for salvation, or Heaven, or immortality. Eventually, even higher desires must go, but not before they have acted the part of a catalyst in the consciousness to help transform some of the baser, lower desires. The eventual result is that Christ will come in and sup in the consciousness, meaning that Christ Consciousness will gain nurturance in the consciousness of the individual, and in turn, offer consolation to him who "hears" and attunes himself to it.

The second part of the promise is that Christ will grant him that overcomes the privilege of sitting down with Him in His throne, just as He is set down with His Father in His throne. This implies that the one who overcomes will share the throne of Christ, whose throne is really the Father's. To sit down with Christ in His throne is to be fully established in Christ Consciousness, and with Christ, to rule the world. What this means is that whosoever overcomes will use Christ Consciousness to wrest the destiny of mankind from the lower, entropic forces.

The rule of Christ is found even today whenever one acts out of a sense of selflessness, purpose, fearlessness, and compassion. For many people, to act in this manner is painful since one has to live consciously, and free of habit and compulsion before he is able to rid himself of all the things that impel one to live below the threshold of Christ Consciousness. For the one who overcomes, meaning the one who is able to hold creative tension in the being until it bears fruits of higher consciousness, purity of being, and clarity of perception, there will be no other way to act. Every action will carry the same deliberateness, compassion, and determination as all others.

Chapter 17

The Philadelphia Letter:
Insight into the Consciousness Beyond Duality

The Letter

King James Version

And to the angel of the church in Philadelphia write; These things saith he that is holy, he that is true, he that hath the key of David, he that openeth, and no man shutteth; and shutteth, and no man openeth;

I know thy works; behold, I have set before thee an open door, and no man can shut it; for thou hast a little strength, and hast kept my word, and hast not denied my name.

Behold, I will make them of the synagogue of Satan, which say they are Jews, and are not, but do lie; behold I will make them to come and worship before thy feet, and to know that I have loved thee.

Because thou hast kept the word of my patience, I also will keep thee from the hour of temptation, which shall come upon all the world, to try them that dwell upon the earth.

Behold, I come quickly; hold that fast which thou hast, that no man take thy crown.

Him that overcometh will I make a pillar in the temple of my God, and he shall go no more out; and I will write upon him the name of my God, and the name of the city of my God, which is new Jerusalem, which cometh down out of heaven from my God; and I will write upon him my new name.

He that hath an ear, let him hear what the Spirit saith unto the churches.

Revised Standard Version

And to the angel of the church in Philadelphia write: "The words of the holy one, the true one, who has the key of David, who opens and no one shall shut, who shuts and no one opens.

"I know your works. Behold, I have set before you an open door, which no one is able to shut; I know that you have but little power, and yet you have kept my word and have not denied my name. Behold, I will make those of the synagogue of Satan who say that they are Jews and are not, but lie—behold, I will make them come and bow down before your feet, and learn that I have loved you. Because you have my word of patient endurance, I will keep you from the hour of trial which is coming on the whole world, to try those who dwell upon the earth. I am coming soon; hold fast what you have, so that no one may seize your crown. He who conquers, I will make him a pillar in the temple of my God; never shall he go out of it, and I will write on him the name of my God, and the name of the city of my God, the New Jerusalem which comes down from my God out of heaven, and my own new name. He who has an ear, let him hear what the Spirit says to the churches." 3:7–13

Interpretation

Introduction

This introduction is quite different from those in the rest of the seven letters. Here, Christ introduces Himself as He that is holy, true, has the key of David, who opens and no man shuts, and shuts and no man opens. It is the least symbolic of Christ's descriptions of Himself, suggesting that there is less of a gulf between the reality of Christ and the state of consciousness represented by Philadelphia.

The reason for this straightforward introduction is that Philadelphia, unlike the other churches, is not caught up in the illusions and dilemmas of existence symbolized by astrological signs and polarities. In the other letters, Christ introduces himself in terms suited to the particular nature of the illusion to which we are prone.

By saying that He is holy, Christ is saying that He is in a state of wholeness. This is the true meaning of holiness, for it stems from a state of integration and completeness. When viewed in this light, it will be seen that the person who is holy is the person who can possess all of his being in harmony. The state of holiness also means that there is no differentiation of the consciousness into conscious and unconscious. The consciousness that is holy, or whole, is that within which God will manifest. As Paul said in the Hebrews' epistle, "Follow peace with all men and holiness without which no man shall see the Lord."[1]

By saying that He is true, Christ is saying that He is Real. He is affirming the authenticity of His own being by saying *I Am*. Anything that is true must have genuineness, a clear identity that sets it apart from everything else. When applied to a person, to be true means that the identity of that person is clear, uncluttered by pretense. To experience trueness as a personal reality, one must first know that it means to "Be"; and to know how to "Be," it is necessary that one first learn what to "Be." This can only be achieved when one has acquired Self knowledge, otherwise what one is expressing may not be true or authentic. Christ knows Himself and in the process has trueness of being or authenticity.

The "key of David" is symbolic of initiation into the secrets of existence, and this power is a natural outgrowth of being holy and true. Being both holy and true, Christ is able to possess all of His being and is able to express this wholeness of being. It is this joint quality that constitutes the key of David, for one cannot be initiated into higher realities unless one has fully assimilated the reality that is his present lot.

Address

Philadelphia is showered with praises in the address. It is told that those who say that they are Jews, but are not, will be made to come and worship before its feet. It also is commended for keeping Christ's word, in recognition of which it will be kept from the hour of temptation that is supposed to come upon all the world to "try them that dwell upon the earth." As a word of caution, it is told to "hold that fast which thou hast, that no man take thy crown."

The lack of rebukes to Philadelphia is due to the fact that Philadelphia represents the consciousness that has elevated itself above astrological influences. It is therefore a state of elevated human existence. And since it is a state beyond the conflicts of self and not-self, it can be said to be a state of Soul[2] realization. In this sense, Philadelphia becomes a holding pattern of growth and transformation. It has completed the work that earthly existence has presented to it, but the present stage of its achievement is not the final outcome.

A study of the praises and promises in the Philadelphia letter gives insight into the consciousness that is beyond duality and astrological influences. First, Christ states that He knows its works and has set before it an open door that no man can shut. This open door means that between the consciousness of the individual who is psychologically at Philadelphia and the reality of Christ, there is an understanding and continuity-of-being. Thus, Philadelphia is also representative of the state of Christ Consciousness. In the psychological state represented by Philadelphia, a person can have communion with Christ. For such an individual, the return of Christ will be an everyday reality. There is similarity between this idea and the open door spoken of in the Gospel of John, where Christ says, "I am the door, by me if any man enter in, he shall be saved, shall go in and out and find pasture."[3]

The open door, which is before Philadelphia, should not be confused with the door under the control of the individual and which is up to the individual to open to the knock of Christ, i.e., as in the Laodicea letter. This door that Christ will leave open is under His control alone, and the action of opening the door to the individual's consciousness will be the much talked about "Second Coming of Christ." It is this knowledge that moved John, the author of Revelation and the Gospel also to write in his epistle, "And we know that the Son of God is come, and hath given us an understanding, that we may know him that is true even his son Jesus Christ. This is the true God, and eternal life."[4]

The "Second Coming of Christ" is not a localized event. It is universal in that it does not take place in a material medium. For this event to meet all the qualifications that the apostles, and Jesus himself laid down for it, this return must be more than an event in time–space. One of the qualifications that the apostle Paul laid down is that there must be individual, personal expectation. He said: "Christ was once offered to bear the sins of many; and unto them that look for him shall he appear the second time without sin unto salvation."[5]

Another qualification is that when Christ shall appear, "all eyes shall see him."[6] This emphasizes the nonlocalized nature of the occurrence. It also refers to the eye of understanding, for when the principle that is Christ is being given expression, He will become visible to all.

The "Second Coming of Christ" is therefore a psychological event, made possible by the expectation that is built up in an individual's consciousness. This expectation is the precondition, for with it come all the mental and behavioral preparations that in themselves give rise to God being more fully expressed in the world. The major difference between the Second Coming of Christ and the "indwelling" Christ of Christian doctrine is that the "indwelling" Christ has no external, corresponding reality of His own, but depends on the cooperation of the individual consciousness. The returned Christ is the Christ that was under incubation in the consciousness and whose growth was fostered by faith. The returned Christ takes over the rule of the life completely and begins to destroy all man-made barriers to the Truth-of-God being expressed on earth. This rule is described as ruling with a rod of iron. This is not to mean a rule of violence, but the rule of inner conviction and an inner sense of purpose.

The commendation of Philadelphia for keeping Christ's word emphasizes that Christ Consciousness is not a matter of cleverness, or luck, but the end result of a process of expressing a particular reality. On this score, Jesus said, "If you abide in me and my words abide in you, you shall ask what ye will and it shall be done unto you."[7] This keeping of the word suggests devotion to the Reality of Christ, albeit in its conceptual and mental form. It is only when the mental reality is thoroughly brought into focus that the emotional reality will manifest.

Philadelphia is also commended for not denying the name of Christ. Not denying the name means that one has uninterruptedly attuned oneself to the consciousness of Christ, since the name of anything in its true sense is the reality that corresponds to it. By also not denying the name of Christ, one is consciously affirming the reality represented by the name. Psychologically speaking, denial is easy, for it only entails living to the lower nature, whereas affirming the name means living to the higher nature. The name of Christ is not a word-name, it is the very consciousness of Christ, the very being of Christ.

The Promise in lieu of Criticism

The first promise made to Philadelphia is that those who call themselves Jews, but are not, will be made to come and worship at its feet and know that Christ has loved Philadelphia. This is quite understandable, for being an open door, and being a "place" where the name of Christ is affirmed, Philadelphia becomes to the world, an opening on matters of the Spirit. Through this opening, people who are concerned with matters of transformation of being, can come for insight as to how to tackle their specific needs. This is what it means for those who claim to be Jews to worship at the feet of Philadelphia. To worship at the feet of Philadelphia does not mean that one needs to venerate the individual whose consciousness is of the quality of Philadelphia. It means that the one whose consciousness is at Philadelphia presents an opportunity to others to raise their energies into higher expressions. This worship will also result in the peaking of the consciousness and the dedication of the being to the work of self-transformation. This is the only way that individuals who want to be conscious can accomplish the task.

The reference to Jews is not to be interpreted as an allusion to the Jewish people. It is a symbolic reference to all those people who have in one way or another claimed to be people of God, or more generally, all those who claim to be on the "path of discipleship," or the "path of Yoga," or "in the church," or whatever the local term might be, whether they be Christians, Jews, Hindus, Moslems, Buddhists, or whatever. When individuals who "claim to be Jews and are not" make outward gestures to indicate that they want to transform their beings, they yet inwardly resist with all their might the work that such transformation entails. Such persons may only want to add to what they already have as if the transformation of being is just another trophy or diploma to be hung on the wall.

The consequence of such a misunderstanding of the spiritual life, and such an ambivalence toward it, is that such persons will realize that if they are to make any headway whatsoever, they will have to seek out a "master," or a "teacher," or a "guru," or whatever the term might be.

To worship at the feet of members of the church of Philadelphia means that it is only there that worship will be effective. Worshippers will find that God does not dwell in temples made with hands, and that He—or It—cannot be found in the scriptures without someone bringing the scriptures to life. The scriptures only take on life in the lives of individuals, and this is the service that Philadelphia provides. Philadelphia gives the ordinary mentality an opportunity to see a working model of what it is supposed to be striving for.

For those who find their way to Philadelphia to worship, they will find the love of God as a personal, tangible reality, not theory or theological speculation. This reality, therefore, is that which seals the promise of Christ that, "If a man love me, he will keep my word; and my Father will love him, and we will come unto him and make our abode with him."[8]

Another of the promises made to the consciousness beyond duality —represented by Philadelphia—is that it will be kept from the hour of temptation which shall come upon all the world to try them which dwell upon the earth. This particular promise is made to Philadelphia because, according to Christ, "thou hast kept the word of my patience." Keeping one from temptation is in fact a figure of speech, for when one is tempted, it is really nothing external that does the tempting, but something inside of oneself that sets up an attraction with something on the outside. It is obedience to this pull that leads ultimately to frustration and suffering. The church at Philadelphia will be kept from temptation because, though it is on the earth, it is not of it. The open door to the Christ Reality enables the "inhabitants" of Philadelphia to let go of material attachments and tune in to their own Divine heritage. Because of this, there is no lust—and all that goes with it.

"All those who dwell upon the earth" is symbolic of all those whose reality is confined to things material. The mind must eventually loosen these self-imposed blinkers and begin to appreciate the vastness and incomprehensibleness of the Real.

Encouragement and Concluding Promise

The encouragement, "Behold I come quickly: hold fast that which thou hast, that no man take thy crown" seems to emphasize that the church at Philadelphia is in a holding pattern. In the true sense of the psychological, a church is a theatre. It is a certain theme in the consciousness that is being played out until the actors have fully assimilated the parts they are acting out. However, no matter how closely an actor plays a part, he is still separate from the identity he is supposed to portray. So too, when one is fully reflecting the Divine to limits of one's capacities, that does not make one Divine. Such a state would involve an irreversible attainment. It is still possible for those at Philadelphia to falter, and this may be the reason why they must be wary lest they lose the opportunity for final realization, which is what the crown symbolizes. The warning against others taking the crown really means that one should not give in to distractions and be robbed of the opportunity to make irreversible and permanent one's attainments in the expression of the higher nature.

The concluding promise to Philadelphia is really a multiple promise:

> *Him that overcometh will I make a pillar in the temple of my God, and he shall go no more out: and I will write upon him the name of my God, and the name of the City of my God, which is new Jerusalem, which cometh down out of heaven from my God; and I will write upon him my new name.*

These promises underscore the fact that the pinnacle of human achievement is just the beginning of the revelation of God in man. For the church at Philadelphia, overcoming should be understood in terms of keeping the door open between it and Christ, or keeping the consciousness receptive. There is no other task. At this stage, the purpose of human life is being consummated, and this is done by the consciousness being made privy to the workings of the Divine Spirit. This is also a give and take, for when it happens, the opportunity is also given to the Divine Spirit to experience and realize Itself in a material setting.

The different promises given to Philadelphia represent different tempos of this joint realization. The first tempo is to become a pillar in the temple of Christ's God. A pillar is a support structure, and a temple is symbolic of a place of worship, meaning, consecration and raising of personal energy. In other words, those individuals who are made pillars in the temple will be conscious participants in the growth and expansion of the Divine Consciousness. The Philadelphian will also become a means of allowing others to come into the reality of true worship, again, meaning that the one whose consciousness is at Philadelphia will make it possible for others to be brought to a point where they can consecrate their own energies. This is perhaps the state that some will call Individualized Consciousness, a state where a person is no longer expressing the collective content of his time and culture, but the uncontaminated content of a Reality beyond time and space. For God to maintain the integrity of His own wholeness in time–space, there must be as many points of personal, individual consciousness as possible for expressing all the facets of the Divine essence, thus the many pillars.

Philadelphia is also promised that it will go no more out. In and out relate to the states of union and separation from God that the Soul experiences. The Soul in union with God will become permeated with joy, and the Soul that goes out becomes separated from that joy to take a particular obligation upon itself. These outs and ins may mean leaving the nonphysical plane for an existence in the physical and vice versa. Each out may occupy a whole lifetime, but not necessarily so. If it does, it may do so by leaving its home in the spiritual to become wrapped up in the antithesis of whatever it is desirous of bringing into manifestation.[9] This way, a bit more of earth becomes spiritualized. The spiritualization of earth takes place when the minds of men become illumined as to how to achieve lasting solutions to long-standing problems of human relationships and purpose.

The idea of ins and outs, or sojourns, may be expressed in various ways. The more common concept used to express this is "reincarnation," which is a cornerstone doctrine for many of the Asian religions. In the Western-Christian tradition, reincarnation is not accepted, and the authoritative doctrine is: "It is appointed unto men once to die, and after this the judgment."[10] Nevertheless, the same Paul who enunciated this doctrine went to great pains to elucidate the doctrine of "Predestination" which supports the concept of the predisposition of the individual to certain situations conducive to, or not conducive to "salvation."

For all intents and purposes, the doctrines of reincarnation and predestination are the same idea expressed from two different perspectives. As such, each of them has its own limitations that can be circumvented only by an understanding of the underlying reality that each tries in its own way to express.

The shortcoming of a traditional view on reincarnation is that it is difficult to know whether someone is discussing the issue from the perspective of the mind, the ego, the Soul, or the All-Pervading and Eternal Spirit. Any notion that something below the Soul level reincarnates encounters difficulties in explaining the heterogeneous nature of what constitutes the human being. And furthermore, such a position takes too mechanistic a view of a Divine process. There is also a danger that there will not be any incentive to grow in consciousness if all favorable conditions are regarded as rewards for deeds in past lives and all conditions of difficulties as punishment for past-life misdeeds. Such a system takes the focus away from what the individual is doing *now* and is able to accomplish from efforts expended *now*.

An outright rejection of reincarnation, without an understanding of the psychological truth it tries to express, is also not doing justice to the Divine process. One is hard pressed with such a hasty rejection to explain inherited privileges, injustices, human suffering, catastrophes, and more, while at the same time espousing concepts of a merciful and just God.

One is able to get around all the above conceptual difficulties when it is acknowledged that what goes in and out is the Soul. This level of reality is beyond some of the dangers of inertia and regression that the lower levels may succumb to when reincarnation is accepted as a reality. At the same time, the despair that many live under becomes unnecessary when it is realized that each one is his own judge at this level of being.

So, returning to Philadelphia, which is the level where the distilled essence of all the conflicts of a material existence is realized, we can safely say that this is the abode of Souls, Individualized Beings,

Divine Helpers. Not going out anymore means that the work of the Soul is to be carried out on other planes beyond the plane of physical manifestation.

The second tempo of realization is that Christ will write upon the Philadelphian the name of His God. This means that in that consciousness there will be a reversal of the direction of effort. First, personal effort and striving were necessary to express the Will of God. Now, with the name of God written upon him, the Philadelphian becomes God's property and as such a conscious expression of God Himself.

The third tempo of realization is that upon the consciousness that is at Philadelphia, the name of the City of God will be written. This is "New Jerusalem." Jerusalem means "possession of peace," and the adjective New is used to emphasize that it belongs to a level of reality not heretofore realized. A city literally means a place where many individuals dwell, and a City of God will imply a "place" where many Individualized beings dwell. To have the name of the City of God written upon one is to share with every Individualized being what is special to each one while expressing this common reality in a unique way.

The final tempo or phase of the realization of the individual is expressed by Christ, by His saying that He will write upon Philadelphia His new name. This promise must be interpreted in light of what has been promised before. First, the consciousness that is at Philadelphia must keep open the door that Christ has set before it. Second, it will be part of the temple of God and will have no further need to go out. Third, upon it will be written the name of Christ's God. Now, Christ will write upon it His new name. This last act in the drama of unfolding means that after the individual has expressed all levels of existence available for individual attainment, he will become like Christ Himself. This is what it means for Christ to write upon the Philadelphian His new name. For in doing so, He will be sealing the individual with His very own identity.

G: *Eventually, no matter what one starts with, one must go to Philadelphia. After Philadelphia all roads are the same.*
R: *Does that mean something?*
G: *Why you ask?*
R: *It makes me snicker, I think it is cute. I wonder how much I see cuteness when you really are trying to say something.*
G: *Everyone must go to Philadelphia. Everyone thinks I mean American Philadelphia. But ... To understand this, they must discover true meaning of "Philadelphia". Everyone must go to "City of Brotherly Love", then all roads are the same.*[11]

Chapter 18

Experiencing the Totality of Ourselves:
The Book of Revelation as a Record of Christian Spiritual Initiation

Spirit of Truth

In the introduction to this book, I suggested that Revelation was written to leave a record of Christian spiritual initiation. Although the preceding material deals at some length with what Revelation entails, it was not possible to discuss this aspect of Revelation as an initiatory record in more detail until now. At this point, we have behind us all the major pieces of the mosaic that characterizes Revelation. From these, we can view the composite and derive some insight into how we might benefit from Revelation's message.

Revelation represents the "untold half of the Truth," or that aspect that Christianity has left unarticulated. As a result, the material found in Revelation cannot be understood within the narrow confines of just the Christian religion. Christian doctrine deals with consciously directed spiritual acts—with repentance and the quest for salvation. Christianity assumes away the need for self-understanding, which requires one to go beyond consciousness and deal with unconscious processes and impulses. Revelation however calls us to account for that part of ourselves that extends beyond the range of conscious observation. In this regard, Revelation has seen to it that Christianity is not unlike most major religious traditions that expound their doctrines at two levels—an outer or exoteric exposition for the causal follower, and an inner or esoteric one for the initiate. Indeed, we find support for this practice in incidents between Jesus and his disciples in the Gospels.

Jesus taught the multitudes in parables but plainly to the disciples, and even among this chosen group, there were those who had access to yet more personalized teachings. We can place Peter, James, and John in this category. Jesus took them with him to the transfiguration (Matthew 17:1) and to Gethsemane (Matthew 26:37). They were also the only ones present at some of the miracles—the miraculous catch of fish (Luke 5:10) and the resurrection of Jairus' daughter (Mark 5:37, Luke 8:51).

We also have Jesus upholding this principle of esotericism by telling the disciples,

> *I have yet many things to say unto you, but ye cannot bear them now. Howbeit when he, the Spirit of truth, is come, he will guide you into all truth: for he shall not speak of himself; but whatsoever he shall hear, that shall he speak: and he will show you things to come.* John 16:12–13

Later on, we find the apostle Paul, who was not among the group of apostles when Jesus was in the flesh, making allusion to the need to split his teaching. He wrote in his first epistle to the church at Corinth:

> *And I brethren, could not speak unto you as unto spiritual, but as unto carnal, even as unto babes in Christ. I have fed you with milk, and not with meat, for hitherto ye were not able to bear it, neither yet now are ye able.*
> I Corinthians 3:1–2

In his Hebrews' epistle, he made similar comments about those who had to be fed "baby food," not being capable of handling adult fare (Hebrews 5: 12–14).

Since the apostles, and Paul in particular, had to package their teachings to suit the various capacities for understanding among their followers, it is likely that a large part of their teachings were passed on verbally. Actually, this was more than likely done out of necessity since it was the practice of the churches to read aloud in church all the apostolic letters. Those things that could not be divulged to all could not be written down otherwise they would have been divulged to those who were unprepared. We get an indication of this practice from Paul's first Corinthian letter where he wrote to the church that "... the rest will I set in order when I come" (I Corinthians 11:34). The verbal part of the teachings was necessary to ensure that those who were ready got the necessary spiritual nourishment, while at the same time protecting those who were not ready.

In Revelation, the principle of esotericism is brought to its zenith, but with a difference. Here, the only factor that separates the inner group from the outer is the level of understanding of each person who reads Revelation. John usually alerts the reader when something has to be read esoterically by saying something of the nature of "This is for him that has understanding," or "He that has ears to hear let him hear." It was because Revelation had to serve the multiple purpose of reaching people at various levels of understanding that John had to use symbolism to convey his teaching.

The esotericism found in Revelation, as is the case with all esoteric teachings, was not intended to last indefinitely. It was intended to last only until such a time when those for whom it was written became capable of assimilating the message contained in it. This time of preparedness is analogous to the descent of "the Spirit of truth" that was promised by Jesus to his disciples. Initiation is the process of becoming acquainted with the Spirit of Truth, or the Spirit of Synthesis or Wholeness.

Spiritual Initiation

At a personal level, a spiritual initiation consists of a set of experiences that can result in the opening up of the mind and the understanding to a perspective on life and the Universe wider than the one with which we were previously acquainted. The experiences that constitute an initiation offer an intense and objective perception of life.

As initiations go, they are not usually the result of conscious choice —they are orchestrated by the Spirit, or the unconscious. An initiation may overturn many of our cherished beliefs, shatter many of our hopes, and ultimately challenge and invalidate our self image and personal notions of who or what God is. Because of this, an initiation is usually accompanied by great suffering.

An individual who is selected to pass through an initiation does not know in advance when his perception of the world will be challenged or how he will stand up to this challenge. For all intents and purposes, this will constitute a time of judgment, a time when he must answer for himself as a human being, when he must face the decision to continue in spiritual darkness or advance to the light.

The experiences that go together to constitute an initiation are different for each person and are based on what we need, in terms of awareness, to round us out. Since the goal of any initiation is to bring about a reconciliation in our consciousness with all that we have intentionally or unintentionally overlooked and inappropriately rejected, the pattern of any initiation is dependent on the illusions we entertain about life and what we have overlooked or repressed in our belief structures. Therefore, the more subjective our view of life is, and the more we have excluded or neglected in our personal view of the Universe, the more intense must the initiation be and the more deeply will our identity be challenged.

Because of the personal difficulties and suffering that may accompany a period of initiation, the individual so engaged will be under pressure to decide what sort of interpretation he should place on the experience. If he accepts the initiatory experience positively, he will regard it as an opportunity for spiritual purification and will consequently consciously cooperate with the process of becoming reconciled with all of life. If he places a negative interpretation on the difficulties, he might believe that he is being abandoned by God and regard the difficulties as the work of the devil. Such a negative interpretation could result in missed opportunities for growth and an intensification and prolongation of the suffering.

Spiritual initiations allow us to expand our consciousness and move us toward the totality of ourselves. Revelation shows us how John becomes progressively acquainted with various aspects of consciousness, albeit in a disguised form. The task for us is to own our various aspects and become acquainted with them.

With the experience of reclaiming one's scattered aspects as a result of having gone through an initiation, one's view of the world is as different as day following night. The initiate understands more and can relate to more than he has before. He now regards less to be not of himself and as a result, becomes more responsible. Part of this new sense of responsibility is that the initiate is able to own various aspects of him or herself previously attributed to God or the devil.[1] This is how the initiate is able to expand his consciousness into the higher spheres of being.

Expansion of Consciousness

As a personal faculty or attribute of the human psyche, consciousness is that which makes us less separate, less self-serving, and consequently less ego-driven. The more of it we have, the more we are concerned with the well-being of others, and the more they will seem to us to form a continuum with our very self.

To the extent that challenges to our self-image force us to release the many constructs through which we view life, we will be able to directly expand our consciousness. This means that each of us is faced with as many opportunities for the expansion of consciousness as we encounter challenges to our subjective images of ourselves. In this regard, all of life can become a progressive initiation. This is the recurring theme of Revelation. It presents a picture of life that is ever pregnant with possibilities for change and growth. In doing so, it is calling us to the experience of adjusting outward and upward, ongoingly, our awareness of the fullness of life.

It is possible to place the process of expanding our awareness in the context of a model of consciousness that characterizes mankind as having capacity to express seven different levels of consciousness.

This model also expresses these possibilities in terms of mankind having the capacity to inhabit seven different *bodies*.

In terms of this model of seven bodies and seven levels of consciousness, we must be careful not to beguile ourselves by the awkwardness of language. For example, when we speak of acquiring higher bodies, we must not understand this in the sense of taking possession of something and making it our servant. Actually, the bodies that we may acquire are really levels or zones of consciousness within which one may become aware. If we are to be accurate in speaking about these matters, we should say that when we become conscious in a higher body or level of Reality, we are in turn possessed by this higher level of Reality.

The concept of a body is, loosely speaking, a metaphor for a level of consciousness that corresponds with different levels of human attention and concerns. The different bodies can be said to be circumscribed by the different spheres that contain one's different concerns. For someone who is only concerned with personal issues and his own physical well-being, the physical body will outline the outer limits of his concerns. His sense of Self will only extend as far as the space occupied by the physical body. For someone whose concerns extend to emotional interactions with others, we can say that such a person has an emotional body. And for the one whose concerns include the world of ideas, that person can be credited with a mental body as well. Although each body correlates with a level of consciousness, it is also possible for one to move between the different bodies depending on the quality of concerns that occupy the attention.

For mankind to have seven bodies means that there are six others besides the physical, outer one. The six higher bodies are all expressed in time–space through the physical one. Indeed, there are areas in the physical body that serve as contact points with the six higher bodies. These areas of interaction are the *chakras*, of which there was a brief mention in the interpretation to the Ephesus letter. We must now look at these *chakras* in greater detail since this concept provides the final step in bringing the pieces of the Revelation puzzle together.

Although the *chakra* concept is of Eastern origin, their locations correlate with the locations and functioning, as far as these can be clinically determined, of seven major endocrine glands. In addition to their relationship to the endocrine system, each of the *chakras* represents a neurological circuit in the human nervous system, being related to the major nerve plexuses in the body. The importance of *chakras* in helping our understanding of what we are as human beings is that the more advanced the individual is in consciousness, the more of these circuits are brought into operation.

For example, one whose concerns are restricted only to the individual physical body would have his consciousness circumscribed to the first *chakra*. Such an individual would be mainly concerned with survival of the body—with eating, sleeping, excretion, and crude sex impulses. At the other extreme, namely, the seventh level, the opposite is the case. Here, the individual experiences what has been referred to as *Cosmic Consciousness*—a state where the whole universe is experienced as the self. At this level, distinctions between oneself and others disappear, psychologically speaking.

An analogy that might help in the understanding of these *chakras* and what they represent, is to view them as a panel of electrical fuses. Just as fuses may be located in an area of a building far removed from the electrical circuits serviced by them, *chakras* are identifiable with certain areas of the body but belong to several modes of being that may be far removed from ordinary states of human consciousness. The similarity may be extended further to include another function of fuses, that is, the controlled passage of an electrical current. A fuse can complete or break an electrical circuit, or to say the same thing, allow a current to flow into a circuit or prevent it from doing so. At the present level of average human development, the higher *chakras* are inactive, and this has the effect of cutting off the circuits they service from being represented in the ordinary expressions of human consciousness.

However, unlike electrical circuitry and fuses, *chakras* undergo interrelated functioning on an ascending scale. This means that as our consciousness grows and as additional circuits are brought into operation, the ones below it become regulated by it and their functions are moderated by the higher ones. Conversely, if the first is to be brought under conscious control, efforts must be made to bring the second into operation, and so on.

When the fourth circuit is functioning, a very important milestone is reached in our human spiritual and psychological development. One is said to achieve contact with the "Higher Self," as the first three *chakras* define an existence that is in the "Lower Self." In the terminology of Revelation, such an existence is said to be "on the earth." An example of this usage is found in the eighth verse of the thirteenth chapter. Here, John is describing the beast that came up from the sea. He says: "And all that *dwell upon the earth* shall worship him, whose names are not written in the book of life of the Lamb slain from the foundation of the world." Also, in speaking about the image that was made to this beast, John says that it was to "them that dwell on the earth" that the beast from the earth gave the command to make an image to the first beast.

It may come as a surprise to some that the underlying concern of most of the New Testament is to get us to elevate our consciousness from the Lower to the Higher Self. It must be stressed that since we are dealing with seven levels, the concept of Higher and Lower relates to the higher and lower groupings of the circuits or *chakras*. This understanding is crucial if we are to get to the core of Revelation's message.

When we first find John in Revelation, he was "in the spirit," according to his own description. This means that he was in meditation, or was communicating with the Higher Self. His consciousness had "left the earth," in a manner of speaking, since his consciousness was elevated into the realm of principles. John's experiences from here on are in the nature of a guided tour, or a *revelation* of ourselves from a spiritual perspective. His encounters show what happens when one goes from the fourth level where he began, to the fifth, sixth, and seventh levels. He did not deal with levels one, two, and three, and this was for a good reason.

Here, we must pause to reflect on the underlying design of the New Testament. From the perspective of the initiation theme, what we find in Revelation is, in a sense, a sequel to the material in the Gospel of Matthew. This makes Revelation a psychological summary of everything that precedes it in the New Testament. For the purpose of continuity, we shall show in the next chapter how the problem of getting the consciousness to move from the first three levels of the being is tackled in the New Testament.

Chapter 19

Progressing from the "Lower" to the "Higher" Self

The Lower Self

As was mentioned before, when someone's consciousness is confined to the three lower *chakras*, that person can be said to be under the influence of the Lower Self. This condition is also defined symbolically in most of the New Testament teachings as being under the influence of Satan. To corroborate this, we need only reexamine the story of the temptations of Jesus as told in the fourth chapter of Matthew. It will soon become clear that these temptations and Jesus' triumph over the Tempter is a demonstration of how we can succeed in raising our consciousness above the "circuits" constituting the Lower Self.

According to the account in Matthew, after Jesus' baptism by John the Baptist, he was "led by the spirit" into the wilderness "to be tempted of the devil" (4:11). If we look at these statements in light of what we have learned from Revelation, we see that when Jesus went "to be tempted of the devil," he really went to purge himself of whatever vestiges may have remained of the Lower Self. Alternatively, we could say that by this ritual act of purification, Jesus was assuring himself once and for all that his consciousness was permanently established in the fourth and successive levels, in the Higher Self. We shall now examine each of these temptations to see how they relate to the advancement of consciousness from *chakra* to *chakra*.

First Level of the Lower Self

Turning now to the fourth chapter of Matthew, we find the following account of how Jesus mastered the energy of the first *chakra*.

> *Then was Jesus led up of the Spirit into the wilderness to be tempted of the devil.*

> *And when he had fasted forty days and forty nights, he was afterward an hungered.*
>
> *And when the tempter came to him, he said, If thou be the Son of God, command that these stones be made bread.*
>
> *But he answered and said, It is written, man shall not live by bread alone, but by every word that proceedeth out of the mouth of God.*   Matt. 4:1–4

It is clear that the line of attack of "the devil," alias the Lower Self, was the first *chakra*—the circuit concerned with basic survival on the material plane. The consciousness that is confined to this level wanted to divert Jesus' attention from his noble calling to looking after basic survival needs such as food. Not only that, Jesus was also being coaxed to use powers of the Higher or Divine Self to serve the needs of the Lower. This would have been, in effect, equivalent to pulling energy downward instead of raising it upward.

Jesus' answer to "the devil" is therefore a clue as to how anyone can overcome the pull created by the perceived needs of this circuit. The individual must respond to such a pull by acknowledging the existence within himself of needs that have a much higher priority since they are concerned with much more than the survival of the physical body.

Second Level of the Lower Self

After triumphing over first *chakra* concerns, Jesus became subjected to the second temptation:

> *Then the devil taketh him up into the holy city, and setteth him on a pinnacle of the temple,*
>
> *And said unto him, If thou be the Son of God, cast thyself down: for it is written, He shall give his angels charge concerning thee; and in their hands they shall bear thee up, lest at any time thou dash thy foot against a stone.*
>
> *Jesus said unto him, It is written, Thou shall not tempt the Lord thy God.*   Matt. 4:5–7

The second temptation was an assault on the second *chakra*, or more accurately, an attempt of the Lower Self to arrest the consciousness at the second *chakra*. Here, Jesus was being enticed to give in to pride by trying to prove that he was indispensable.

The confinement of consciousness to the second *chakra* shows up as the need for emotional nourishment, the need for acceptance. Usually, this need is met in sexual differentiation and attraction. Because of this, the second *chakra* is generally referred to as the Sex Center. However, in this temptation, the expression of this *chakra* is demonstrated in terms more general than that of the sex function. With this temptation, the expression of this *chakra* is represented as the need to prove one's specialness, or individuality, or indispensability. In other words, it functions essentially in terms of using polarity or separateness as a vehicle for emotional gratification.

Third Level of the Lower Self
Finally, we come to the third temptation. We read:

Again, the devil taketh him up into an exceeding high mountain, and showeth him all the kingdoms of the world, and the glory of them;

And said unto him, All these things will I give thee if thou wilt fall down and worship me.

Then said Jesus unto him, Get thee hence from me Satan: for it is written, Thou shalt worship the Lord thy God, and him only shalt thou serve.

Then the devil leaveth him, and behold, angels came and ministered unto him. Matt. 4:8–11

The third temptation was an attack through the third *chakra*, the circuit that is related to "will" in the individual. In a transformational sense, will is not the power to wield force, but the ability to organize the energy at one's disposal for the good of the whole being rather than just part of it. Until the higher circuits are open, the energy at the disposal of the individual is misused by the third *chakra*. For one whose consciousness is arrested here, the mode of being is one that enjoys displaying power in the form of ruling others and lording over them.

The exchange that Jesus was asked to make here was that of giving up his high calling for material power. What must be understood here is that the temptation comes from the devil in the medium of ideas, meaning that ideas that are part of the expression of the Lower Self may intrude into consciousness, coaxing the individual to depart from the ideals he has set for himself. For example, Jesus knew that his mission was not to seek earthly power, but one of planting powerful ideas in the hearts and minds of men and women. Thus, any thoughts, no matter how fleeting, that invaded his mind to present a "second-best" solution were a temptation of the devil, the Lower Self.

No doubt, consciousness imprisoned by the Lower Self would have been able to rationalize the event of Jesus using his powers to political ends. It would have been easy for him, should the consciousness have been arrested here, to believe that he was doing so for the good of humanity. When Jesus replied to the devil that he should "serve the Lord thy God, and him only shalt thou serve," he was really saying that the Lower Self should serve the Higher, that the lower circuits should be controlled by the higher ones, and not vice versa. At this point "angels came and ministered to him"— meaning that this is the point at which one rises into the Divine realm. Even the angels pay homage to one when the consciousness triumphs over the lower circuits.

It was with this victory that Jesus then set about his business of teaching his disciples to teach others how to move into the zone of the Higher Self and to successively higher levels of being.

The Levels of the Higher Self

In Revelation, it was not necessary to repeat the demonstration of what the three lower circuits represent, so when we find John, he is already at the fourth level to finish the conducted tour begun by Jesus in the temptation episode.

Since each of the *chakras* can be said to relate to a "body," it can be said that when John began to experience the visions, he was in the "fourth body." Various occult traditions have given names to these bodies, making it possible to cross-reference the details of mystical experiences given by various individuals about these bodies.

We can back up a bit here to look at the bodies related to the Lower Self before we deal with those of the Higher Self. With respect to the lower bodies, we have, of course, the physical body. Next there is what is called the energy or *etheric* body. Third, there is the *astral* body, and fourth, the *mental* body. In terms of this categorization, John was in his *mental* body when we find him. As he advances to each successive level, certain cues are provided to tell us of his point of entry into the higher bodies. He always begins his descriptions from the new vantage point by saying something of the nature of, "I was in the Spirit," or "He carried me away in the Spirit." Since by his own admission he was in the Spirit to begin with, such comments relating to being taken in the Spirit can

Table 19-1. Properties of the Various Levels of Being

Level of Being or Body	Point of Encounter in Revelation
IV—Mental	1:10: "I was in the Spirit."
V—Causal or Soul	4:2: "Immediately, I was in the Spirit."
VI—Spiritual	17:3: "So he carried me away in the Spirit."
VII—Divine	21:19: "And he carried me away in the Spirit."

only relate to the experience of going beyond a previously attained level.

We shall now look at Table 19-1 to get a bird's eye view of how Revelation is organized around the properties of the various levels of being or bodies within which John's point of consciousness becomes anchored. These references to being taken "in the Spirit" listed here are the only ones in Revelation. We shall now look at the different levels in this grouping and briefly examine the significant "events" in Revelation structured around each of them.

Fourth Level of Consciousness or First Level of the Higher Self

It was at the fourth level, the level of the *mental* body, that John received the letters to the Seven Churches, which as we have already seen, are symbols for the six zodiacal polarities and their common point of resolution. The mental body opens up the door for one to begin knowing by direct experience. This happens because it allows an individual, for the very first time, to get a sighting on the purpose of life in its utmost clarity. It offers us an overview of the whole process that is not colored by our own desire processes.

It will be remembered that the letters to the Seven Churches dealt with the way we could deal with the conflicts that arise in the consciousness from our attempts to come to terms with conflicting energies, symbolized by pairs of opposites. Human functioning at this level, therefore, deals with gaining an understanding of the ideal of a thing or a situation, or alternatively, with the blueprint of a thing to be built. In this case, the thing to be "built" is a level of consciousness that expresses life from the Divine perspective. Astrology belongs to the fourth body since it helps us to accept responsibility for ourselves and to work at changing our destiny through a change of consciousness.

Fifth Level of Consciousness or Second Level of the Higher Self

The fifth level of being, the *Causal* or Soul body, was opened up to John by the angel saying to him "Come up hither." To this invitation he realized, "Immediately, I was in the Spirit." This level of being is where John discusses the principles behind the functioning in the human psyche, of the twelve astrological signs as individual energies. He also gives an unveiling of the forces that are struggling to dominate the human psyche and take command of our attention. On one hand, there is the false sense of self (the dragon) and the false sense of belonging and identification that results (beast from the sea), the materialistic intellect (beast from the earth), and the focus of these three into a false mental picture of what constitutes progress (the image to the first beast). On the other hand, we have the forces that give rise to Christ Consciousness—humility and sacrifice—operating in the saints.

The reason for naming the fifth level of the body the Soul has to do with this being the level of being at which we gain mastery over the Elements. The Elements refer to Fire, Earth, Air, and Water, which as we saw on several previous occasions, are also symbols for the manifestation of consciousness in the material world. When we've gained mastery over the Elements, we gain the power to refashion the inherited conditions of our existence.

This control or mastery is what was symbolized by the Woman with child whom we encountered in the twelfth chapter of Revelation. She was clothed with the sun, the moon was under her feet, and she had a crown of twelve stars. All these signify that the forces of life, feeling, and mentality were all coming together to form a new synthesis, the child. Also, this controlled mastery was what was symbolized by the saints overcoming the dragon (Fire), beast from the sea (Water), beast from the earth (Earth), and the image of the beast from the sea (Air).

Mastery over the Elements has its concrete expression also. It means that we do not allow the material conditions of our life to dictate the level of our consciousness. Another way of viewing this is to see this mastery as the ability to understand the hidden principles of nature so that we can live harmoniously with life. Consequently, one special feature of this mastery is that one is able to act from the perspective of the Soul and is able to work for its own sake and not from the anticipation of reward. In other words, one lives in the domain of causes and not in the domain of effects. One's life is not bound up with just dealing with the effects of past actions, but rather with setting causes into motion. This is why the Soul level is called the Causal level: it is the level at which one takes charge of one's own destiny.

The Causal or Soul level is what is demonstrated in all the events recorded from the start of the fourth to the end of the sixteenth chapter of Revelation.

Sixth Level of Consciousness or Third Level of the Higher Self

The sixth level of being is that which we are introduced to in the seventeenth chapter. John introduces the scenes that are related to the sixth level by describing how this particular intensification of the vision came about. He says:

> *And there came one of the seven angels which had the seven vials, and talked with me, saying unto me, Come hither; I will show unto thee the judgment of the great whore that sitteth upon many waters:*
>
> *With whom the kings of the earth have committed fornication, and the inhabitants of the earth have been made drunk with the wine of her fornication.*
>
> *So he carried me away in the spirit into the wilderness;*
>
> Rev. 17:1–3

From here on, John describes the woman and the beast upon which she sits. But before we go into this, we must first say something about the sixth level or sixth *chakra*—the abode of the Spiritual body.

This center is also described as the seat of Christ Consciousness. An individual who has succeeded in bringing this circuit into consciousness is able to experience impersonal love, or charity, as Paul labels and describes it in his Corinthians epistle (I Corinthians 13). At this level, the ego is truly sublimated and the individual is able to become a true co-creator with God. With the ego now sublimated, all our personal actions are undertaken, not for personal gain, but for the good of humanity, whether these be material, psychological, or spiritual. In other words, this center is the seat of true sacrifices.

When this center is not brought into conscious functioning, however, it becomes the source of self-love and vanity. Also, with this self-love come false ideas about one's accomplishments, which in turn become the basis of false hopes. Basically, we are dealing with the antithesis of everything that this center is when it is brought under conscious expression. This is why the malfunctioning of this center is equated with the behavior of a harlot. A harlot misinterprets and misapplies her female endowments. In similar manner, this center in its malfunctioning misinterprets the energy that is accessible here. This misinterpretation takes place when the center of gravity of consciousness is still on the earth, meaning below the fourth level.

As we return to John for a fuller description of what goes on here, he says:

> *And I saw a woman sit upon a scarlet-colored beast, full of names of blasphemy, having seven heads and ten horns.*
>
> *And the woman was arrayed in purple and scarlet colour, and decked with gold and precious stones and pearls, having a golden cup in her hand full of abominations and filthiness of her fornication:*
>
> *And upon her forehead was a name written* MYSTERY, BABYLON THE GREAT, THE MOTHER OF HARLOTS AND ABOMINATIONS OF THE EARTH.
>
> *And I saw the woman drunken with the blood of the saints, and with the blood of the martyrs of Jesus.* Rev. 17:3–16

This woman is a symbol for both a personal and a collective misappropriation of psychic energy. The beast upon which she sits is the same in characterization as the one we encountered earlier that was described as coming from the sea. We identified this beast with the false emotional nature—with the identification and attachment impulse. The fact that the woman is sitting upon it means that she has her existence outside of the beast but is dependent upon it. She exploits it to her advantage.

Just as conscious exercise of the sixth center means that one subordinates one's personal needs to collective needs and thus becomes a co-creator with God, the unconscious expression also involves a certain subordination to the collectivity. But this subordination occurs more in the manner of a *force majeure*: the individual becomes a cork in the ocean of collective psychic energy. This occurs because, in its unharnessed functioning, the energy of the sixth center is the source of what is generally called civilization, culture, and the various forms of institutionalized religions. All these forms of expression give mankind assurances that he is successful (feeds his vanity), that he is making progress (nourishing false hopes), and that he has evolved past his ancestors (nourishing self-love). From the point of view of Revelation, the only true progress is, of course, success at the transformation of being—elevating the point of consciousness from lower to higher centers or overcoming the devil, the Lower Self.[1]

By calling the woman "Babylon the Great," John is saying that what Babylon stood for is quite aptly represented in her, remembering that she is a symbol for the malfunctioning of the sixth center. Babylon was a center of ancient wisdom, and it certainly did its part to nurture false hopes and self-love. The story of the Tower of Babel, as it is recorded in the Bible, has indelibly impressed the idea in people's minds that Babylon tried to usurp the place of God by trying to build a tower to heaven. However, from what we know of Babylon from historical and other archaeological findings, this idea of Babylon is correct with one significant exception. The transgression of Babylon did not take place on the three-dimensional plane but on higher ones.

As far as the biblical story of the Tower of Babel goes, we must accept it as an allegory of the working of the linear mind. This is the mind that views reality from its own center, from its own point of view—which is conditioned only by what it has experienced. Literal towers, or ziggurats as they are known, were important places for observing the heavens and probably for conducting other forms of observances. We now know that astrology, for example, was developed in Babylon and can safely surmise that the clear, unobstructed views of the heavens that the ziggurats provided made charting the stars and planets possible. However, we cannot say that it was astrology per se that identified Babylon with vain hopes. What was wrong about Babylon and the woman that now represents it has to do with the proper use of knowledge.

For example, astrology, as it has the potential for existing today, was nonexistent in Babylon. What astrology represented then was prediction or divination. Consequently, to the extent that the Babylonians used astrological information to predict the future, they "in effect" tried to ascend to heaven. Because, in being able to predict the future with success, they would have "deciphered the Mind of God." This is quite likely what the Old Testament authors, who recorded these events, felt. In their estimation, for mankind to know the future is not consistent with the process of the evolution of the human psyche through the growth of consciousness. In some Old Testament passages, the soothsayers, the astrologers, Chaldeans, and the magicians are severely ridiculed.

The psychological basis for this apparent prejudice against these customs is that if mankind were preoccupied with knowing the future, he would lose sight of the power resident within him, to create the future. He would become blind to the fact that the events he was trying to foresee were really the consequences of the causes that he himself has set in motion through some previous action. For one to try to see the future with the view of taking evasive action of foretold events is equivalent to that person presumptuously trying to evade the consequences of events that he himself has placed into motion through some previous action. And to try to evade the consequences of actions that one has put in motion is to live in false hopes.

As was mentioned in the Introduction, properly employed, astrology should help one to understand the past and to use that understanding to gain some perspective on the present, to find out where one "is at." After this perspective is accomplished, astrology must be left behind and one must press forward in growth of being.

Another characteristic of this Woman that should interest us is that she was drunk with the blood of the saints and the blood of the martyrs of Jesus. Revelation uses the term "saint" for anyone engaged in and successful at the processes of raising consciousness to higher levels. Those individuals earning the title of "saint" are also engaged in efforts to raise the level of awareness of humanity at large. To be drunk with the blood of the saints is to siphon off and divert the efforts of all of these individuals to advance mankind spiritually.

The most effective way that this subversion is done is for this "Woman," this process in the collective psyche of man, to ignore the lessons of the "saints" and to be blind to the examples they have set. This is done even as society venerates them and pays homage to their memory. Because of this, the work of the "saints" may have the opposite effects to those intended. Their efforts can simply add to the sense of false hope that individuals at large entertain.

It is this growing sense of false hope that is portrayed by the Woman becoming drunk. This imagery is quite apt, for just as being drunk places one in a stupor such that one is unable to function, false hopes place one in a situation where one does not work on one's being. Instead, one thinks that one already has that which is to be striven for. Such is the functioning of the energy of the sixth *chakra* in its unharnessed mode.

Seventh Level of Consciousness or Fourth Level of the Higher Self

The seventh level of consciousness is portrayed in Revelation 21:1 to 22:5. This level is formally reached by John after he was invited by one of the angels, who had the seven plagues, to go see the Lamb's wife. John says of this event:

> *And he carried me away in the spirit to a great and high mountain, and showed me that great city, the holy Jerusalem, descending out of heaven from God.* Rev. 21:10

Before this formal introduction took place, John is already discussing this reality that he is being made privy to. This expose is found at the start of the twenty-first chapter where he says:

> *And I saw a new heaven and a new earth: for the first heaven and the first earth were passed away, and there was no more sea.*
>
> *And I John saw the holy city, new Jerusalem, coming down from God out of heaven, prepared as a bride adorned for her husband.* Rev. 21:1–2

Here, we have a most curious symbol to represent the bride of the Lamb—a city. It is called holy, new, and is said to come down from God out of Heaven. In dealing with this symbol, we shall first examine the appropriateness of using the concept of a wife or a bride to represent the seventh center. After this, we shall look into the appropriateness of using the concept of a city to represent the bride of the Lamb.

Before we proceed to look at characteristics of this center, we must pause to reflect on the enormity of the task before us. When we looked at the other centers, we were able to learn of their characteristics even by inference. We were able to do this by virtue of those centers being dual—by their having a positive and a negative expression. However, the seventh center is non-dual and the only way we can get an idea of its functioning is to examine the symbols used to represent it.

The most outstanding feature of the seventh center is that it is the center of rest, a state of withdrawal from purposive activity. However, this rest can be said to be dynamic rest, by which I mean that there is no subject–object separation, and therefore no "conscious" doing. Yet, there is growth and expansion of awareness, of being. The secret of this puzzle is that whatever goes on here emanates from the secret recesses of the "heart of God." The individual does not act, but causes things to happen because of the alignment of his heart and will with universal values.

The concept of the Lamb's bride is used to describe this center because the Lamb, as we saw earlier, is the consciousness that is whole, yet allows itself to be subjected to humility and sacrifice in time–space—i.e., earth life. But here, beyond time–space, is the counterpart to this reality in the form of the Lamb's bride. This symbol, therefore, represents the principle of consummation, of celebration, and of rapture. The picture we get here is the unification of complementary parts. The bride is the other half of the self-same reality, which in another realm—the realm of time–space, was subject to sacrifice and suffering.

The message here is that should one, dwelling in time–space, embrace the sacrifice and suffering that are characteristic of the consciousness of the Lamb, that person will also automatically be included in the celebration that is characterized by the marriage of the Lamb. The celebration of the marriage of the Lamb goes with the sacrifice and suffering of the Lamb and is really just their echo. This is why the consciousness characterized by the seventh center has been described as the state of the *Mystical Marriage*.

The idea of describing this reality as a city and calling it Jerusalem with such adjectives as *holy* and *new* also has a symbolic function. First, the etymological meaning of the name Jerusalem is "possession of peace." This reinforces the explanation of the seventh center as a place of rest. Also, *new* and *holy* imply that it is beyond time–space, beyond ephemerality and beyond fractionalization. The concept of *new*ness relates to the lack of a temporal past, something not here-to-fore realized. And *holy* means that it is a reality that is defined by wholeness or Collective Consciousness.

We can now pursue this explanation further by pointing out that a city is really a place of collective habitation. This explanation emphasizes that the seventh center is a personal as well as a collective, well-orchestrated state of awareness. The idea of a collective state is also implied in the opening verse of the twenty-first chapter where John says that he saw a new heaven and a new earth and that the first heaven and earth had passed away. He also tells us that "there was no more sea" (21:1).

The passing away of heaven and earth suggests a realignment of boundaries between what might be considered to be spiritual (heaven) and what might be considered material (earth), or between what is perceived as conscious and what is unconscious. The addition of the phrase "that there was no more sea" suggests that boundaries disappear—islands of consciousness in a sea of unconsciousness cease to be the norm, in a manner of speaking.

It is significant that astrological symbolism persists to the very end in Revelation. Here, at the seventh level, the condition upon which an individual can partake of this reality are enumerated in astrological terms. This enumeration seems to emphasize that the attainment of the seventh level of consciousness must begin with conscious efforts to synthesize the principles of life as one encounters them. Here, at the end of the Revelation message, John gives the condition under which one will be able to partake of the consciousness that characterizes this center. He states:

He that overcometh shall inherit all things; and I will be his God, and he shall be my son.

But the fearful, and unbelieving, and the abominable, and murderers, and whoremongers, and sorcerers, and idolaters, and all liars, shall have their part in the lake which burneth with fire and brimstone: which is the second death.

Rev. 21:7–8

As we saw previously, this listing of faults really has to do with a lack of assimilation of the principles represented by astrological signs: Fearfulness relates to Aries–Libra, unbelieving to Virgo–Pisces, abominable to Cancer–Capricorn, murderers to Leo, whoremongers to Scorpio, sorcerers to Aquarius, idolaters to Taurus, and liars to Gemini–Sagittarius. To talk about these shortcomings as crimes of individuals is a way of saying that the consciousness that is characterized by such "lumpiness" will not be able to blend smoothly into the collective state of the Mystical Marriage.

As far as the second death is concerned, we are told that "... death and hell were cast into the lake of fire. This is the second death" (20:14). This is saying that whatsoever is not transformed through conscious striving and made part of the Collective Consciousness will be "melted down" and put back into the process. It will no longer be feasible for unprocessed energies to take refuge in death or the unconscious, for even the unconscious too will cease to function as a repository for all that mankind is not willing to face. We have already seen that the passing away of the old heaven and earth implies a shifting of boundaries between what is considered to be conscious and unconscious. Thus, to twist a well known cliché, "Whatsoever is not part of the solution will not be permitted to be part of the problem."

Notes

Introduction
1. Carl G. Jung: *Memories, Dreams, Reflections*, (New York: Vintage Books, 1965), p. 333.

Chapter 1
1. Dane Rudhyar: *The Lunation Cycle—A Key to the Understanding of Personality*, Shambhala Press, Berkeley and London, 1971, pp. 3-4.
2. Manly P. Hall: *The Secret Teachings of All Ages*, The Philosophical Research Society Inc., Los Angeles, California, 1977, p. 55.
3. Elisabeth Haich: *Initiation*, The Seed Center, Palo Alto, California, 1974, p. 250.
4. William Barclay: *The Revelation of John*, Vol. I in the series, The Daily Study Bible, Revised Edition; G. R. Welch Col., Ltd., Toronto, 1976; pp. 160-1.
5. It is peculiar that the association of the Four Beasts with the Fixed signs of the zodiac should have escaped Jung of all people, as well-versed as he was in astrology.
6. Elisabeth Haich: *Sexual Energy and Yoga*, ASI Publishers Inc., New York, 1975, p. 64.
7. Entry by C. G. Howie in P. L. Gerber and R. E. Funk, *The Interpreter's Dictionary Of The Bible*, Volume 2, Nashville and New York: Abingdon, 1962, pp. 205–213.
8. C. W. Ceram: *Gods, Graves, and Scholars—The Story of Archeology*, Second Revised Edition; translated from the German by E. B. Garside and Sophie Wilkins, Bantam Books, 1972, p. 291.

Chapter 2
1. This anecdote is related in the book *Astrology for the Millions*, by Grant Lewi (see page 3). The original citation is given as an article by Dr. Morris Jastrow in the Eleventh Edition of Encyclopedia Britanica.
2. Clement of Alexandria, "The Stromata, Or Miscellanies," Book V, Chapter VI. From *The Ante-Nicene Fathers*, Grand Rapids, Mich., Wm. B. Eerdmans Publishing Co., 1979, p. 453.

NOTES 213

3. Gerber and Funk, vol. 2, 905.
4. Arnold Toynbee, ed., *The Crucible of Christianity—Judaism, Hellenism, and the Historical Background to the Christian Faith*, New York and Cleveland: World Publishing Co., 1969, 273.
5. This quote is taken from *The Crucible of Christianity*, but the original source is given as Clementine Recognitions VI, 37.
6. The meaning of Bartholomew's name—i.e., "furrowed, ready for seed"—was obtained from the *Metaphysical Bible Dictionary*.
7. Gerber and Funk, Vol. 4, 357.

Chapter 3

1. See C. G. Jung's *Psychological Types*, vol. VI of *The Collected Works of C. G. Jung*, Princeton, N.J.: Princeton University Press, Bolligen Series xx, 1956.

Chapter 4

1. Jeff Mayo, *Astrology*, London: Teach Yourself Books, 1975, 55, 59, 65, 71.
2. After writing this piece identifying the role of the Cancer and Capricorn sign energies as the reversal of entropy, I found the following in R. Buckminster Fuller's *Utopia or Oblivion: The Prospects for Humanity* (New York: Bantam Books, 1972, p. 15):

   I am confident that the difference between animal brains and the human mind lies specifically in man's unique ability to generalize to progressively compounding degrees of abstraction. I think that this is man's unique function in universe—antientrophy. The physical universe is entropic; that is, energies escape from local systems and the "fallout" is described as the Law of Increase of the Random Element, and that increase of diffuse energies brings about the expanding physical universe; in superb balance with which the human mind continually probes for and discovers the order in universe and continually contracts the descriptions of the separate orderly behaviors discovered in nature and combines the generalized observations in progressively comprehensive generalizations whereby the metaphysical universe cofunctions equally with the physical universe *as its* contracting-universe *and* increasing orderliness *counterpart. Man is the great antientropy of universe. The famous "Second Law" of Thermodynamics propounds entropy. But the human mind discovered and described and harnessed in orderly fashion this disorderly propensity of nature. Einstein's mind discovered and generalized the comprehensive law of physical energy universe as $E = Mc^2$ and the process of metaphysical mastery of the physical is irreversible."*

Chapter 6

1. S. J. De Vries, an entry on calendars in *The Interpreter's Dictionary of the Bible*, vol. I, 483–88.
2. It is impossible to completely describe what spiritual realization is and how it is attained since it comes as an act of Grace and is different for everyone. However, Grace usually comes when we have exhausted ourselves by fully taking advantage of the opportunities available in life for

214   MEDITATIONS ON THE APOCALYPSE

spiritual development. Thus, for a consciousness to discover its completeness—i.e. become spiritually realized—it must first discover its own limitations which it cannot do until it has been fully committed and engaged in living life to its fullest capacity.
3. Clement of Alexandria, 499.
4. For example, in the book *Kundalini Yoga* by Swami Sivananda, *kundalini* is described as "an electric fiery occult power, the great pristine force which underlies all organic and inorganic matter." Additions to this description go as follows: "This mysterious *kundalini* lies face downwards at the mouth of the *Sushumna Nadi* on the head of *Svayambhu Linga*. It has three and a half coils like a serpent" (pp. 63 and 64). Also, C. W. Leadbeater, in his book *The Chakras*, says: "Kundalini is described as a devi or goddess luminous as lightning, who lies asleep in the root chakra, coiled like a serpent three and a half times around the *Svayambhu linga* which is there, and closing the entrance to the sushumna with her head" (p. 116).

Chapter 7

1. A good example of a "glimpse of Truth" that might be misused is the oft quoted statement from St. Augustine, "Love God and do what you will." This is mystical truth, which, if we are able to understand it to its depths, can lead to spiritual freedom and liberation, but which, if we understand it only with the materialistic intellect, can lead to greater bondage to the senses.
2. "Drawing energy downward" describes a dynamic in consciousness where we use higher faculties to serve the lower ones. For example, we might regard spiritual abilities as something that might give us an advantage in life's various arenas of achievement—fame, money, power, prestige. The opposite dynamic of "drawing energy upward" means that the lower faculties serve the higher, such that the resources of body, mind, and will are utilized to further our quest for spiritual understanding and realization regardless of the opportunities we might miss to become a "success" in the eyes of others and society.
3. Namely, the attainment of a certain level of spiritual insight and realization that is just enough to inflate the ego but not enough to cause one to go all the way, i.e., full surrender of the personal will to the Will of God. Egoic pride sets up a defense that aborts the process of psychospiritual integration.
4. The word money is used here to mean not only currency, but the whole idea of stored up power, or privilege. Money functions as a *numeraire* for all that is transferable in a society—material goods, services, homage, authority, in short, privilege. Even in societies that do not regard themselves as monetized, there are always other means of conferring status and the privileges that go with it.

Chapter 8

1. Sir William Ramsay, *The Letters to the Seven Churches of Asia*, (London: Hodder and Stoughton, 1904).
2. The circular road mentioned refers to the location of the seven cities on a circular route comprised by "The Great Road" connecting Ephesus to Pergamum and then by "The Imperial Post Road" to Laodicea as they were connected in the first century A.D.
3. Ramsay, 188.
4. Ramsay himself recognized and addressed some of the inconsistencies that his position gave rise to. The most significant of these, and also the most relevant for us, is the apostolic custom of pointing out in their letters the places besides the one addressed where the letters were to be read. For example, in the epistle of Paul to the church at Colossae, he pointed out that his epistle was to be read at Laodicea as well. John did not give any such indication that his letter was to be read elsewhere besides the Seven, and therefore, if Ramsay's position that the Seven were representative of seven districts was correct, John would have committed an oversight in mentioning the churches where the letter was to be read. Ramsay, however, attempts to solve this problem by saying that John took it for granted that the letter would have been automatically dispatched to the other churches in Asia outside the group of Seven. He also tries to reconcile this position with the custom of the Pauline letter by postulating that the communication network was not in place in Paul's time, being a latter addition.
5. Ramsay, 41.
6. Ibid.
7. It was customary at the time for Asian cities to have a deity to whom the inhabitants looked for divine protection. This is confirmed by Franz Cumont in his book *Astrology and Religion Among the Greeks and Romans*. He states: "The cities of Syria often stamp on their coins certain signs of the zodiac to mark the fact that they stood under their patronage" (p. 46).

Chapter 9

1. Geoffrey Parrinder, ed., *Man and His Gods: Encyclopedia of the World's Religions* (London: The Hamlyn Publishing Group, Ltd., 1971), 83, 127.
2. Robert Graves, *The Greek Myths*, Vol. I and II (New York: Penguin Books, 1955), 31.
3. Edith Hamilton, *Mythology*, (New York: New American Library, 1942), 40.
4. Michael Stapleton, *A Dictionary of Greek and Roman Mythology*, (New York: Bell Publishing Co., 1978).
5. Ramsay, 221.
6. An abstract representation is more "direct" since it encourages us to look beyond a fixation on an image to the principle behind the image. On the other hand, a representation that is more realistic, such as a human-form statue, is less direct since it may detract from the principle

it represents by encouraging admiration of the form to the neglect of the principle the form represents.
7. Ramsay, 223.
8. Ramsay, 252.
9. Jack Lindsay, *Helen of Troy—Woman and Goddess*, (London: Constable and Co., Ltd., 1974), 309–10.
10. Lindsay, 310–11.
11. Graves, 125.
12. Parrinder, 135.
13. Parrinder, 125–26.
14. The Three Avenging Spirits—The Furies of Roman Mythology: Alecto (unresting), Megaera (jealous), Tisiphone (avenger). See J. E. Zimmerman, *Dictionary of Classical Mythology* (New York: Bantam Books, 1966), 98.
15. Lindsay, 31.
16. Robert H. Mounce, *The Book of Revelation*, (Grand Rapids, Mich: Wm. B. Eerdmans Publishing Co., 1965), 95.
17. Walter Scott, *Exposition of the Revelation of Jesus Christ* (London: Pickering and Ingles, Ltd.), 39.
18. Gerber and Funk, Supplementary volume, 654.
19. It must be remembered that these planets are those designated in astrology as rulers of the signs Sagittarius and Gemini respectively, a factor that further cements the links between these signs and Pergamum.
20. Ramsay, 281–82.
21. Mounce, 95.
22. Ibid.
23. The origin of this staff is given in the myth that Hermes struck, with his staff, a pair of serpents in combat with one another. The blow tamed the serpents which wound themselves around it.
24. Ramsay, 281–82.
25. Hamilton, 40–42.
26. Ramsay, 326.
27. Ibid.
28. Parrinder, 139.
29. Hamilton, 34–35.
30. Hamilton, 29–30.
31. Ramsay, 326.
32. Ramsay, 364–65.
33. Ramsay, 357–58.
34. Ramsay, 362.
35. Ramsay, 363.
36. Ramsay, 365.
37. For example, William Barclay, C. G. Jung, and *The Interpreter's Dictionary of the Bible*.
38. Tacitus, *Annals Of Imperial Rome*, vol. XIV: 27 (New York: Penguin Books, 1956), 326.
39. Ramsay, 417.
40. Ramsay, 418–19.
41. Ibid.

NOTES 217

42. For example, Arnold Toynbee, *The Crucible of Christianity*, plate 50.
43. Here, Jung elaborates in a footnote: "The difference between this and the Mithraic sacrifice is significant. The dadophors are harmless gods of light who take no part in the sacrifice. The Christian scene is much more dramatic. The inner relation of the dadophors to Mithras ... suggests that there was a similar relation between Christ and the two thieves"—Jung's *Symbols of Transformation*, vol. V, 120.
44. This refers to Franz Cumont, author of *The Mysteries of Mithra*.
45. Jung says in a footnote; "For the period from 4300 to 2150 B.C. So, although those signs had long been superseded, they were preserved in the cults until well into the Christian era."—Jung, *Symbols of Transformation*, 201.
46. Jung, 201.
47. Ramsay, 392.
48. Jung, *Modern Man in Search of a Soul*, (New York: Harcourt, Brace and World, Inc., 1933), 196–97.
49. Ramsay, 397.
50. Ramsay, 398.

Chapter 11

1. The feeling principle represents a consummation of our human experiences because through it, we are able to express our various capacities to empathize, to nurture, to love, to forgive, and to hope.
2. This means that one receives so that whatever is received can be channeled to where there is need. In a sense, the Christ principle is the principle of living not to oneself, but to be a channel of life.
3. See *The Chakras* by C. W. Leadbeater and *Kundalini Yoga* by Swami Sivananda, referred in the Bibliography.
4. For example, in order to fulfill personal ambitions in the material world, an individual has to organize his mental, emotional, and physical energies to identify and fill existing needs in the world. The "conspiracy" takes the form of the psychological factors that go to form personal ambitions—the desire to build up self-esteem, status, reputation, and so on.
5. Luke 14:26.
6. I Corinthians 3:3–7.

Chapter 12

1. Matthew 15:11.
2. Matthew 12:34.

Chapter 13

1. Matthew 15:11.
2. Matthew 12:34.
3. Ephesians 3:17; see also Ephesians 3:11–19 for full context.
4. Numbers, chapters 22, 23, 24, and 25.

5. Numbers 22:20.
6. Numbers 22:22.
7. Numbers 25:1–3.
8. See Joshua 13:22, 24:9–10; Neheimiah 13:2; Micah 6:5 in the Old Testament; and II Peter 2:15, Jude 11 in the New Testament.
9. Numbers 24:16–17.
10. At the level of existence where the *oneness* of the Universe is comprehended, everything becomes *Real*. For someone who has experienced such a *Vision*, there is nothing that is out of place, so even something done in jest would unleash energy just as potent as if it were done with the utmost sincerity.
11. I Corinthians 10:7.
12. Although the act of sex is solemnized by the marital commitment, the nature of the act itself is not changed by marriage as a *legal* arrangement. Indeed, the morality of sex is not based on the legal aspects of marriage, but rather the *spiritual quality* of a relationship. Marriage is a symbol of this spiritual quality. If this spiritual quality is lacking in a marriage, the sex act can be as "immoral" as any outside of marriage.

Chapter 14

1. John 5:22.
2. This association is attributed to the medieval alchemists only in the sense that they provide a ready source for the information as it has come down to us. In fact, alchemy goes back to before the time of Christ. Titus Burckhardt, in his book *Alchemy*, states:
   Alchemy traces its descent back to a priestly art of the ancient Egyptians; the alchemical tradition which spread all over Europe and the Near East, and which perhaps even influenced Indian alchemy, recognizes as its founder Hermes Trismegistos, the 'thrice-great Hermes,' who is identifiable with the Egyptian God Thoth, the God who presides over all priestly arts and sciences ..." (pp. 15–16, see bibliography).
3. True reason and rationality are gifts of the Spirit and are inseparable from Will, without which rationality degenerates into an unlimited capacity to make excuses and reason becomes delusionary.

Chapter 15

1. Integration can occur at various levels of the being, depending on where one's center of gravity is located. Integration is therefore less difficult at lower levels than at higher ones. For example, the criminal without a conscience is exhibiting a level of integration of sorts by being able to commit various crimes without any moral qualms. Should he reform, he would have to seek integration that also incorporates a conscience where he might enjoy a level of peace of mind comparable with his prior state.
2. II Timothy 1:7.
3. Matthew 8:21–22.
4. Matthew 13:12.

5. Basically, not making conscious contact with Christ amounts to living life without awareness or acknowledgment of the debt of gratitude that we owe for our individual, personal existence.
6. Paul describes this process in the following manner: "... God was in Christ reconciling the world unto himself..." (II Corinthians 5:19).
7. I Peter 4:18.
8. In this context, *charity* is not simply kindness or generosity. It is closer to *equanimity*—a state where we act out of principles rather than personal motives. Personal motives, no matter how noble, can never lead to true *charity* since behind every kind gesture may lurk some expectation of compensation, even the expectation of earning "salvation" or a way to "heaven."
9. One sets up "enforcement factors" in the sense that by declaring oneself publicly, others will either ridicule or insist upon outward proof that the claim one is making is true. For example, to verbally proclaim one's allegiance to Christ is to challenge oneself to live up to all that this allegiance implies. It is in the sense that the individual is giving others a standard by which his actions will be evaluated that he is setting up "enforcement factors" in his environment.
10. Matthew 10:32–33.

Chapter 16

1. This is not to be taken as a literal support for the idea of reincarnation. The idea of growth achieved through more than one lifetime is paradoxical. First, this idea implies that when a person dies, the essence of that person continues as consciousness. However, it does not necessarily mean the consciousness that results from a life that has been lived continues into another life as an integral being, or to say the same thing, that the person is reborn. In my personal view, continuity of existence does not necessarily imply a personal aspect. The essence of a life can be reborn in whole or in part with the sole purpose of undergoing a refinement. Basically, this does not constitute reincarnation since it is not accompanied by a personal element.
2. Rev. 3:15–17.
3. Recall that in the commentary on the Sardis letter, white clothing was said to symbolize psychological integration that is based on one's spiritual ideals. Integration at such a level brings at-one-ment in the psyche and results in various fruits of the Spirit being realized in consciousness.
4. Ramsay, 419.

Chapter 17

1. Hebrews 12:14.
2. The term "Soul" is used here in the sense of a "dynamic process" rather than a fixed entity. A concept that is parallel to that of Soul is that of personality. However, Soul, unlike personality, involves a level of organization where actions are orchestrated for considerations other than personal fulfillment.

3. John 10:9
4. II John 3:20.
5. Hebrews 9:28.
6. Revelation 1:7.
7. John 15:7.
8. John 14:23.
9. For example, if the Soul desires to make a contribution toward the elimination of human oppression, it might choose a birth in a situation where the yoke of oppression may be directly experienced. Part of its task of assisting humanity to grow might include inspiring others by example to get rid of oppressive situations.
10. Romans 8:20–31, 28–31.
11. *Secret Talks with Mr. G.* (The Institute for the Development of Harmonious Human Beings, Inc., 1978), 104–5. "G" refers to G. I. Gurdjieff.

Chapter 18

1. Indeed, one of the lessons we learn through spiritual initiation is to release our definitions of God and move toward the True God. The initiate realizes that whatever is conceived in our minds cannot be God, as God is beyond knowing; that God cannot be circumscribed in our experiences, as God is more clearly "experienced" by the absence of experience. The initiate knows that we must surrender all our idols, all our preconceived notions of God before God can be realized in our consciousness. Even then, we realize God only indirectly, by moving to the very limits of our known being.

   Likewise, the initiate would have deepened his or her understanding of evil and of the devil. He or she sees evil as our collective conspiracy against Truth and the devil as the coalition—i.e., his name is "legion," meaning many—of unconscious psychic energies, beginning with our native pride in our individual differences. The initiate understands that the devil has no life of its own and only comes into being when we lose our connectedness with God, or when we step back from what is Real and fix our allegiance on what is un-Real.

Chapter 19

1. The energies of the higher *chakras* are expressed in an unconscious and a conscious mode. Expressed unconsciously, they feed into the unconscious, collective body of humanity and impact on the individual at an unconscious level. When one is unconscious of the energies represented by these *chakras*, one simply interprets their energies in terms of the level of conscious development one has attained. The goal is to become conscious of the energies of the higher *chakras* by taking responsibility for these energies. This is done by increasing the spheres of one's concerns or acquiring higher bodies.

Bibliography

Astrology
Cumont, Franz, *Astrology and Religion Among the Greeks and Romans*. New York: Dover Publications, Inc., 1960.
Mayo, Jeff, *Astrology—Teach Yourself Books*. London: The English Universities Press Ltd., 1975.
Rudhyar, Dane, *The Lunation Cycle—A Key to the Understanding of Personality*. Berkeley and London: Shambhala, 1971.

Bible Concordance, Dictionaries
Gerber, P. L. and Funk, R. E., *The Interpreter's Dictionary of the Bible—An Illustrated Encyclopedia*, vols. I–V, 1962, Supplementary volume, 1976. Nashville: Abingdon Press.
Metaphysical Bible Dictionary, Unity Village, Mo.: Unity School of Christianity.
Young, Robert, *Analytical Concordance to the Holy Bible*, Rev. ed. London: United Society for Christian Literature, Lutterworth Press, 1939.

Bible Translations
King James Version. Nashville and New York: Thomas Nelson Inc., 1970.
Revised Standard Version. *The New Oxford Annotated Bible*, ed. Herbert G. May and Bruce Metzger. New York: Oxford University Press, 1977.

Commentaries
Barclay, William, *The Revelation of John*, Vol. 1 in the series, *The Daily Study Bible*, Rev. ed. Toronto: G. R. Welsh Co. Ltd., 1976.
Clement of Alexandria, "The Stromata, or Miscellanies," *The Ante-Nicene Fathers*, Translations of The Writings of the Fathers Down to A.D. 325, vol. II. Grand Rapids, Mich.: Wm. B. Eerdmans Publishing Co., 1979.
Mounce, Robert H., *The Book of Revelation: The New International Commentary on the New Testament*. Grand Rapids, Mich.: Wm. B. Eerdmans Publishing Co., 1965.
Ramsay, Sir William, *The Letters to the Seven Churches of Asia*. London: Hodder and Stoughton, 1904.

Historical References

Ceram, C. W., *Gods, Graves, and Scholars—The Story of Archeology*, 2nd Rev. ed, Translated from the German by E. B. Garside and Sophie Wilkins New York: Bantam, 1972.

Kitto, H. D. F., *The Greeks*. New York: Penguin Books, 1951.

Parrinder, Geoffrey, General Ed., *Man and His Gods—Encyclopedia of the World's Religions*. London: The Hamlyn Publishing Group Ltd., 1971.

Tacitus, *Annals of Imperial Rome*, vol. XIV: 27 (1956) Translated by Michael Grant. New York: Penguin Books, 1971.

Tenney, Merrill C., *New Testament Times*. Grand Rapids, Mich: Wm. B. Eerdmans Publishing Co., 1965.

Toynbee, Arnold, ed., *The Crucible of Christianity—Judaism, Hellenism, and the Historical Background to the Christian Faith*. New York and Cleveland: World Publishing Co., 1969.

Mythology

Campbell, Joseph, *The Masks of Gods—Occidental Mythology*. New York: Penguin, 1964.

Graves, Robert, *The Greek Myths*, vols. 1 and 2. New York: Penguin Books, 1955.

Hamilton, Edith, *Mythology*. New York: New American Library, 1942.

Homer, *The Odyssey*. Translated by E. V. Rieu. New York: Penguin Books, 1946.

———, *The Iliad*. Translated by E. V. Rieu. New York: Penguin Books, 1950.

Lindsay, Jack, *Helen of Troy—Woman and Goddess*. London: Constable and Co. Ltd., 1974.

Stapleton, Michael, *A Dictionary of Greek and Roman Mythology*. New York: Bell Publishing Co., 1978.

Zimmerman, J. E., *Dictionary of Classical Mythology*. New York: Bantam, 1966.

Psychology

Burckhardt, Titus, *Alchemy—Science of the Cosmos, Science of the Soul*. Baltimore: Penguin Books, 1971.

Jung, Carl G., *Symbols of Transformation, Psychological Types*, vol. VI. Translated by R. F. C. Hull, vol. V of *The Collected Works of C. G. Jung*, Bollingen Series XX. Princeton: Princeton University Press, 1956.

———, *Modern Man in Search of a Soul*. Translated by W. S. Dell and Carey F. Baynes. New York: Harcourt, Brace and World, Inc., 1933.

———, ed., *Man and His Symbols*. New York: Dell Publishing Co. Inc., 1964.

Other

Fuller, R. Buckminister, *Utopia or Oblivion: The Prospects for Humanity.* New York: Bantam Books, 1972.

Haich, Elisabeth, *Initiation.* Palo Alto, Calif.: The Seed Center, 1974.

———, *Sexual Energy and Yoga.* New York: A. S. I. Publishers Inc., 1972.

Hall, Manley P., *The Secret Teachings of All Ages.* Los Angeles, Cali.: The Philosophical Research Society Inc., 1977.

The Institute for the Development of Harmonious Human Beings, Inc., (I.D.H.H.B. Inc.), *Secret Talks with Mr. G.*, 1978.

Leadbeater, C. W., *The Chakras.* Wheaton, Ill.: The Theosophical Publishing House, 1974.

Sivananda, Swami, *Kundalini Yoga.* India: The Divine Life Society, Yoga Vedanta Forest Academy Press, 1971 edition.

Stanley-Alder, Vera, *The Finding of the Third Eye.* New York: Samual Weiser, 1968.